Studying Local Churches

Studying
Local Churches:
A Handbook

Edited by
Helen Cameron, Philip Richter,
Douglas Davies and Frances Ward

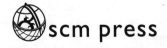

© Helen Cameron, Philip Richter, Douglas Davies and
Frances Ward 2005

British Library Cataloguing in Publication data

A catalogue record for this book is available
from the British Library

0 334 02960 0

First published in 2005 by SCM Press
9–17 St Albans Place, London N1 0NX

www.scm-canterburypress.co.uk

SCM Press is a division of
SCM-Canterbury Press Ltd

Printed and bound in Great Britain by
William Clowes Ltd, Beccles, Suffolk

Contents

List of contributors   ix

Introduction   xiii

1 Why Study the Local Church?   1

1.0 Introduction   1
1.1 You, the Reader . . .   2
    Local Church Leaders   2
    Ministerial Training Students   3
    Students in Higher Education   3
    Local Policy-Makers   4
1.2 An Overview of Congregational Studies   5
1.3 Conclusion   11

2 How to Study the Local Church   12

2.0 Introduction   12
2.1 Introducing the Four Disciplines: *Anthropology*;
    Sociology; *Organizational Studies*; *Theology*   13
2.2 Methodological Approaches   19
2.3 Methods   26
2.4 The Research Process   35
2.5 Conclusion   42

3 Perspectives on the Local Church   43

3.0 Introduction   43
3.1 Global and Local Context   43
     Anthropological Strand – Simon Coleman   44
     Sociological Strand – Linda Woodhead   54
     Organizational Studies Strand – Helen Cameron
     and Stephen Pattison   65
     Theological Strand – Chris Baker   76

3.2 The Worship and Action of the Local Church   89
     Anthropological Strand – Martin Stringer   89
     Sociological Strand – Mathew Guest   98
     Organizational Studies Strand – Stuart Jordan   109
     Theological Strand – Jan Berry   122

3.3 The Resources and People of the Local Church   135
     Anthropological Strand – Peter Collins   136
     Sociological Strand – Sylvia Collins   146
     Organizational Studies Strand – Helen Cameron   159
     Theological Strand – William Storrar   174

3.4 Power in the Local Church   187
     Anthropological Strand – Douglas Davies   188
     Sociological Strand – Paul Chambers   198
     Organizational Studies Strand – Margaret Harris   209
     Theological Strand – Frances Ward   221

4 Where next in the Study of the Local Church?   234

     Local Church Leaders   234
     Ministerial Training Students   236
     Students in Higher Education   238
     Local Policy-Makers   240

Conclusion 243

Bibliography 245

Index of Subjects 257

Index of Names 266

List of contributors

Chris Baker is Research Director for the William Temple Foundation based in Manchester, a member of the Scargill community in North Yorkshire, and teaches urban theology at the University of Manchester and the Luther King House Theological Partnership.

Jan Berry teaches practical theology within the Ecumenical Partnership for Theological Education in Manchester. She has a particular interest in feminist liturgy, and is currently researching women's rituals of transition.

Helen Cameron is Visiting Research Fellow at the Wesley Centre, Westminster Institute of Education, Oxford Brookes University. She is Senior Tutor for an MA in consultancy for mission and ministry. She is a member of The Salvation Army.

Paul Chambers is a research fellow at the University of Glamorgan and is the author of a number of congregational studies and articles relating to religion and identity in Wales.

Simon Coleman is Professor of Anthropology at the University of Sussex. His work includes study of Swedish Pentecostals.

Peter Collins is a lecturer in Durham University's Department of Anthropology. His research includes studies of Quaker groups.

Sylvia Collins is Senior Lecturer in Sociology at Kingston University, teaching social research methods and sociology of religion, and currently researching the influence of Christian-based youth work on young people's worldview and faith development.

Douglas Davies is Professor in the Study of Religion at Durham University's Department of Theology and Religion. His research focuses on Mormonism, death studies and Anglicanism.

Mathew Guest is lecturer in theology and society at Durham University's Department of Theology and Religion. He is a co-editor of *Congregational Studies in the UK: Christianity in a Post-Christian Context*.

Margaret Harris is Professor of Voluntary Sector Organization at Aston Business School, the author of *Organizing God's Work: Challenges for Churches and Synagogues* (Macmillan, 1998), and a member of a Reform synagogue.

Stuart Jordan is a Methodist minister, currently Secretary of the London Committee. He has a PhD in the reception of liberation theology and a Masters in church-based consultancy.

Stephen Pattison is head of the School of Religious and Theological Studies at Cardiff University and a member of the Church of England.

Philip Richter is a Methodist minister, sociologist and theological educator. He is Director of Education at the Southern Theological Education and Training Scheme (STETS), based in Salisbury.

William Storrar is Professor of Practical Theology at Edinburgh University. With a background in parish ministry, his research interest is in changing patterns of ministry and mission in congregations. He has recently co-edited *God and Society* (2003) and *Public Theology for the 21st Century* (2004).

Martin Stringer is Senior Lecturer in the Anthropology and Sociology of Religion in Birmingham University's Department of Theology. He has extensively studied various Christian congregations in England.

Frances Ward is a parish priest in the diocese of Manchester. She is the editor of *CONTACT: A Journal in Practical and Pastoral Theology*. Her latest book is *Lifelong Learning: Supervision and Theological Education* (SCM Press, 2005).

Linda Woodhead is Senior Lecturer in Christian Studies at Lancaster University. Her recent publications include: *The Spiritual Revolution: Why Religion is Giving Way to Spirituality* (with Paul Heelas, Blackwell, 2005).

Additional case studies contributed by:

Graham Dover is a management consultant, specializing in non-profit organizations, and has an MSc in voluntary sector organization. His most recent work has been with the Willow Creek Association UK.

Ian D. Johnson served as a Methodist Connexional Property Secretary and then as Local Mission Development Secretary until his retirement as a Methodist minister in 2004. He is a part-time consultant.

Virginia Luckett MSc works for Oasis Trust, an international Christian charity, as the Community Action Development Manager and has wide experience of Christian social action.

Research assistance provided by Philip Coull.

Introduction

Now is an exciting time to be involved with local churches. They have always been there, a significant aspect of life in any local community, but often rather hidden and taken for granted. Churches are where people come together to worship God and serve the neighbourhood, gathering in a particular place because it is the parish church, or because it is the Baptist church where they were brought up, or because a local Alpha course drew them into a new way of looking at life. A group of people of varying interests and backgrounds who meet because they have something in common; who share fellowship, a sense of vision for the world, who struggle with life at times, who welcome the opportunity to be thankful. And now, for one reason or another, as explored below, there is increasing interest in local churches. This book, written for church leaders, students and policymakers, contributes to that growing perception of the significant part that the local church plays in life today.

Perhaps, as they say, researchers only become interested in things when they are dying. While there is a great deal of concern about falling numbers of worshipping Christians, and much anxiety among church leaders about fewer and fewer potential ministers offering themselves for training, there are also signs of real vitality. Certainly old patterns of church life are changing, but there is much to suggest that different ways of being church are emerging that meet the various needs of people living in today's network society of transient populations and complex lifestyles.

There is a longer history of studying congregations in the United States, and a number of reasons why this is the case, which are explored in Section 1.2 below. This book emerges from the British context. Its editors share a common fascination with local churches as communities that reflect and engage with life and social trends in Britain today. How can we think more about the ways churches develop their patterns of worship and engagement in the neighbourhood? What ways are there to research the people and resources, such as buildings and financial aspects of a church community? How do local churches organize themselves? How can power be understood, institutionally and at the local level? These questions and more are explored in this book.

The editors believe that local churches are interesting phenomena for study in their own right. But, increasingly, faith communities are perceived to have potential to provide resources in partnership with local government in terms of voluntary activity and social contribution. As places of belonging and believing, they can offer much to enhance and strengthen the fabric of society in a multicultural world.

Consider how the local church can share in Christianity's long history. Each denomination possesses its distinctive appropriation of it. Catholic and Orthodox Churches identify with the earliest Christians by stressing the handing on of tradition. Many Protestant denominations root themselves in the Reformation of the sixteenth century. Others try to jump the centuries to draw on the biblical scenes of the Acts of the Apostles. These choices reflect theological outlooks and are reflected in forms of church organization. Many churches also possess a strong sense of local history covering a relatively brief span of time and colouring current biases and policies. Or think about how architecture reflects and imparts Christian traditions. Early Christians built churches around the graves of their martyred dead and elaborate buildings followed. These were called into question in periods of scrutiny as in the Iconoclasm Controversy of the Greek Orthodox Church in the eighth century, and with the Puritans and their destruction of many religious images after the Protestant Reformation. Some contemporary charismatic churches, for example, prefer to meet in halls or more secular structures than in the Gothic buildings of traditional Christianity. Some have seen Christianity as a pendulum that swings from 'temples' as sacred places where God dwelt and which worshippers attended in a spirit of awe, to 'meeting houses' that accommodated the faithful with simplicity of style (Turner, 1979). Such a perspective provides a rich background for the debate you will often hear on whether church is 'building' or 'people'. Then again, because doctrines and teaching often influence architecture, differences and changes in doctrinal emphasis will be reflected in architecture and buildings.

Art, too, will reveal much about the life of a local church. Accumulated treasures and contemporary banners and posters show the elements of the Christian story valued by particular churches. From a theological perspective, art is a valuable way of embodying an understanding of the incarnation, the belief that because God became human in the person of Jesus of Nazareth, God's being can be seen in the material things of the world. The local church will often also value music. It has flourished at times of religious vitality as at the Reformation, the Methodist Revival and the rise of the charismatic movement of the 1970s, and is a vibrant way in which the local church shares in the universal community of faith. Hymns and music often reflect social life: compare the many nineteenth-century hymns on death with the paucity of such themes in twentieth-century Christianity.

There are many way in which interest in the local church can be triggered – as varied as the aspects of life that the community of faith touches. The four editors bring particular ways of understanding with them as they turn their attention to the local church in this book. We are an anthropologist, a sociologist, an analyst of organizations and a theologian, but believe that we need to engage across different disciplines if we are to do justice to our study of the local church. At times it is necessary to draw on the expertise of the geographer, for instance, if a deeper grasp of the local environment is called for, as a church struggles with changing patterns of employment in a local area. Or perhaps the ethicist has a contribution to make as a church seeks to make decisions about issues of value and human worth in a complex world where national, family and sexual life are under scrutiny. Or again an economist or political advisor might engage with, or help the local church about matters relating, for example, to war, the exploitation of people through unfair labour agreements, or ecological matters that raise questions for the local church about their stewardship of the earth.

Local churches have much to offer as communities seeking to respond to God and make a difference in the world. To do this as a community, rather than solely as an individual, will be central to the approach of most local churchgoers, and is particularly important in a world of many cultures where diversity needs to be celebrated. Making common cause, for example, over ethical issues of social justice and human flourishing can bring a church into deeper relations with other religions and faith communities in their area.

This book cannot cover everything. Still the editors hope to offer perspectives and approaches that will stimulate you in further research and deepen your appreciation of the local church and its place in contemporary society. We have structured the book around four broad questions:

- Why?
- How?
- What?
- Where to, now?

The 'Why' section locates this book within the growing field of congregational studies. The 'How' section focuses in detail upon different research methods, approaches and processes that will be useful in studying local churches. The 'What?' section offers 16 different perspectives on the local church, organized by these themes:

- context
- worship and action
- people and resources
- power.

Each theme is considered from the approaches the editors represent: anthropology, sociology, organizational studies and theology. The fourth section suggests ways in which the study of the local church can be taken forward.

   Most sections contain further reading you can follow up. Throughout the book, references to other writers are indicated by the surname of the author and the year of publication – these can be looked up in the bibliography at the back. There is a website associated with this book where you will find further resources, advice and examples: *www.scmpress.co.uk/studyinglocalchurches*.

Why Study the Local Church?

1.0 Introduction

In the world of theological education, there is an increasing number of courses on offer that explore ways in which the local church can be studied, aimed at those who are pursuing an interest in religious studies, or are training for ministry. For them the literature of 'congregational studies' is not large, and is mainly drawn from the United States. For leaders within the local church there is a great deal of material that is geared towards fostering church growth and health, often written from the particular perspective of one denomination, but little that will help them carry out a piece of research to the depth that this book offers (Resourcing Mission Office, 2001; Warren, 2004). For policy-makers who wish to engage with local faith communities there is very little reading material that offers an intelligent, non-confessional approach to studying the local church. There is a need for a handbook like this. It draws together current research in an accessible way and offers a practical emphasis to a wide readership.

At times it will be clear that the editors are addressing 'you' as the reader, adopting a style often used in distance-learning materials where the style is informal, direct and accessible. In other sections of the book contributions from leading researchers have kept their style, revealing the particular approach of their own discipline, be that anthropology, sociology, organizational studies or theology, and offering a rich feast of different voices and perspectives. Each comes with a sense of excitement about the local church. As editors we are encouraged by the development of interest from these different disciplinary perspectives, and the creativity generated by involvement in the local church. You will find that there are recurring themes and methods throughout the text, and that the four approaches and four topics that we have used to structure the book cross-fertilize and interlink with each other.

Throughout this book the editors have reflected upon the reasons for studying the local church in the hope that you, as reader, will find something of use. We have assumed four different types of reader: a local church leader, a person training for ministry, a student in higher education, a local policy-maker. Between us we work in local churches, train ministerial students and teach students and policy-makers so we have tried to imagine the different questions you might ask as you use this book in your particular context.

1.1 You, the Reader . . .

Local Church Leaders

Frances Ward

Anyone immersed in a local church and exercising leadership, whether as a lay or ordained person, will find this book offers ways to under-stand the dynamics and particularities of their own situation. Perhaps your congregation faces a time of change, or is in a crisis of identity, or is in the middle of a vacancy and seeks to discern the future more clearly. Any number of questions can emerge from such situations, or generally in the ongoing life of a church. This book is for those who have just such an interest in shaping the life and priorities of the faith community to which they belong.

For lay and ordained leaders, including church secretaries, church wardens, deacons, pastoral assistants and ministers at the local level of any denomination, this book is a useful resource to help shape future strategies and visions, to manage change and yet honour past traditions and congregational history. Perhaps you are concerned about how leadership itself can be understood in the light of bibli-cal injunctions and changes in society. Perhaps your congregation, in planning its mission and outreach, wishes to think more clearly about how its members can meet the needs of the local community. Perhaps you have responsibility for understanding the place and future of the local church within the wider institutional life of the denomination, for example, when faced with pastoral reorganization at provincial, circuit or deanery level, or closure, or church-planting in a given con-text. The book will provoke further thought by offering different methods of approach and ways of doing theology to carry forward reflection and action in the local or regional context.

Ministerial Training Students

Philip Richter

This book is also designed for those in ministerial training, either within initial ministerial formation or as part of ongoing ministerial development. It will enable student ministers to achieve a degree of critical distance from the local church in which they are training, especially if this happens to be their home church and perhaps overly familiar. The book will help ministers orientate themselves when they move to a new appointment and ministerial context. The various approaches in this book will enable ministers to be more objective as they seek to understand the local church, rather than relying on, for instance, under-informed hunches, folk wisdom, accounts of the church from those with vested interests or, indeed, their own personal prejudices. Ministers will be encouraged to take seriously the uniqueness of each local church and to be attentive to the social and theological dynamics of the church in particular times and places. There is sometimes a temptation to assume that styles of ministry suitable for one place can be readily transferred to another place. This book is intended to ease ministers away from such a 'one size fits all' philosophy and to enable them to see the particularities of their situation more clearly, the negative as well as the positive features. Seeing the 'warts and all' can help avoid idealizing the church, and allow for a balanced appreciation of its finer points within God's economy. This book will also, however, help ministers recognize characteristics common to many local churches. Ministers may well find it liberating to understand that some factors are characteristic of certain types of church and may, or may not, be within their control in a given situation.

Students in Higher Education

Douglas Davies

Students increasingly have opportunity for practical research on churches through a degree dissertation or a professional report on a practical placement. While it makes sense to focus upon a familiar denomination – especially if you intend to work in it in some professional capacity – it is sometimes wise to study a different group to gain a sense of comparison. Those not belonging to any church can also find such study appealing for its intellectual interest and the challenge of unfamiliar territory. It is important, at the outset, to seek clarity on your reasons for study and on the way the project relates to your degree's aims and objectives. Also never forget the importance of your course tutor and others involved in your project.

Why study local churches?

- To relate theory and practice. Academic disciplines often compartmentalize life's complex unity whereas practical study helps integrate them. In a two-way process theoretical ideas gain from practical information just as data come to make more sense when interpreted by theories.
- To bring some realism to the often misplaced ideals of pure theory. Scholars who never engage in work with people and groups can hold some unrealistic views and theories.
- To add to the store of knowledge and to contribute new ideas.
- To afford a degree of distance from overly familiar experience by bringing new perspectives and insights to bear.
- To help change and develop the student.
- To help develop the transferable skill of working with people, assessing their views and relating this information to an organization, to history and to society as a whole.
- To help the church studied to gain some distanced evaluation of its own life and the way it fosters or hinders its own goals.

Local Policy-Makers

Helen Cameron

Increasingly, faith communities are being drawn into local policy-making. In all parts of the UK, local strategic partnerships seek to bring together those who represent and serve local people. In areas that receive regeneration funding, government is keen to involve faith communities as ways of mobilizing local people and reaching hard-to-serve client groups. This builds upon the longstanding engagement of many local churches with social action and their involvement with political and economic life.

You may be coming to this book to prepare yourself for working alongside faith communities or to help you reflect on your work and the distinctive challenges that it has presented. It will help you gain an appreciation of the issues that face local churches and the ways in which they seek to make sense of them. You will see that it is possible to make use of both theology and the social sciences in studying congregations and that there is considerable potential for developing a dialogue between the different approaches. Since this book deals only with the Christian tradition it is important not to assume that its lessons translate automatically to other faith communities.

On a practical level, this book can help you commission and participate in research that paves the way for faith communities to engage in local policy implementation. Similarly, if you need to set up evaluations of projects or partnerships involving local churches you will be able to do so in a way that is sympathetic to their perspective. It may be helpful to use the handbook as a tool you share as you debate an appropriate course of action. For example, the congregation might decide to engage in a process of theological reflection and enquiry that parallels research using social scientific disciplines.

Finally, the book will assist you in becoming a 'critical consumer' of research about faith communities and point you in the direction of some existing effective studies.

1.2 An Overview of Congregational Studies

This overview uses the terminology of 'congregational studies' which is the term most often found in academic circles, especially in the United States, from where it has been imported to the UK. We've used the term 'local church' because we feel it is more encompassing.

Tracing the Study of the Local Church

Mathew Guest

Interest in the local church has always been shaped by wider contexts and questions, not least the perceived significance of the church as a whole and the shifting theoretical interests internal to academic disciplines. These factors have produced distinctive patterns on each side of the Atlantic, so that the UK and US literature reflects cultural and academic differences (Farnsley, 2004; Guest, Tusting et al., 2004). In recent years, these differences have arguably broadened, so that the assumptions and interests underpinning local church studies represent two separate orientations. The UK fosters an approach mainly concerned with understanding local cultures; the USA focuses on how the local church may contribute to solving wider social problems. These divergent traditions shape how studies are funded, which agenda is served, and which methods are deemed most appropriate.

In the early twentieth century, many commentators shared the assumption that modernity was corrosive of community, and especially that those living in urban areas were vulnerable to forces which threatened to undermine a sense of common identity. Efforts at postwar reconstruction echoed this call for a renewal of community. Ventures such as the Institute of Community Studies, based in 1950s London, focused on this problem and assumed that local churches had a significant part to play in its resolution. Related studies portrayed the local church as a site in which wider social forces were at play, and as a means of renewing healthy, social relationships. Similar efforts appeared in the USA, not least the Lynds' portrait of *Middletown* (Lynd and Lynd, 1929), although this was a self-consciously anthropological account, seeking objectivity and critical distance.

Work of a similar kind emerged among church leaders, although here exhortations that the church be fostered and celebrated as the centre of local community were coloured by shifting theological traditions. Studies drew from a 'parish and people' ethos and often focused on how the specifically Christian resources of the church could be mobilized in an attempt to tackle social fragmentation. Michonneau's *Revolution in a City Parish* (1950) channelled European influences, inspiring Southcott's *The Parish Comes Alive* (1956), while Bishop E. R. Wickham (1957) applied his missiological concerns to congregational reform in industrial Sheffield. Roman Catholic studies adopted a similar agenda, although by 1958, C. K. Ward was questioning the viability of the 'parish' as an organizational unit within urban communities (Ward, 1958).

Throughout the 1970s and 1980s, studies of the local church evolved in response to a different set of questions, posed by different disciplines. Many adopted what James Hopewell (1987) called a 'mechanistic' approach, that is, they proceeded from the assumption that congregations function according to a set of rules, which, when mastered, reveal opportunities for reform and improvement.

For example, studies inspired by church growth theory either examined individual congregations as a means of developing principles for church growth, or observed the implementation of church growth strategies among local churches (McGavran, 1955; Wagner, 1976). Such studies assume an evangelical understanding of growth, centred on numerical expansion and the saving of souls, although some, such as Bruce Reed's *The Dynamics of Religion* (1978), combine ideas from church growth literature with a focus on the responsibility of the church to the local community.

Since the 1980s, a further systemic approach has been developed by scholars in the field of organizational studies. Often based in departments of management or social policy research, scholars advocating this approach are interested in how local churches achieve a different set of goals, for the most part shaped by government initiatives. Studies such as Margaret Harris' *Organizing God's Work* (1998) focus on issues of social capital, civic responsibility and the capacity of congregations to serve as welfare providers. However, such studies do not assume that congregations constitute a special force for good. Rather, local churches are analysed alongside other institutions fostering voluntary action and community service, and this has encouraged a healthy use of interdisciplinary theory.

A concern for how local churches may be nurtured and developed is reflected in a burgeoning US literature that can be traced back to Carl Dudley's *Building Effective Ministry: Theory and Practice in the Local Church* (1983). Dudley's work drew together academics, church growth experts and congregational leaders, and its thorough empirical approach was offered as a template for others wishing to enhance the life of their own church by studying it. This approach was developed by Carroll and others whose *Handbook for Congregational Studies* was revised and updated by Nancy Ammerman in 1998 (Ammerman, Carroll et al., 1998). This persistent 'church health' literature builds on broad theological assumptions about the local church being a force for moral and social good. Moreover, Ammerman's (1997) argument that local churches thrive best when they successfully adapt to changes in their local context, contains an implicit liberal theology concerned with welfare provision and social capital, rather than an evangelical one focused on numerical expansion. A more explicitly theological agenda is evident in Don Browning's *A Fundamental Practical Theology* (1991). Here, doctrinal issues are explored from the starting point of the local church, treated as a site within which practical reason and wisdom are continually constructed and revised in the light of human experience.

In the UK, Elaine Graham's work provides a bridge between the US literature and a more sociologically critical strand emerging among British writers. Her *Transforming Practice: Pastoral Theology in an Age of Uncertainty* (Graham, 1996) adopts Browning's concern for the practicalities of church life, but criticizes his tendency to present the local church as merely a collective of rational individuals, engaged in constructing a moral universe. Graham brings our attention back to the multiform complexity of local church life, caught up in values that are expressed in worship, teaching and social action, in practice as well as moral discourse. She also stresses that values are constructed at a local level, in dialogue with local circumstances, and shaped by differentials of power and authority in relation to gender, age and ethnicity.

But the dominating trend among more recent UK studies of the local church suggests a move away from broader questions – whether grounded in theology, social science or social policy concerns – to a focus upon the need to re-present local churches in ways that are faithful to their cultural identity. In some respects this shift reflects the broader 'cultural turn' in the social sciences, favouring interpretative accounts of cultural phenomena rather than objective, scientific analysis. It also reflects the related perception – heightened by globalization and postmodern relativity – that things are best understood when their particularity is properly taken into account. These 'cultural' studies of local churches provide a portrait of the congregation on its own terms and for the sake of understanding it better.

Such studies can be traced back to James Hopewell's *Congregation: Stories and Structures* (1987), which pioneered a narrative approach, emphasizing how each local church expresses its own meaning in a story. Hopewell follows anthropologist Clifford Geertz in seeking a 'thick description' of local church cultures, and in so doing stresses the need to understand the particularity of congregations if we are to address their needs. Hopewell's approach – ethnographic, sensitive to the voices of parishioners, building models of the local church from the ground upwards – has been highly influential on both sides of the Atlantic, but its key emphases have been more enduringly embraced by scholars in the UK.

In his innovative study of worship in four congregations in Manchester, Martin Stringer (1999) draws from Hopewell's comments on narrative as constitutive of congregational identity. David Clark's *Between Pulpit and Pew* (1982), and Timothy Jenkins' *Religion in English Everyday Life* (1999) both present ethnographic portraits of church life, set within the context of local patterns of belonging and identity construction. Al Dowie's (2002) study of 'Riverstane' church in Scotland adopts a similar sensitivity to local culture, but sets his findings within the context of questions from pastoral theology. Dowie also incorporates insights from the 'new anthropology', acknowledging that the researcher plays an active – not dispassionate – part in the production of knowledge, an issue also grappled with by Frances Ward within the context of her relationship to a congregation in Manchester (Ward, 2000).

This British strand, characterized by a focus on local specifics, indigenous voices and cultural sensitivity, is showing signs of growth and development. Many of the essays in *Congregational Studies in the UK* (Guest, Tusting et al., 2004) reflect – indeed radicalize – Hopewell's vision, seeking to understand congregations apart from any external agenda or wider social concern. This tendency is in part reflective of differences in funding. US projects are often financed by endowments which have particular interests, perhaps in the health of local churches or their capacity as generators of social capital. UK studies are almost uniformly isolated, locally specific and funded by government subsidized research grants that come with fewer ideological strings attached.

But the resurgence of interest in the local church in recent years has also occurred in less disinterested circles. Theological colleges affirm a renewed interest in practical and pastoral theology, on the assumption that ordinands will achieve greater insights into congregational life through empirical study (Lyon, 2000). The results of this reorientation can be seen in the plethora of empirically based Master of Ministry (MMin) and Doctor of Ministry (DMin) theses produced in recent years, especially out of centres like the Lincoln Theological Institute, now based at Manchester, or at Cliff College near Sheffield.

Why is the Study of Local Churches Important Today?

Congregational studies is finally taking off in the UK, and there are indications that the emerging literature is only the tip of an iceberg. Students in various university departments, theological colleges and clergy themselves are beginning to explore in greater depth the local church as a centre of identity, community and religious belonging.

There are several reasons why the study of local churches is particularly important at the present time. First, as sociologists keep reminding us, we exist as isolated individuals in a fragmented postmodern world, incredulous of tradition. Aside from instilling a rather dark picture of modernity, this trend has triggered a change of focus among many people, and a corresponding shift among academics observing them. There has been a resurgence of community, with individuals forging new communal relationships in order to make up for the dislocation of the postmodern experience. One of their options is the local church, which provides ready-made social networks and systems of support, and which is therefore of key interest as a potential haven of community.

This relates to the second reason: social capital. Robert Putnam's *Bowling Alone* (2000) brought to wider attention the issue of the decline of community, particularly in relation to civic responsibility. His work has had a shaping influence on academic agendas as well as on New Labour policy-makers, and this has shifted the spotlight onto local churches as potential providers of welfare within British cities, towns and villages. Indeed, this echoes provisions in the USA introduced by the Clinton administration, and followed up by Bush, with respect to faith-based organizations. Recent work in organizational studies has taken up this issue, and persistent government interest ensures a continuing examination of the role of the local church in addressing problems of urban and rural deprivation.

Third, there is an argument for the topicality of local churches based on social theory. When the secularization thesis dominated the sociology of religion, scholars were preoccupied with issues of grand theory – macro-social processes spanning history and cultural boundaries. The so-called 'cultural turn' within the social sciences shifted attention to the culturally specific, exemplified in ethnographic studies of neglected groups located at the margins of society. This turn has arguably encouraged an approach to religious groups which is under-theorized, and which fails to engage in wider debates about the changing nature of collective identity. The influence of postmodernism has also triggered a focus on particularity – on what differentiates individuals, at the expense of what unites them. Religious identity is not always discussed within the context of institutional or communal structures, and issues of locality have often been overlooked. Penny Becker has begun to address this problem in the USA, analysing congregations as social institutions within specific local contexts (Becker, 1999). There is much more work to be done in the UK, not least on the part that local factors play in fostering or impinging on Christian identities. The local church is at the heart of Christian religion in Britain, and thus deserves to be at the heart of its analysis.

1.3 Conclusion

Chapter 1 has attempted to answer the question 'why?' study the local church. As editors we have tried to imagine what issues and questions different readers might have as they read this book and seek to relate it to their local churches and contexts. With an understanding of why there is increasing interest in churches and faith communities, it is possible to see the creative potential they have. Local churches are particular and distinctive organizations that are local manifestations in time and place, many and varied in today's world. In order to do justice to that diversity, we offer in the next chapter a wide range of research approaches and methods, as we seek to answer the question 'how?' to study local churches.

How to Study the Local Church

2.0 Introduction

This chapter offers a 'hands on' approach to the question of how a local church can be studied. By the end of it you should have a good grasp of the different ways and methods that can be used, and further understanding of the processes of developing your own research project. The editors bring four different perspectives to the study of the local church and each of the disciplines they work from has particular methodological emphases that we outline here. We were aware that there are other approaches that could also provide fruitful avenues of exploration as in architecture and art, or geography, for example. We suggest that if you want to come to the local church with another interpretative lens, then you will need to familiarize yourself with the academic discipline in question, its main approaches and methods, and use them in creative dialogue with what you find in this book.

Chapter 2 contains the following sections. 2.1 introduces the four academic disciplines we are using, namely, anthropology, sociology, organizational studies and practical theology. 2.2 explains the way in which our four chosen disciplines approach research, a topic known as methodology. 2.3 introduces a range of methods that are used in the four disciplines and which you could use in undertaking your study. 2.4 offers some guidance on the process of undertaking research.

2.1 Introducing the Four Disciplines

Anthropology

Douglas Davies

Anthropology is the study of humanity. As a discipline it branches into physical and social/cultural anthropology. Physical anthropology is largely biological and deals with human evolution and physical diversities and is not relevant to this book. Our focus is within social or cultural anthropology, and although the British often prefer to speak of social anthropology and the Americans of cultural anthropology, for our purposes they are equivalent.

Anthropology began in the late nineteenth century when British scholars such as E. B. Tylor and J. G. Frazer turned their attention from traditional classical studies to the question of human evolution, following the discoveries of Charles Darwin. There was an explosion of knowledge about peoples, often called primitive tribes. As the empires of the European states developed, government officers, merchants, missionaries and travellers produced accounts of apparently strange civilizations. Anthropologists in the USA, without an empire as such, turned their attention to the many groups of Native Americans. This first phase of the discipline was, then, both evolutionist and colonial in outlook. Its evolutionism involved much speculative guesswork about the stages or phases through which humanity had passed from its 'primitive' origins to its 'civilized' present. European scholars considered themselves 'civilized', and regarded tribal peoples as 'primitive', as retaining something of humanity's early condition. Some anthropologists assumed that by studying different kinds of tribes it was possible to understand the evolutionary stages through which humanity had passed. Religion was thought to have originated in primitive magic and it was assumed by some that it would give way to science.

The twentieth century witnessed major changes in anthropological thought, for example, 'evolutionism' was replaced by 'functionalism'. Instead of a focus upon origins and evolutionary pathways, functionalists tried to understand how a particular contemporary society worked or functioned. Emphasis was placed on the institutions, like marriage, religion, politics and economics, which channelled the biological and social needs of people. To collect data about such matters, anthropologists stopped depending on the reports of others and developed the method of participant observation. As a participant observer, the anthropologist would live among a people for some time to understand the underlying pattern of values and beliefs: how they viewed the world, coped with life, produced or bought food, reproduced, managed human and sexual relations and dealt with death. Questions of festivity and aesthetic life, of ritual and symbolism were studied as aspects of religion, along with the myths and stories of a people.

Anthropology as a discipline is generally agnostic about belief in God – it is more interested in what people say about God than in God's existence.

Sociology

Philip Richter

Sociology seeks to understand why people behave and believe as they do, as members of particular societies, social groupings and in relation to established patterns of human interaction. It is different from politics or economics in that its subject matter is the whole of social life, rather than just one aspect of it. It also differs from, say, psychology, in its interest in social regularities rather than individual variation.

Sociologists can be divided into three types, functionalists, conflict theorists and social action theorists. Functionalists tend to understand society as a stable interdependent organism whose cohesion and reproduction rests on moral consensus. By contrast, conflict theorists tend to understand society in terms of social divisions, grounded in competing vested interests and sustained by mechanisms of social control, including dominant ideologies. The social action theorist focuses instead on small-scale human interaction and its meanings for the social actors concerned, reflected, generated and developed in the course of that interaction, including the unanticipated consequences of that activity.

A functionalist will try to discover, among other things:

- how society is structured
- how social institutions, such as marriage or organized religion, regulate behaviour
- how individuals are socialized into society's norms and values.

Conflict theorists will want to know:

- how society is stratified
- how inequality is sustained
- how conflict is contained and how mechanisms of social control break down.

Social action theorists will research:

- how individuals interact with each other and society
- how their identities are socially formed, sustained and modified
- how the meanings attached to situations and people are negotiated in the course of social interaction.

Some sociologists have interpreted religious beliefs and practices as merely social in origin; others have an irreligious agenda, dismissing the truth claims of religion. Others have bracketed-out the metaphysical premises of religion as off-limits to sociological inquiry, without necessarily questioning their validity. So, therefore, you could draw correlations between church attendance and, for example, age or generational variables, without thereby reducing churchgoing to social factors. In studying local churches, sociology can enable you to locate the local church and the beliefs and activities of members on a broader map, understanding the church as a social, as well as a theological, body. It can offer ways to interpret the church both in terms of its internal more micro-level social interaction and in relation to wider social processes.

Sociology is a discipline that questions taken-for-granted reality and discovers that things may not be quite as they seem. The awareness of social factors can liberate and enable us to see that things can be different.

Organizational Studies

Helen Cameron

People who work in churches or in voluntary organizations often greet the idea of studying organizations with suspicion; sometimes, hostility. To study an organization can be equated with 'management', and can evoke powerful emotions for those who think that management does not adequately describe what they do in their work. It feels reductive and does not fully capture their experience of grappling with theological and ethical issues. These feelings can be well-founded. The purpose of this section is to set out the range of approaches to studying organizations so you can critically evaluate what you read about them.

The 'management' approach to organizational studies originates from business schools and commercial consultants. It is the source of many of the paperback books that fill airport bookstalls, and reflects the world of large business where managers need to appear confident and in control. Such has been the impact of these ideas on popular culture that some writers describe it in terms of 'managerialism': an ideology that effective management can cure all society's ills (Pattison, 1997). Some academics who study public sector organizations would say that this ideology has swept through public institutions (like schools and hospitals), making exaggerated claims to transform performance. As a reaction to the assumptions that 'big business' makes about management, a group of academics in the USA and UK has, in the last 20 years, looked at the particular issues that face voluntary organizations. It is their work that the strand of organizational studies draws upon here.

So far, I have mentioned three types of people engaged in the study of organizations:

- business schools
- scholars of public sector management
- scholars of voluntary sector management.

Although fewer in number, there are also scholars from the social sciences who have taken the organization as a focus for study. They examine organizations from within the concepts of their own disciplines in order to reflect critically upon the role they play in society. They include psychologists (Katz and Kahn, 1978), sociologists (Collins, 1998; Parker, 2002), anthropologists (Wright, 1994) and psychotherapists (Gabriel, 1999).

This strand of the handbook, then, is not about 'management'. It will show how local churches can be analysed as organizations, within this large and diffuse area of academic enquiry which has many contributors and perspectives.

A helpful book for gaining an overview of the field of organizational studies is: Morgan, G. (1997) *Images of Organization*, London: Sage.

Theology

Frances Ward

As the editors met to plan and edit the book, it quickly became clear that theology offered something different to the other three strands, with their distinctive sets of analytical tools and range of theories. Theology as such does not provide obvious methods of enquiry (like those outlined in section 2.3) that could be used in a straightforward way to study the local church. The editors had to think carefully about some quite basic questions. Can it be said that someone who studies the local church is necessarily a theologian – as if there is something intrinsically theological about researching a faith community? But then what of the agnostic student who approaches the local church as a sociologist? Can it be said that she is 'doing theology'? Not necessarily. The authors were convinced that theology needed to be there as a discipline – but in what capacity? To answer this question it is necessary to think further about the nature of theology, and the way in which it has been changing over the last decades of the twentieth century and into the twenty-first century.

Traditionally theology, as an academic subject, has divided into a number of subdisciplines: systematic or dogmatic theology; philosophical theology; biblical studies, for instance. Over the last 40 years or so, in many departments of theology and religious studies, the traditional area of 'pastoral studies' has mutated into practical theology and the emphasis has shifted from a concern with the hints and tips of ministry to the development of new ways of relating theological enquiry to the concerns and issues of contemporary times: the relationship between church and society, religion, ethics and politics, public life and economics are explored. The theological emphasis in this book falls most naturally within this growing field of practical theology. So what is practical theology?

As a discipline, practical theology is distinctive in the following ways:

- It is interdisciplinary, welcoming the insights and skills of other disciplines in the search for understanding. This book itself is a good example of different approaches coming together in dialogue.
- This interdisciplinary nature can also be found as practical theologians draw upon insights within the different subspecialties of

theology itself. For example, a practical theologian interested in the local church might turn to biblical studies, or to church history, to research faith communities at different times of history.

- It attends to the way knowledge is produced. Practical theologians will often say that there is no point in doing theology from the ivory tower of pure theory: you need to be immersed in culture and contemporary issues and let your theological reflection make a difference in the world. That difference will mean that it is important to take seriously questions of responsibility and ethics in the production of knowledge.
- Practical theologians will examine the values they bring to research: their own precommitments. These often go unacknowledged, but they influence the perspective of the theologian and therefore influence the knowledge produced. Let us think for a moment about the different reasons why you might be reading this book. Perhaps you want to find ways to enhance the growth of your church. Or perhaps as a student you don't belong to any faith tradition, but are really interested, say, in the provision offered to children by a neighbourhood church as you train to be a local policy-maker. Or perhaps in a senior management role in the church you are concerned with the deployment of ministers in an institutional church that is finding new ways of using its paid ministry. The reason for your interest will colour your reading of this book, and your engagement in the life of the local church.
- A practical theologian will want to reflect upon their practice and develop it through disciplined study and reflection. Reflective practice as an ongoing method of learning holds together action and reflection in a continual cycle of doing, being and thinking.

The editors concluded their discussions about the place of practical theology in this text by agreeing that it offers different models, and you will find three developed below: praxis, critical correlation and corporate theological reflection. These models use a wide range of methods from other social sciences, depending on what is appropriate to the theological exploration of the local church.

Further reading

Two accessible introductions to practical theology are:
Ballard, P. and J. Pritchard (1996) *Practical Theology in Action*,
    London: SPCK.
Green, L. (2000) *Let's Do Theology*, London: Mowbray.

2.2 Methodological Approaches

In this book we make the distinction between *methodology*, *method*
and *model*.

'Methodology' is best regarded as the study of different approaches
to research within an academic discipline. It offers more abstract and
theoretical exploration of how to carry forward the research. It allows
you to weigh up the advantages and disadvantages of one method
over and against another as well as giving an account of the rationale
behind particular methods. The term 'method', on the other hand,
applies to the actual use and implementation of an approach. People
often talk about methodology when in fact they are really referring to
a particular method and its use.

As we saw in Section 2.1, the practical theologian takes seriously the
methodological issues involved in doing theology, and will draw upon
other disciplines for methods appropriate to the research in hand. As
a theologian she will welcome the opportunity to work with other
disciplines, and will use particular 'models' of engagement to make
the theological nature of the research explicit. In what follows you will
find an introduction to the different *methodologies* of each discipline,
a wide range of *methods* from each of the academic disciplines, and
three theological *models*, praxis, critical correlation and corporate
theological reflection.

Methodological Approaches: Anthropology

Douglas Davies

Methodologically speaking, anthropology describes, compares and interprets. To do this it employs key methods which are fieldwork, participant observation, comparative analysis and cultural interpretation.

Fieldwork and *participant observation* are closely related. Field-work involves living and working with the people studied. Participant observation is what happens as you both participate in and observe the group. This raises issues of neutrality and objectivity. Many anthro-pologists recognize that there is no such thing as a neutral observer: you will always come with your own preconceived ideas, and will have an impact upon the group you study. But it is surprising just how resilient people are to someone in their midst, especially over a length of time. 'Observation' is not simple and takes practice to achieve. It is usually necessary to take field notes that describe your observations and which become the basis for your analysis at a later date. Studies using these methods are often called 'ethnographies'.

The *comparative method* is fundamental to anthropology. It involves comparing the group you study with other groups which either you have studied yourself or which you find in the ethnographies of other anthropologists. Using material from field notes, drawing upon relevant comparative material and making use of established anthro-pological theories produces the final ethnographic study. Sometimes anthropologists distinguish between 'emic' and 'etic' explanations (see *ethnography* below on p. 29).

An important part of this total process is *cultural interpretation*. This happens as the cultures of the researched and the researcher come into contact and interpret one another. Although there will always be some dialogue between the different cultures, the culture of the researcher is usually the one that informs the interpretation.

Methodological Approaches: Sociology

Philip Richter

Sociology is a social science, so shares some, but not all, of the method-ological approaches of the natural sciences. It is grounded in empirical investigation. Social data are carefully observed, regularities are noted, differences within and between societies are captured, changes over the course of time are identified. And, as in the natural sciences, find-ings are interpreted in relation to wider theoretical frameworks and in terms of potential causes and effects. Sociologists seek to develop their theories in objective and systematic ways, regularly cross-checking the accuracy of their findings and allowing for their own biases.

Sociology also differs from the natural sciences, because its subject matter is radically different. Human beings, unlike, say, chemical molecules, do not simply respond automatically to external stimuli. They attach meaning to their behaviour. The sociologist seeks insight into the subjective meanings behind human action. Indeed, some sociologists would claim that there are no objective social facts, that social causes and effects cannot be gauged, and that the most a sociologist can do is to intuit the meanings given by people to specific phenomena.

There are two main methodologies outlined here. The positivist approach to sociology tends to focus directly on observable human behaviour, rather than its meanings, and assumes that, as in the natural world, behaviour is a reaction to external stimuli. Society in this view has patterned regularities and is governed by principles of cause and effect that can be discerned and differentiated by careful objective observation and measurement of social data, in relation to particular research issues. A positivist will look for regular correlations between different variables. Where such correlations are identified, he will then seek to discern whether or not there are causal connections between the variables, such that one is affecting the other, by filtering out and 'controlling' other possible factors.

A quite different methodological approach focuses upon the meanings attached to human behaviour. This methodology is more intuitive. You cannot directly observe individuals' thought processes, nor read motives from their behaviour, but you can elicit how individuals interpret their own behaviour, values and beliefs and are, in turn, understood by other social actors. This sort of research is typically called qualitative (the study of different qualities, or 'soft data'), rather than quantitative (study using quantities, statistics, 'hard' data). In qualitative research, a sociologist will prefer to undertake a modest number of extensive, probing interviews, rather than a large-scale 'number-crunching' survey. The results will have a richness and depth of understanding, although it may be more difficult to generalize the findings and apply them in other situations. In qualitative research, the sociologist needs to be aware that the human subjects may be aware they are being studied, and therefore present themselves differently, sometimes seeking to please, or even mislead, the researcher.

Methodological Approaches: Organizational Studies

Helen Cameron

As Section 2.1 indicated, organizational studies is a diffuse area of academic study spanning a range of purposes and approaches. Many study organizations (particularly under the banner of management) in order to improve performance. Other academics study them to reflect critically upon the role organizations play in society and human relationships.

If the organization is a local church, the purpose of the research will have a significant impact on the methods chosen and how those methods are implemented.

- Researchers who aim to influence what a local church does and how it does it, will need to think about introducing and building support for the project by involving people in the research and discussing the results. The researcher will adopt particular methods such as action research or consultancy (see Section 2.3 for definitions).
- Researchers who study the local church as a social phenomenon are more likely to use methods that will yield the data that addresses their research questions. The interpretation of their findings will be theirs alone, and not dependent on whether their research respondents agree with their conclusions.

All the methods described in Section 2.3 can be used in an organizational study. As with other disciplines care is needed to match appropriate methods to the research question. Will the chosen methods allow the researcher to find out what she really wants to know? For example, if the research question is about attitudes to an issue, what methods are most likely to get people to express honestly their attitudes? Will a combination of methods be needed to get a full picture?

The choice of methods may also reflect the underlying assumptions of the researcher about the nature of organizational life.

- An objectivist viewpoint (maybe one that sees organizations as systems that can be improved) might seek data about whether aspects of church life are meeting the needs of participants.
- An interpretivist viewpoint (maybe one that sees organizations as cultures that are resistant to change) might seek stories from

participants about incidents which illustrate change taking place, whether for better or worse.

Participants in church life bring experience of other organizations with them and these often mean they have mental models of 'how organizational life should work'. Discovering whether these mental models overlap or clash can be helpful preparation for organizational research or can be included as part of the research process.

Whatever research is tackled it is likely to involve meetings in organizational contexts. Preparing, conducting and following through such meetings repays careful thought and the following book can be recommended:

Widdicombe, C. (2000) *Meetings that Work: A Practical Guide to Teamworking in Groups*, Cambridge: Lutterworth.

Methodological Approaches: Practical Theology

Frances Ward

The praxis model of doing theology

In this model the whole process of research is seen as theological. Sometimes referred to as the *pastoral cycle* (Green, 2000), it can take a simple form called *see, judge, act*, which will be familiar to many ministerial students.

This model can be divided into four stages: *experience, exploration, reflection* and *action*.

- It begins with the *experience* that forms a research question, perhaps a problem facing the local church . . . (the *see* stage)
  For example, the nature of leadership in your church sparks your interest, and you ask questions such as these that will lead you into the next stage of *exploration*:
  - Why am I interested? (Examine your precommitments.)
  - Why is this important in the life of the church? (Is the current style of leadership impeding the growth or health?)
  - What other styles of leadership are there? (Turn to other disciplines, like organizational studies or sociology.)

- You have begun already to move into the *exploration* stage.

- You need to read further literature relevant to the question, seeking guidance from others if need be.
- You could set up a research project. Using sociological or anthropological methods, you gather data to enable you to compare the different styles of leadership in yours and the other churches in the vicinity, for example.

- When you have gathered enough data and read sufficiently about the topic, you are ready for the *reflection* stage . . . (the *judge* stage)
  - Here you could draw on theological or biblical resources to reflect further about leadership.
  - Or you could form a small group to examine relevant biblical and other material on leadership. Such an exercise might well provoke questions and alternatives in the church, potentially changing the practice of leadership.

- And so you find yourself moving into the *action* stage, where the issue you have studied has an impact upon the practice of your local church . . . (the *act* stage)

The outcomes of your research project may well have repercussions for decades to come as the local church you belong to benefits from the discussions you have initiated. Things change – perhaps not monumentally – but in significant ways for the better, if only in a greater understanding of leadership within the community.

   If such a project is done carefully, with responsibility and an understanding of the ethics of research, a practical theologian would argue that the whole process has been 'theological'. You have been 'doing theology' (see Green, 1990; Reader, 1994). The process begins and ends in practice, and hopefully leads to better practice and more just outcomes. As a method, the roots of *praxis* lie in liberation theology. Ballard and Pritchard (1996) offers a very good introduction if you want to read further.

The model of critical correlation

Depending on the particular experience facing a local church, the researcher selects a traditional theological doctrine or biblical text (for example, the incarnation, or a particular understanding of the nature of church, or an aspect of christology). The insights of tradition are brought into dialogue with the contemporary situation. As the text or doctrine and the contemporary situation correlate with each other, a dialogue, or conversation, develops as traditional understandings interplay with contemporary explorations.

This method of critical correlation owes much to the work of Paul Tillich in the 1960s, and has been taken forward by a number of theologians since who have been particularly interested in the processes of interpretation that are implicit in this approach. How we understand the Bible, how we use social sciences to research, how we understand the perspective and precommitments of the researcher are all important questions that require consideration. Don Browning offers a good example of critical correlation in his book *A Fundamental Practical Theology* (1991). Nothing remains static in this process of critical correlation: new insights emerge that broaden or deepen the previous understanding (Beckford, 2004).

The model of corporate theological reflection

The two main models outlined above assume the researcher is the prime person engaged in the enterprise as an individual. There is another important way in which theology is 'done' in the local church and that is by the congregation itself. Corporate theological reflection is often overlooked by individuals engaged in research projects, but is full of interest in terms of the range of methods used. If you return to the praxis model above and the example given about leadership in the local congregation, you will see how the researcher encouraged a group of congregational members to reflect further for themselves. This is corporate theological reflection. It needs to be done carefully and properly. A practical theologian might well draw in some of the insights of adult education in groups, or the literature on reflective practice.

A very good example of both the praxis model and the corporate theological model is found in Laurie Green's book *Let's Do Theology* where he describes a knitting group working its way through the stages of the pastoral cycle (2000, pp. 36–7). It shows how a church group was enabled together to reflect theologically on their own situation, *corporately*. It gives a good illustration of the *praxis* model in operation, using a spiral of doing theology where, through exploration and reflection, an original experience becomes a new experience open in turn to further and different exploration and reflection. It also shows how empowering this model of doing theology can be for participants.

Further reading

Ballard, P. and J. Pritchard (1996) *Practical Theology in Action: Christian Thinking in the Service of Church and Society*, London: SPCK.
Graham, E., H. Walton and F. Ward (forthcoming 2005) *Theological Reflection* (two volumes), London: SCM-Canterbury Press.
Green, L. (2000), *Let's do Theology*, 2nd ed., London: Mowbray.

2.3 Methods

Action Research

Action research is an approach to research in which the external researchers and internal organizational members work together in partnership. They jointly define the problem to be researched, decide how to investigate it, undertake the investigation and analyse the data. Together they propose and implement new ways of working and then evaluate how effective the new practices are in addressing the problem they originally identified.

The external researchers bring to the research knowledge of what is already known about the problem and experience of appropriate research methods. The organizational members bring their experience of the problem and their desire to find more effective ways of working. Both objective and subjective perceptions of the problem are respected and the problem is usually seen to have individual and group dimensions.

Adequate time, space and permission from all involved are needed for this approach to succeed. It can be a successful way of bringing about change because it blends research, participation and action. It can be derailed by imposed agendas, unrealistic timescales or an attempt to assert the supremacy of one particular perspective on the problem.

Further reading

Coghlan, D. and T. Branwick (2001) *Doing Action Research in Your Own Organization*, London: Sage.

Studying Artefacts

Ethnography can include the study of the artefacts made or used by a group, which range from buildings to temporary notices. Artefacts are included in what Cantwell Smith called the 'cumulative tradition' of a church (Smith, 1963) and offer valuable access to how people reflect upon their history, beliefs and current work and how they engage with or avoid wider society. Artefacts can show how past members related to the church through donations, and may recall someone whose family is still influential in the congregation. Churches acquire standard artefacts of their denomination such as altars, bells, Bibles, candles, chairs, fonts, hymn books, icons, organs, photographs and pictures, tables, pews, pulpits, stained-glass, vestments and many other things. Comparing new with old versions of objects is a means to evaluate change, or to assess increase or decrease in wealth or shifting doctrinal emphasis. Familiarity with an object can cause it to be overlooked, so always note the obvious and strive to use the comparative method to ask why some artefacts are absent here when present in other churches.

Consultancy

Consultancy comes in many guises and is a method of obtaining help with research. It is a means of buying in expertise about the problem being addressed, and can range from the recruitment of a critical friend who will advise on the best process for undertaking the work but leave it to the participants to determine the purpose of the research and the questions to be addressed, to more formal expertise and facilitation. Another distinction is between external and internal consultants. External consultants come from outside the organization and usually undertake consultancy as their main line of work. Internal consultants are people already in the organization with the necessary expertise or skill, prepared to stand aside from their normal role in order to act in the role.

It is helpful if organizations think through what type of help they need and it is always advisable to write a contract so that consultant and consultor have clear expectations about the help to be provided.

Further reading

Block, P. (2000) *Flawless Consulting: A Guide to Getting Your Expertise Used*, San Francisco, CA: Jossey-Bass/Pfeiffer.
This provides insights into the expert model of consulting but with much helpful advice on process.

Lovell, G. (1994) *Analysis and Design: A Handbook for Practitioners and Consultants in Church and Community Work*, London: Burns and Oates.
This provides insights into non-directive process consulting.

Documents

'Documents' include those that already exist, or can be specially created for the purposes of the research. The former include histories of Christianity, denominations and local groups, biographies and autobiographies of leaders and members. They afford special insight into congregational change over time. Records of national, regional and local church meetings, special commissions, committees and other reports often exist at church headquarters or within libraries. Local or national press archives can be another source for documentary data on local churches. For many practical purposes recent church registers and records are invaluable for accessing the numbers attending and nature of services and meetings, as well as sermons and talks given by church leaders who often keep collections of them. Photographs and paintings provide their own record of a church, as may video or other films taken at various events.

Documents are often generated by researchers through social surveys, including the transcription of interviews or through diaries and journals. Various specialist methods, including computer programs, exist for the analysis of all such written documents whether pre-existing or gathered by the researcher.

Ethnography

Ethnography, the descriptive interpretation of a people, originated as the key method in early twentieth-century anthropology before spreading into other social sciences. In practice it is difficult to separate description from interpretation because the very way we describe things is strongly influenced by how we interpret the world.

Anthropologists favour long periods of fieldwork in order to grasp something of a people's worldview. The local interpretation is often called the 'emic' view of life. When the researcher moves to a further stage of interpretation, using theories and models, this represents the 'etic' level of analysis. Sometimes emic and etic explanations are similar, sometimes very different. For example, an emic explanation of spirit possession might be grounded in belief in supernatural powers. The anthropologist's etic theory might explain it as a means of attracting attention or expressing powerlessness on the part of the possessed.

The final ethnography can be seen as an act of cultural interpretation as the researcher interprets the society studied to people who are unfamiliar with it. An effective example would be: Heskins, J. (2001) *Unheard Voices*, London: Darton, Longman and Todd.

Evaluation

Evaluation is the name for research which specifically aims to assess the effectiveness of a particular programme of work, activity or organization. It can be done in a number of ways. Effectiveness is usually judged by asking those involved what their starting objectives were and using them as the criteria for making assessments. Sometimes an external evaluator is commissioned as an expert in the area of work under question who can make comparisons with other situations. Sometimes workers evaluate their own work and can seek advice on the process of doing so. When external funding for projects is made available to local churches, it is likely they will be required to monitor and evaluate outcomes more than previously.

Further Reading

First Steps in Monitoring and Evaluation (2003), London: Charity
Evaluation Services.

Pattison, S. and J. Woodward (2000) 'An Introduction to Evaluation
in Pastoral Theology and Pastoral Care' in *The Blackwell Reader in
Pastoral and Practical Theology*, J. Woodward and S. Pattison (eds),
Oxford: Blackwell.
Here it is argued that evaluation needs to be appropriate for the
context and not over-elaborate. It also contains helpful questions
about the purpose of evaluation.

History

History concerns the past and its interpretation. Basic documents
include written accounts in records and registers, diaries, archives, autobiographies and biographies and earlier written histories. For churches,
sermons and published books may be important. Complementing individual products are formal church documents of specialist doctrine or
liturgical committees and public statements, which may have been discussed regionally or locally, as well as minutes for committees, synods
or councils. For example, The Society of Friends has kept detailed
records of meetings; many individual Mormons keep extensive personal journals and Anglican parishes hold extensive local records.

The interpretation of such documents is the concern of the historian
and demands a historical sense of the influences upon the original
authors that will be reflected in the way they have written or presented
information. Oral histories within local churches are also of considerable importance to show how personal views frame the interpretation
of events. Such oral histories may be collected, recorded and interpreted in the study of the local church.

Interviews

Interviews with individuals

Interviews are data-gathering conversations, guided by the researcher,
with selected individuals from a particular target population. The
sample is usually determined either by setting quotas to represent key

known characteristics of the population, or by 'snowballing', where contacts recommend other contacts. Interviews can be highly structured with a predetermined interview schedule, although this may discourage subjects from raising other relevant issues, or unstructured and free-flowing, which can yield richer data, but be more difficult to analyse. Semi-structured interviews use schedules, but with flexibility and openness to the interviewee's agenda. The interviewer needs to set the interviewee at ease and encourage participation, yet be able to probe and clarify. It is important to avoid using leading questions; otherwise interviewees may merely echo the researcher's own agenda. Normally interview material will be treated confidentially and with anonymity. With the subject's permission, interviews can be recorded and later transcribed for analysis. Analysis of the interviews entails careful coding of the data in terms of themes and concepts, which is often best done collaboratively, looking for emergent patterns and taking into account, even revising, one's original research question.

Interviews with groups

Group interviews entail interviewing a number of people at the same time. As with individual interviews, the questions and responses are usually an exchange between researcher and interviewees, except 'focus groups', which are topic-led group discussions. Group interviews can be quicker and more effective than a series of individual interviews. Interaction with other participants can help individuals, as in real life, flesh out and nuance their viewpoints, making for richer, more differentiated data. It can be easier for individuals to volunteer emotionally charged or painful information in the context of a supportive group; on the other hand, peer group pressure can sometimes inhibit responses: male teenagers may, for instance, be reluctant to talk about their religious beliefs in front of their friends. The researcher may find it difficult to control the direction of the discussion. Recording and analysis of group interviews can be challenging: it can be difficult to differentiate individual voices, especially when individuals interrupt and talk over each other. It is preferable to have two interviewers, with the first concentrating on facilitating the discussion and the second recording the data.

Further reading

Berg, Bruce L. (2001) *Qualitative Research Methods for the Social Sciences*, London: Allyn and Bacon.

Journaling

Keeping a journal aids awareness of oneself as a researcher and helps identify the precommitments that are brought to the research. A journal enables continual reflection upon practice by turning lived experiences into a written account which then becomes available for further analysis. Those who use this method will try to write regularly. They will often include other material, like newspaper cuttings, passages from novels or reflections on films and creative writings that throws a different light on the research question. A journal can offer the opportunity for theological reflection by providing the opportunity to engage with biblical or theological writing. To gain the most from this method of reflection during a research project, it is important regularly to review what has been written to identify recurring patterns and to allow new insights to emerge. In a journal crucial questions can emerge that can be referred to a supervisor, tutor or other 'sounding board' as part of ongoing analysis and reflection.

Further reading

Osborn, L. (1988) *Dear Diary: An Introduction to Spiritual Journalling*, Nottingham: Grove Books Limited.
Coffey, A. (1999) *The Ethnographic Self: Fieldwork and the Representation of Identity*, London: Thousand Oaks, New Delhi: Sage Publications.
Graham, E., H. Walton and F. Ward (forthcoming 2005) *Theological Reflection*, (two volumes), London: SCM-Canterbury Press.

Reflective Practice

Reflective practice describes an approach to research and learning that encourages the development of critical thinking in research and professional practice. It is based on the assumption of lifelong learning: that practitioners continue to learn and develop by reflection on experience. Reflective practice can foster creative interaction between experience and learning, enhance professional practice and problem-solving skills, and develop self-awareness and creativity. It can take a number of forms. A group working together can provide good cross-fertilization of ideas and aid problem-solving. Creative writing (Bolton, 2001) is another valuable way of deepening the quality of lifelong learning in a given situation. Keeping a journal or using the stages of the praxis cycle outlined above are other recognized methods. Reflective practice facilitates a questioning attitude that is able to identify and challenge assumptions and explore other perspectives.

Further reading:

Bolton, G. (2001) *Reflective Practice: Writing and Professional Development*, London, California, New Delhi: Paul Chapman Publishing.
Brookfield, S. (1987) *Developing Critical Thinkers*, Milton Keynes: Open University Press.
Moon, J. (2000) *Reflection in Learning and Professional Development: Theory and Practice*, London: Kogan Page.
Schön, D. (1983) *The Reflective Practitioner*, New York: Basic Books.
Ward, F. (2005) *Lifelong Learning: Supervision and Theological Education*, London: SCM-Canterbury Press.

Surveys

Surveys collect standardized data about people's characteristics, behaviour, attitudes or opinions, normally by means of questionnaires. Survey data, if properly collected, should be reliable and repeatable and can be statistically analysed to test hypotheses, detect patterns and correlations and investigate potential causal links. If it is impracticable to survey all the individuals relevant to the research, a representative sample is surveyed. Researchers should be well-informed about their research area, in order to formulate appropriate questionnaire items. The design of the questionnaire is driven by the research question conceptualized by potentially relevant factors.
Individual questions translate these key concepts into areas for

objective measurement. It is important to avoid leading questions, which lead the respondent in one direction, or ambiguous ones that ask two or more things simultaneously. If possible, the survey should be pre-tested in a small-scale pilot study. Questions may be *open*, for respondents to answer as they wish, or *closed*, with a restricted choice of answers. Closed questions are standardized and easier to quantify, but may be differentially interpreted and fail to capture fully nuanced responses. Survey reliability is increased by having a large enough sample and by maximizing the response by following up non-respondents.

Further reading

May, T. (1997) 'Social Surveys: Design to Analysis', in T. May (ed.) *Social Research*, Buckingham: Open University Press, pp. 81–108.

Time Line

A time line enables a local church to reflect upon its history and present corporate identity. The researcher draws together a diverse cross-section of members to pool their memories of a particular period in the life of the church. A piece of plain wallpaper, affixed to a wall, with time segments marked vertically, will cover the period under discussion. It is best to stay within living memory, although key dates in the more distant past, which had a decisive impact upon the congregation can also be included. The paper needs also to be divided horizontally to denote the local, the denominational, the national and the global.

The exercise works best if participants are encouraged to work as a group and contribute their memories as they occur, stimulating each other to remember. If the time line is left in place, others can be asked to contribute on future occasions. When the time line is completed, time can be spent with the original group or with the whole congregation exploring the significance of what has been charted.

Further reading

Ammerman, N., J. Carroll, et al. (1998) *Studying Congregations: A New Handbook*, Nashville: Abingdon Press, pp. 209ff.

A Vicinity Walk

A very useful exercise to deepen knowledge of the vicinity of the local church is to walk around the area, or around the church itself, to observe the local context. This can be particularly helpful if the area is overfamiliar, as things taken for granted can be seen with new eyes. It is important to take a notebook, and write down any observations. For other perspectives it can enrich your observations to take with you someone who does not know the area, or someone who is elderly, or a parent with a young child, and ask them what they see, what they like, what they find difficult. This exercise can be repeated at intervals over a number of months or years, and comparisons made, to provide a record of the changing context in which the church is located.

Further reading

Ammerman, N., J. Carroll, et al. (1998) *Studying Congregations: A New Handbook*, Nashville: Abingdon Press, pp. 47–50.
de Certeau, M. (1984) *The Practice of Everyday Life*, Berkeley, CA: University of California Press, Part 3, 'Spatial Practices', and Chapter 7, 'Walking in the City'.

2.4 The Research Process

Helen Cameron

This section is intended as an annotated checklist for planning research. It recognizes that those using this handbook will come with different levels of experience. The editors have thought about what is distinctive about conducting research in local churches, and the checklist reflects that emphasis. Not all the items will be relevant to all situations, so three books are recommended that offer further reading.

There are two common problems in the timing of research. One is to underestimate the amount of time it takes to set up a research project and get the necessary permissions and agreements. Another is to underestimate the time needed to analyse and write up the results. Often there is a period when the researcher is overwhelmed by data and needs time to see the wood for the trees. This section is presented as a sequential list, but in real life some steps may take place at the same time, or in a different order, or need to be repeated.

Who Will Conduct the Research?

For university students studying a local church in order to write a dissertation, it is likely they will conduct the research alone. The research is most likely to follow the academic agenda of the student rather than the interests of the church. This may also apply to those training for ministry although there is a greater likelihood that, with them, the church will want to be involved in setting the purpose of the research and getting feedback on the results. When ministers, lay leaders or members of a local church decide to study some aspect of their own life together, the decisions about who to involve will carry more significance for the impact of the research. Should someone from outside the church be involved either as an expert or companion? Should a group from within the church steer the research? Who should be on such a group? Who has the skills, time and motivation to gather data, analyse and give feedback?

Finally, the research may be initiated by another organization seeking to work with the local church. It may want to control the purpose of the research or it may want to agree the purpose collaboratively. The church will need to think about the most appropriate way to respond to such an approach.

Agreeing the Purpose of the Research

Churches do not often see themselves as subjects of research. They might be reluctant for fear of intrusion into the private lives of members, or be uncertain about why they could be of interest to a researcher. Clarity about the purpose of the research can help its acceptance. Three purposes are suggested here, but there may well be others, and some research may have more than one purpose:

- To add to the store of academic knowledge about the local church.
- To assist in the training of someone who will work in the local church.
- To stimulate reflection about some aspect of the life of the local church with the aim of making changes.

Identifying a Research Question

Deciding what you want to find out gives focus to the research. It prevents time wasted gathering data that will not be used. It ensures that the research project is realistic given the time and resources available. The research question will need to relate to your overall purpose in conducting the research, and it will shape the methods you use.

The best research questions tend to emerge from discussion and debate. 'What is it we really want to find out?' is a question that can helpfully be asked a number of times.

Reviewing What Is Already Known

It is always worth reviewing what is already known about your research question. It saves duplicating work and can suggest new questions and methods you hadn't considered earlier. In Chapter 3 below, the contributors discuss the existing research on local churches and point to other material they have found useful, although this is necessarily a limited overview of what has been published, mostly as academic research. You may also find unpublished studies or the dissertations of students useful.

Selecting Disciplines and Methods

This handbook uses four academic disciplines (anthropology, sociology, organizational studies and practical theology) to study the local church. Each discipline has different insights to offer and tends to favour some methods and models of enquiry over others. Reading Sections 2.1 and 2.2 will give you an overview of possibilities. So for example, if you are interested in church members' attitudes to evangelism, theological and sociological approaches may be particularly helpful. If you are interested in the way in which the church building supports or hinders the mission of the church, the anthropological and organizational approaches may have something to offer.

Your initial decisions are to help you focus the research. You may come back to other disciplines and ideas as you seek to interpret your data.

Learning or Piloting the Methods

Where there is more than one researcher or the solo researcher is new to research, it makes sense to learn how to undertake the research methods before embarking on the main research project. Even experienced researchers pilot their project to spot any pitfalls before beginning the full research venture. Piloting can test things such as the wording of questions, the time it will take to fill in a questionnaire, or the best way of recording data.

Gaining Access to a Local Church

For those already attached to a local church it may be tempting to skip over this point and assume you have the permission to proceed. However, all researchers need to be aware that local churches will have different decision-making processes and varying expectations about who should be consulted before research is undertaken. Failure to seek permission and negotiate about confidentiality, research questions and research outcomes may well undermine the success of your research. Find out at an early stage what the timescales are likely to be for reaching a decision. Some committees may only meet once a quarter and this can build delays into the research. Don't assume that because the minister is supportive of the research no further decision-making processes will be required. If you are a student you will also need to check whether your research proposal needs to be cleared by a university or department ethics committee.

Agreeing Confidentiality

It can be important to agree appropriate levels of confidentiality if people are going to talk frankly. However, don't promise more confidentiality than can realistically be offered. Offering confidentiality to individual respondents is fine, but there are often key people who will be able to be identified by their replies. If replies are analysed statistically there may be some small numbers that enable individuals to be identified. Offering confidentiality to local churches who are part of a larger study or who will be mentioned in an academic publication is also fine, but it can be very difficult to disguise the identity of an individual church. My own experience is that I had to withhold the name of the town in which congregations were located to be sure their identity couldn't be guessed.

If the purpose of the research is to help a church reflect upon itself, it may be important that responses are from named people so that it is clear who would support new developments.

Agreeing the Research Question

The extent to which the research question is negotiated with the church will depend upon the purpose of the research. A student may want a high level of control of the research question and the church may be happy to grant that control, having negotiated the level of confidentiality offered. Research undertaken to further the work of the church will need to be negotiated more thoroughly.

Agreeing what Benefits the Church will Gain from the Research

As a matter of courtesy, feedback on the results of the research should always be offered. Respondents should know what will happen to the data they provide and how the church will learn about the final results. If the purpose of the research is to further the work of the church then planning how the research will be discussed and acted upon needs to be part of the discussions.

Attending Worship

Most local churches see the services of worship they provide as their most important activity and one which conveys their beliefs and values. Most worship is open to the public. This raises questions as to whether researchers who do not belong to the church concerned should attend worship during the course of the research. It will be important that the researcher makes it clear whether they are attending worship in order to observe it as part of the data collection or whether they are attending as a way of familiarizing themselves with the church. My experience was that congregants appreciated the researcher making an effort to attend some services of worship, seeing it as a sign of respect for something that was important to them. However, I also realized that it was impossible to attend worship without making some observations that influenced the research.

Conveying the Researcher's Identity and Purpose

Most local churches seek to be friendly and welcoming places. People often know each other well and so are quick to spot newcomers. Because relationships in local churches are seen as part of people's private lives, people will be quick to ask newcomers personal questions about their family life and associations with church life. Researchers need to reflect what information about themselves they wish to share and how they will describe the purpose of the research. Where the researcher is already involved in the church, it may be important to be clear when they have their 'researcher' hat on so that congregants know which conversations will count as 'data'.

Gathering Data

Section 2.3 offers a range of methods that can be used to gather data and points to further reading. During the process of gathering data, it is common for ideas to arise about its interpretation. A research journal can record these thoughts so they can be reviewed during the data analysis.

Analysing Data

For the solo researcher this may be done alone and conclusions drawn before any feedback is given. For collaborative research and research aiming to stimulate action it is valuable to get a group of people to look at the data. It is important to ensure that conclusions drawn can be justified by the data and that findings are not exaggerated.

Making Links back to what Is Already Known

A helpful part of analysing data can be to relate it to what is already known. At this point, links to other ideas and disciplines not envisaged at the outset may become apparent and they can be used to enrich the presentation of the research. A common outcome of research is that the problem is understood differently and new questions arise which then change the way people think about the situation.

Presenting the Research

If the research is done for academic purposes there are likely to be clear guidelines. If there is to be feedback to the church, careful thought is needed about what will be accessible and what will be effective. Are people comfortable with statistical data? Will people read a document? If so, how long should it be? Or would a verbal presentation and discussion work better?

Fulfilling Commitments Made to the Church

As the research draws to a close, it is important to revisit the purpose of the research, the research question and any undertakings that have been given to the church about confidentiality and research outcomes. To fail to fulfil commitments can make it more difficult for research to be done in the future. It will also make it difficult for the outcomes of the research to gain sufficient respect to form the basis for action.

From Research to Action

If the purpose of the research was to stimulate action then the process by which the outcomes of the research are considered is vital. It is too easy for a research report to gather dust: perhaps because it is too long; doesn't reach clear conclusions; isn't expressed in a way which the congregants can grasp; or hasn't been open to challenge throughout the process. If key people change during the research process then it may be necessary to loop back to the stages of access and negotiation. If theological reflection has not been built into the process of the research, it can be valuable to undertake it at this point.

Further reading

If you have access to a university library you will easily locate other similar books if these ones are not available.

Bell, J. (1993) *Doing Your Research Project: A Guide for First-Time Researchers in Education and Social Science*, Milton Keynes: Open University.

A popular guide used widely by students.

Dawson, C. (2002) *Practical Research Methods: A User-Friendly Guide to Mastering Research Techniques and Projects*, Oxford: How To Books.

A straightforward guide, low on jargon and useful for those not doing research for academic reasons.

Denscombe, M. (2002) *Ground Rules for Good Research*, Buckingham: Open University Press.

A more detailed discussion of what makes good research. It contains helpful checklists that would guide a larger research project.

2.5 Conclusion

We hope this chapter of the handbook will have introduced you to the practicalities of research. Local churches are distinctive organizations, and offer a wide range of exciting possibilities for study. The purpose of research needs careful thought if questions are to be formulated with clarity and the processes of data-gathering, analysis of outcomes, feedback and consequent action are to work effectively for all concerned. In the next chapter you will discover more about how others have studied the local church, with different perspectives on

* the context
* worship and action
* people and resources
* power,

four different aspects of church life, each considered within the four disciplinary approaches that inform this handbook.

3

Perspectives on the Local Church

3.0 Introduction

While Christianity's adaptability has afforded missionary success over the centuries, degrees of creative tension often accompany periodic desires for revitalization, reform, reorganization and renewal. This is true today. To offer some grasp of the forces at work in this complex life of local churches, this chapter brings together diverse yet complementary perspectives derived from anthropology, sociology, organizational studies and theology. Though these possess a style and particular theoretical concerns of their own, together they provide a cluster of ideas to help see how local churches worship, manage resources and handle power through local church organization while maintaining a sense of universality.

3.1 Global and Local Context

Christianity's complexity lies partly in the fact that believers speak of it both as a single, unified faith and as a diverse set of churches, denominations, sects and movements. In this section, an anthropological view explores these points through the narrative stories churches tell of their place in the world, while the sociological emphasis falls on the national context of local congregational studies. Organizational studies highlights a series of ideas of how local networks may be conceived and managed, while the theological account reaffirms the universal framework for local Christianity through a novel view of catholicity.

Anthropological Strand – Context

Simon Coleman

Introduction

In many ways, churches are perfect places of study for anthropologists. Our discipline focuses on the small-scale study of 'bounded' groups; and we use 'participant-observation' to observe human behaviour, which means that we engage intensively with a group for up to a year or more, attempting to understand and appreciate the rationale behind other people's ways of thinking and acting, even – or perhaps especially – if they are different from our own. I remember once as a young PhD student, studying a Pentecostalist church in Sweden, meeting an elder of the church in the congregation's café and hearing (with a combination of gratification and embarrassment) him praise 'our English brother' for his constant presence in church and willingness to help out on all occasions. The gratification was caused by the sense that I was becoming a part of the 'culture' I was studying, even though it certainly was not my own; but the embarrassment came from my awareness that anthropology must always have a double motive: I was happy to participate in church activities ranging from translating sermons into English for visitors, to tobogganing with the church's youth group, but I was also there to observe, to gain a rounded picture of the church before converting my observations into an ethnographic text.

Such a technique of study involves developing a relatively close relationship with informants. As such, it is qualitative rather than quantitative. Anthropologists do use statistics and occasionally we generate testable hypotheses, but our main aim is first to interpret the cultures we study, to attempt as far as possible to see such cultures 'from the inside' as well as in their social, economic and political contexts; and then, second, to compare cultures across time and space. Thus, in studying a contemporary church in Sweden, I was also comparing it with a newer charismatic church in the same city; with other Pentecostal churches in Sweden, past and present; and even with churches and religious rituals from other parts of the world. The aim was to see what was unique to the church, and what was more general to human worship elsewhere.

Such comparisons illustrate the opportunities but also the problems associated with the idea of studying a local church. What exactly does 'local' mean? Any given congregation is of course 'located' in a given place, but it will have many frames of reference that extend beyond its own borders: to other churches of the same denomination, or for instance to Christians whom it might have sent out for missionary purposes. Ultimately, the members of a congregation may well feel a kinship with the whole 'body of Christ'. They are naturally likely to feel allegiances to a region and nation, but these allegiances may be contradicted by adherence to the tenets of a world religion such as Christianity, whose truths and texts are believed precisely to transcend time and space in their relevance and application. Issues relating to identities and identifications are grist to the mill of anthropologists, who are concerned with such topics as social and cultural boundaries, forms of belonging, local meanings, identity and language. They also underlie much of what I shall be writing here, as I try to show how the insights of anthropologists – indeed, of all those who write ethnography – can be used not only for the benefit of other academics, but also for people who live and work in congregations as active Christians.

I need to make one more introductory point before going on, and it relates to the issue of 'belief'. As social scientists, no matter what our personal convictions may be, we must remain as theologically neutral as possible: our discipline is concerned to understand the social functions and effects, rather than the truth-value, of any given religion. Let me refer to a famous definition of religion, now almost a century old, by a social theorist who greatly influenced sociological and social anthropological studies of religion. Emile Durkheim (1858–1917) was the son of a rabbi who broke with the Jewish religion, but who remained concerned to understand the societal importance of religion. He concluded in his classic *The Elementary Forms of the Religious Life* (Durkheim, 1915/1995) that religion was a system of beliefs and practices relative to sacred things, which united adherents into a single moral community. Notice what Durkheim focuses on in this definition. He does not talk of God, but of a kind of action – the tendency of religion to divide between the sacred and profane. Moreover, religion is shown to be about practice as well as belief, actions as well as ideas. And we see how religion is said to function to create social integration: it is defined not in terms of specific dogmas, but in terms of what it does. The effect of the definition is not to deny the existence of God, but simply to deny the relevance of the question to the social sciences.

How, then, can we trace the anthropological analysis of the church? Following Durkheim, we need to look at how churches create particular kinds of social world that perform certain functions – functions which may or may not be immediately obvious to members. We also need to understand how such social groups are part of wider cultural and societal contexts. Perhaps unlike Durkheim, we need to realize that any social grouping, even a church, is likely to be characterized by internal tensions and contradictions as well as attempts at integration.

In the following, I focus my comments on the topics of narrative, memory and place within local and global contexts. Each of these will be concerned with the social and cultural significance of churches as organizations. Interestingly, anthropologists do not have a long history of writing about Christianity. For many scholars throughout the century-long history of the discipline, Christianity was simply too close to home – seen as a religion of western culture rather than of the people to be studied. However, not only are Christianity and its churches increasingly evident in societies around the world, but we have come to realize that our own institutions are just as 'exotic' – in need of explanation and contextualization – as anybody else's.

Narrative

Why study narrative? First of all, let us establish what is meant by the term. Put briefly, narrative analysis looks at how people construct and deploy stories to interpret the world. As such, narratives are invaluable to anthropologists who are keen to understand how a culture appears from the perspective of those whom they study. Thus, ethnographers do not listen to narratives assuming that they are factually 'true' (although they may be): they see them rather as socially constructed forms that reflect the cultural assumptions of the speaker or writer. Everybody tells stories, whether they are at the top or the bottom of any given social hierarchy, and such stories help to construct a person's individual or group identity, representing themselves to themselves and to others. Social life can therefore be said to be 'storied', with some narratives becoming public property, to be circulated and perhaps subtly altered in each telling and retelling.

One might argue that church life is built around one, central narrative: that of the Bible. Biblical narrative not only provides the subject for sermons and readings, it also lies at the basis of the organization of the church year. It therefore provides a prime source of other narratives that Christians tell each other and, on occasion, non-Christians. The ways in which a believer, or set of believers, tell biblical stories can reveal much about the theological, as well as the cultural, assumptions of the speaker.

Here, however, I want briefly to explore one way in which the Bible becomes 'storied' in any given church, and I do so by reference to a key term: indexicality. This term marks the extent to which a statement refers to the specific context in which it occurs, to the circumstances, assumptions, concerns and even history of the listener or listeners. Consider the stark contrast between two forms of speaking that may go on in a church service. In one form, the priest talks in Latin to a 'flock' who do not understand what is being said, but know that the language used is sacred and ancient. Here, words may refer to the Christian story but it can be argued that their primary function is to establish a sense of legitimacy and even awe in relation to liturgy. In the other form, a preacher may say to his or her congregation: 'God is a father to humanity, just as you are fathers and mothers to your children, as we discussed last week when we were talking about Mr and Mrs Brown and their son John, who is here with us today . . .' Here (risking bathos), the preacher is not only referring to assumptions held in common by the congregation, but explicitly building connections between biblical example and contemporary circumstances – and moreover not only referring to listeners' general role as parents, but also to statements that were made to the same group of people only a few days earlier.

The contrast between these two forms of speaking reflects more than just possible theological differences: it reveals the different strategies that may be used at different times by an authoritative speaker – whether to appeal to the generic and the more obviously transcendent, or whether to appeal to the particular and indeed the local. The former refers in a sense to the body of Christ; the latter to the specific body of people gathered there 'today': each creates and reinforces different kinds of social boundaries. The very fact that the speaker does not need to explain who 'Mr and Mrs Brown' are acts as a means of reminding the community, even if implicitly, that they hold much personal history in common.

In a way, this contrast is also embodied in two of the ways that the Bible is used in many church services: simple readings from the Bible present biblical language without comment; sermons, on the other hand, are precisely ways in which the preacher acts as a mediator between biblical narratives and congregational narratives, linking the two in ways that can be seen as indexical.

Similar shifts have been evident in debates over Bible translations in this and other countries. For instance, the move from a King James Version to a much more up-to-date translation is likely to remove the 'awe' from the text, but will also make it more readily accessible in the present. This act of moving between the generic and the particular is perhaps presented in its most heightened form in the conversion narrative commonly deployed by evangelical Protestants. Often, the speaker tells a story of how 'Jesus came into my life', in effect juxtaposing the self with a biblical exemplar, before, of course, moving from the first person into the second person: 'Are you ready to take Jesus into your life?'

More generally, and across theological divides, it might be said that narratives are drawn on by ordinary members of churches in more fragmentary but still significant ways. People do not have to sermonize to invoke the biblical narratives that are important in so many churches: they may simply mention half a biblical verse, call somebody else a 'Good Samaritan', and so on, for a range of shared references to be evoked. Furthermore, we should not assume that all of a congregation's sustaining narratives will refer to the Bible. As communities of people that are often relatively stable, churches create funds of narratives that are resources of commonality (though sometimes also of tension).

The argument has also been made that any given congregation develops a coherent and unique 'story' of its own, giving a pattern and coherence to all of the church's activities, placing it into a wider context, and giving meaning to adherence. Naturally, members may plug into such a common narrative to a greater or lesser extent, so that processes of inclusion inevitably go along with those of exclusion.

Memory

This sense of a common fund of stories links to my second characterization of churches: as 'sites of memory'. Some social scientists would argue that churches act as key repositories of historical consciousness for society as a whole. According to this logic, the fact that western society seems (from one perspective) to be becoming progressively more and more dechristianized is not necessarily because we have suddenly become self-conscious rationalists, but because our society is no longer able to sustain the collective traditions and memories it once had. Ironically, in such circumstances churches are both more threatened and in a sense more important than ever before in providing possible ways in which to challenge our progressive societal amnesia.

Here, I want to pursue the idea of memory in two slightly different ways, however. The first refers to churches not only as repositories for stories that may reinforce a sense of mutual belonging, but also to rituals and other embodied actions that are key to the maintenance of community. Here, I invoke a concept taken from, among other people, the French anthropologist Pierre Bourdieu (1977): that of the 'habitus'. The word, which sounds rather like 'habit', is meant to refer to a person's basically stable 'dispositions' – beliefs, recurrent and unconscious scripts for behaviour, body movements and postures that are likely to guide that person's choices of action in any given situation. Bourdieu points out that one's habitus is not a form of behaviour that can be switched on or off by the person, nor is it entirely unique to each individual since it represents inherited structures of thought and action. My point here is to note that churches can themselves inculcate aspects of a person's habitus (especially when the person grows up within the church). Membership of a congregation can mean far more than just participating in rituals in church: it may involve a wide range of ways of behaving, from the language that one speaks to the clothes than one wears.

Habitus in this sense comes close to the idea of a congregational narrative as described above. In both cases, we see how understanding the culture of a congregation goes far beyond looking at the formal Bible readings or structures of ritual: there is an inherited texture to social life within a church that is often unconsciously articulated, but still very much 'there'. I experienced this point when carrying out fieldwork in the Pentecostal church described above: members of the church 'just knew' when a member of the rival, charismatic church was sitting in the café or taking part in services, since the embodied ways of participating in worship, speaking in tongues, even holding one's Bible, were distinct.

My final perspective on the idea of memory moves me in the direction of rather more overt conflict within any given church. Again, I invoke classic social theory that has influenced both anthropologists and sociologists. The German scholar Max Weber (1864–1920) talked of the various ways of justifying authority and action in the modern world. One was 'tradition', in the sense that it is possible to appeal to history and precedent; another was 'charisma' – embedded perhaps in the personality of a particularly powerful leader; and finally, there was what one might call 'rationality' – an appeal to the most efficient way of achieving a given goal. Clearly, any social situation is likely to involve a combination of these orientations, but they are often given particular flavour in the context of churches. Think, for instance, of how a Roman Catholic appeal to the historical church might contrast with a charismatic appeal to the revelation granted 'just now', perhaps through the medium of a particularly 'anointed' pastor. In reality, these are, of course, caricatures of church life, but they do point to some occasionally conflicting assumptions in decision-making: what is to prevail – the past, the character of a person, or supposedly disinterested efficiency? And which might represent God's will?

Place

Narratives, rituals, memories and so on are not articulated in a vacuum, either social or architectural. Collective worship usually 'takes place' in a building, and is therefore rooted in a physical context. The connections here with habitus are clear, and deployment of Bourdieu's concept therefore allows us – in one sense – to bypass theological differences between different senses of place. Of course it is true that, for instance, relics are important in Catholic and Orthodox contexts, invoking a sacrality associated with material culture that is mistrusted by Protestants, but even the latter may come to appreciate the memories associated with a given church building. Once one has been baptized in a building, perhaps married in it, it takes on important associations no matter how plain and functional its architecture.

The shape of a building may even change along with the attitudes of the congregation. In one non-conformist church I have visited in Sweden, I was struck by the way in which the well-established congregation used the building of a new church in 1983 to articulate a new relationship not only to theology, but also to the wider context in which the church was situated. Members of the Swedish Mission Covenant Church in Uppsala were conscious of the way in which their Pietist heritage was encased in their old church, a building whose small windows and isolated position expressed a sense of separation from the people of the city. By moving the church closer to the centre, opening out its foyer to visitors and, for instance, painting a mural of a tree in the church that echoed the trees visible outside through large windows, the congregation consciously changed its boundaries with the outside world, and perhaps even its collective habitus.

The Local and the Global

So far, I have tried to show how any church – no matter what its theological orientation – can be seen as a community encouraging its own ways of speaking, behaving and dressing. The focus has been on churches as sub-cultures within society at large. However, what happens when we examine the contemporary role of churches in the context of western societies such as the UK? What are the factors that might have an impact on churches, and how can we characterize the responses of churches to such challenges?

Only a few related points can be made here. First, there is the changing nature of community itself – what has come to be known as the idea that people continue to 'believe' in some kind of God in our society, but do not necessarily perceive the need to 'belong' to an organization that may represent a form of hierarchy, or require a regular commitment, that they are not prepared to countenance. Second, there is the fact that personal mobility has grown greatly in recent decades, enabling people to move within and even out of the country, and thus experience a series of 'localities' over time. Finally, one might argue that the consumerist ethic evident in the West has encouraged a wider assumption of choice in all areas of life, including one's church. All of these tendencies reflect wider anthropological conceptions of the impact of globalization, as belonging to a given place is now constantly called into question by increased awareness of what it might be like elsewhere.

Such developments need not imply the death of the local church, however. Rather, they represent new challenges calling for adaptation, in contexts where 'locality' might be seen as both an anachronistic constraint on cultural cosmopolitanism and a scarce resource in a world of often frightening change. A classic distinction between types of human organization can be drawn here: a 'community' or parish church is one that is concerned to look after all those within a given area, so that social action becomes as important as worship; an associational or voluntary church is one that attempts to attract people to its message – even if they must travel many miles to do so. These tensions between place and choice, locality and mobility, are – in common with Weber's forms of authority – always likely to be present in mixed form in any real-life case.

Practical Ways of Studying Churches

Participant observation as I have described it is, on one level, simply a matter of 'hanging out' in a given context such as a church. The fieldworker almost becomes part of the fabric of the place, so that informants are no longer self-conscious in the presence of a researcher. However, such hanging out is not quite as simple as it sounds, though it can be immensely rewarding. In ethical terms, the researcher needs to ensure that others are as aware as possible of what they are doing, and normally anonymity is guaranteed those discussed in an ethnography. In methodological terms, it is important for the anthropologist to gain as rounded a picture as possible of a church. It is all too easy to concentrate on obvious, visible activities such as Sunday morning services, and forget the more personal forms of piety that might be practised in smaller and more intimate circles. In churches that might be divided on theological grounds, it is important not to become too associated with any one faction, in order to ensure that all opinions are covered. Similarly, it is necessary to make sure that one does not ignore any one gender or age group. It is often a good idea to carry out participant observation for a given period, so that church members come to trust the researcher and so that key research questions can be identified, before carrying out more formal interviews or questionnaire surveys. As far as possible, congregation members should also be shown the resulting ethnography. If the researcher is already an 'insider' to the church, then the same rules apply except that the person needs to learn how to 'distance' him or herself from the church, in order to see it as a sub-culture whose assumptions need to be explained.

Case Study

Paul Chambers (2004) has written in practical terms about the relative fate of three Anglican congregations in the Welsh town of 'Dockside' (a pseudonym). His general message is that in an environment of relative religious decline, the churches have succeeded in maintaining a continuing presence in the working-class community. One congregation, 'St John's', has even experienced significant numerical growth: Why?

The answer has a number of dimensions:

- A vicar who appears to come from the same kind of community as the parishioners, and who understands the call of family as opposed to church on many occasions.

- A recognition that internal divisions within the church, e.g. between liberals and evangelicals, need to be managed so that conflict does not become endemic.
- The use of group projects such as improving buildings, not only to develop facilities, but also to restore confidence and encourage participation on the part of parishioners.
- Allowing local social networks based on kinship, friendship and neighbourhood to achieve expression in the church.
- Permitting local community use of church resources, including educational and recreational activities.
- Mission through sustained contact with the local congregation, rather than aggressive missionizing.

Of course, this recipe for success is based on a particular kind of church in a particular kind of area, but it does illustrate the importance of a social principle that is central to many of the viable social contexts examined by anthropologists: the existence of cross-cutting ties between people. In contexts where the church – as has been suggested in this contribution as a whole – can become a multidimensional place where people can co-operate and realize interests on a number of levels, a greater level of stability is likely to occur.

Further reading

Guest, M., K. Tusting and L. Woodhead (eds) (2004) *Congregational Studies in the UK: Christianity in a Post-Christian Context*, Aldershot: Ashgate.
  Contains chapters on a variety of congregations, mostly in the UK, and includes a useful summarizing introduction in which British and American work on congregations is described and assessed.
Hopewell, James (1987) *Congregation: Stories and Structures*, London: SCM Press.
  Written by an American theologian, puts forward the idea that every congregation has its story and set of distinctive meanings.
Jenkins, Tim (1999) *Religion in English Everyday Life*, New York and Oxford: Berghahn Books.
  Written by an Anglican anthropologist, presents a broadly

Durkheimian case for the close integration between congregation and local community.

Riessman, C. K. (1993) *Narrative Analysis*, London: Sage.
A useful introduction to the field of narrative analysis.

Toulis, N. (1997) *Believing Identity: Pentecostalism and the Mediation of Jamaican Ethnicity and Gender in England*, Oxford: Berg.
An ethnographic account of African-Caribbean Pentecostalism in Birmingham, focusing on issues of identity and secular versus spiritual citizenship.

Sociological Strand – Context

Linda Woodhead

Introduction

Congregations do not exist in isolation. Even those that try hardest to shut out the potentially disruptive influences of the outside world cannot help but be affected by the wider contexts in which they find themselves. These contexts may be viewed as a series of concentric circles, ranging from the local to the global.

Accordingly, we begin by looking at the salience of the local context for congregational studies, before moving on to the national context. The possible meanings of both the 'local' and the 'national' will be considered, and examples of possible engagement with these contexts will be introduced. Moving upscale, we introduce 'western culture' as a context that can often be of relevance to congregational study, and isolate some recent cultural trends that the latter may take into account, including the shift to 'Post Materialism' and the 'subjective turn'. Next the 'global' context comes under the spotlight, and some examples are given of studies that situate their congregations in global contexts.

With the journey through the possible contexts of congregational study complete, we profile the debate between those who believe that congregations should be viewed in context, and those who prefer an 'intrinsic' approach that focuses more exclusively on the life of the congregation itself. We end with examples and suggestions for those who wish to study congregations in context.

The Local Context

All the contexts within which a congregation may be located are socially constructed. Rather than being straightforwardly determined by physical features of a landscape, human beings decide what is to count as the local, the national, the cultural and the global – and the boundaries are often contested. Christianity has played an important part in constructing the idea of a 'local' context, with a key role being played in England first by the Catholic Church and then by the Church of England. The parochial system that gradually came into existence during the Middle Ages divided up local space into a comprehensive network of ecclesiastical oversight. The boundaries of the parish gradually came to define the boundaries of the local; in many rural areas today they still do. But the growth of towns and cities complicated the churches' neat division of the country into parishes and dioceses and created new sorts of local boundary. Today people in smaller towns are likely to identify the local with the town boundaries, while city-dwellers will often have in mind the area around their home with its own small 'centre', perhaps a shopping area or a park, and array of essential institutions – school, doctor's surgery, supermarket and so on. For others, of course, 'the local' is the pub!

In studying congregations, it is usually best to consider the local context as the area most residents consider 'local'. This will usually be roughly co-terminous with the catchment area of a congregation, even though there will always be some people who are willing to travel further distances to go to church. Cathedrals and 'megachurches', for example, draw on much larger areas. Local contexts are of relevance to congregations and those who study them, precisely because they contain the majority of a congregation's actual and potential clientele. For this reason they are of particular interest to those who are interested in church growth. The massive 'Congregations in Changing Communities' project in the USA, whose findings were published by Ammerman (1997), furnishes a good example of an academic project which looks in detail at a range of congregations and the local contexts in which they are situated. The study concludes that a congregation's ability to adapt to the changing needs of its local population, or some significant section of it, is a key factor affecting growth or decline.

For 'community studies' the local area is *the* main focus of concern, and congregations are studied for the light they can shed on communities rather than vice versa (as in Margaret Stacey's study of Banbury; Stacey, 1960). Tim Jenkins' *Religion in English Everyday Life* (1999) is influenced by this approach as well as by anthropological method, and studies two congregations as integral parts of the communities in which they are situated. The theoretical underpinning of Jenkins' method derives from the work of Emile Durkheim, who understood religion as the place where a society affirms its core values and consolidates itself through collective action and emotion.

Although local society might once have been a place where residents lived out the main part of their lives together with friends and kin, this can no longer be assumed. Individuals may now work and spend leisure time outside their local area, and their networks of friends and family may be vastly more extended. This does not mean that the importance of religion as a focus of local social cohesion necessarily disappears, but it does mean that this function is likely to be of reduced relevance for a large number of congregational members and potential members. For those studying congregations it means that the importance of the relationship between congregation and local context must be investigated rather than assumed.

The National Context

If this were a handbook for congregational studies in the USA rather than the UK, it might be more natural to progress from looking at the local context to considering the national context. There are historical reasons for this. American religion and the American nation developed hand-in-hand, as both grew up in an era of nation-states. By contrast, Christianity established a dominant place in Britain before nationhood in the modern sense had been established. In the pre-Reformation era the Catholic Church was supranational rather than national, and the Reformation attempt to create a national church (the Church of England) was never completely successful – not least because more than half the churchgoing population have been 'dissenters' since at least the mid-nineteenth century. For this and for other reasons, including rapid church decline since the 1960s and the creation of the European Union, Christianity in Great Britain is somewhat less closely bound up with national identity than in the USA.

Congregational studies from either side of the Atlantic often reflect this difference. In the USA they are often concerned not only with the health of the church but with the health of the nation. Robert Bellah and co-authors' *Habits of the Heart* (1985) was an attempt to take the moral temperature of American society, and research within religious congregations was an integral part of the study. Similarly, Nancy Ammerman's *Congregations and Community* (1997), mentioned above, concludes with a long discussion of congregations' ability to provide 'social capital' in the USA. Studies like the latter are often funded by trusts that give money for the express purpose of supporting congregational life in order to strengthen American society.

Although this pragmatic concern with congregations as building blocks of a stable and 'healthy' society is much less common in the UK, there are a number of studies that look at congregations within a national context. Their concern is not with the health of the nation, but with understanding how what is happening to congregational religion relates to the broader national picture. Michael Hornsby-Smith's studies of British Catholicism, such as *The Changing Parish* (Hornsby-Smith, 1989), furnish one example, though such work inevitably has a pan-national denominational as well as a national focus. Paul Heelas and Linda Woodhead (2005) also relate their study of congregations in the town of Kendal, Cumbria, to what is happening in Britain as a whole. They are particularly concerned to relate patterns of congregational decline at the local level to the national level. Such contextualization has been greatly assisted by the large-scale surveys of churchgoing in England, Scotland and Wales that have been carried out by Peter Brierley every ten years since 1979 (e.g. Brierley, 2000).

Even if attention is paid to the national context, it is worth remembering that what counts as national within the British Isles is far from straightforward. Since constituent parts of the United Kingdom are nations in their own right, it may be as appropriate to consider congregations in a Welsh, Scottish or Northern Irish, as in a British context.

The Context of 'Western Culture'

What is happening to congregations at the local level may be bound up not only with national trends, but also with wider cultural change. For this reason congregational studies may wish to broaden their focus beyond the local and even the national to consider what is happening at the scale that may be referred to as that of 'western culture'.

Without denying local and national differences and specificities, the idea that there are more widely shared cultural norms and values has been given empirical grounding by studies like those of Ronald Inglehart (1997), based on analysis of successive rounds of European and World Values Surveys. Inglehart discovers the growing influence of a shared set of 'Post Materialist' values which have more to do with improving the quality of one's own subjective life and experiences than with accumulating material goods and security. The numbers of Post Materialists in western society have grown with every generation since the early babyboomers (born in the immediate post-Second World War period). Generation X (born after 1960) is the most Post Materialist generation yet. While Post Materialists are more concerned with 'meaning of life' issues than Materialists, and more open to spirituality, they are less likely to attend church.

Findings like these concerning broad cultural trends in advanced industrial societies can be helpfully related to what is happening to congregations on the ground. Close empirical study at the local level may help confirm, or fail to confirm, claims about wider trends, thereby helping to highlight what is actually happening within the congregational domain. In the study mentioned above, for example, Heelas and Woodhead relate the idea of a 'subjective turn' in modern culture to what is happening to associational forms of religion and spirituality at the local level. On the one hand they find that congregations' reluctance to accommodate the widespread demand for the cultivation and enhancement of unique individual lives seems to be a major factor in their decline. On the other hand, they find that new forms of holistic spirituality which offer individuals help in understanding, coming to terms with, and developing their own unique subjective lives – in relation to the spiritual dimension of life – have been proliferating (and that congregations which offer most by way of subjective satisfaction are also doing best within the congregational domain).

The idea that broad cultural and social trends may have a decisive impact on the fate of congregations is nothing new, for it underlies the 'secularization theories' that have long dominated the sociology of religion. Such theories appeal to general processes of modernization such as pluralization, rationalization, and detraditionalization to explain what is happening to religion, usually Christianity, on the ground. Until recently, however, such work has been mainly theoretical. Congregational studies have an important role to play in testing out theories of secularization by way of in-depth empirical research. It is possible that new theories about processes of 'postmodernization' may also be tested in this way, for example, the idea that religion is becoming a 'pick and mix' or 'bricolage' of elements constructed by individuals according to their own personal needs.

The Global Context

Is it enough to consider only the local, national or cultural contexts in which congregations are situated? In a globalizing world, should we not also be thinking of the global context? The answer seems to be that there is not one global context, but several, and that their relevance to congregational studies depends upon the type of congregation, or congregations, under consideration.

In his study of the Word of Life congregation in Sweden, British anthropologist Simon Coleman (2000) is ineluctably drawn to consider the global context, since he finds that the sort of charismatic Christianity with which he is dealing can only be properly understood as a global movement. It is universalistic in its theology and its outlook (not least its desire to convert the whole world), global in its culture (with influences drawn from charismatic Christianity around the world), and global in its contacts. But the global context in this case is not the whole of human culture, but charismatic Christian culture. If one were looking at another form or denomination of Christianity, say an Anglican congregation, the 'global' context might take a very different form, with the worldwide Anglican communion of churches being the main referent.

It is interesting to consider the work of the British sociologist of religion David Martin in this context, for Martin has always painted on a broad canvas. His early work refined and qualified existing secularization theories by showing how the churches' fate in a particular territory was bound up with their relationship to political power. In terms of the scheme we are using here, this work indicated the significance of national contexts for congregational life. But in later works Martin extended his perspective even further, becoming one of the first to study the upsurge of charismatic Christianity in the southern hemisphere (see, for example, Martin, 2002). The global perspective he adopts to interpret this upsurge is an interesting one, for it draws a parallel between charismatic Christianity in the developing world today and Methodism in the West in the era of industrialization. What Martin's work reminds us is that congregational studies may work with not one but two dimensions: not only the geographic but also the historical – and that these may interweave in interesting ways.

Contextualization and its Critics

Not all congregational studies pay attention to the wider contexts of the congregations being researched. In some cases this is a matter of theoretical preference, based on the belief that intrinsic factors having to do with the congregation's own life are more important than contextual factors. The debate about the relative importance of intrinsic and contextual factors was provoked by the publication in 1977 of Dean Kelley's *Why Conservative Churches Are Growing*. Kelley argued that 'strictness' and 'sincerity' were the most important factors influencing the fortunes of particular congregations, and accordingly strict congregations were doing better than laxer, more liberal ones. The implication was that it is what goes on in a congregation's own life that shapes its fate. It is interesting to note that the 'intrinsic' assumption is often shared by congregations themselves, and is particularly evident in the way in which periods of success or failure in congregational life may be attributed to the actions and regime of particular clergy.

Dean Hoge and David Roozen (1979) attempted to test Kelley's assumption by using mainly quantitative studies to gauge whether there was a stronger correlation between intrinsic or contextual factors and congregational growth or decline. Their results tended to suggest that contextual factors (particularly widespread value commitments) were somewhat more important than intrinsic factors, but their findings were somewhat inconclusive. The difficulty in adjudicating the matter lies, in part, in the fact that contexts are often very difficult to disentangle, not least because widespread cultural influences are often mediated through national and local institutions and media.

As well as being of academic interest, this issue is of considerable importance to congregations themselves for according to the 'intrinsic' approach, congregations and clergy are largely responsible for their own fate. According to the 'contextual' approach, however, there may be little that a congregation can do if wider contextual factors are conspiring against it. The latter can point out that congregational fortunes are largely the function of factors beyond an individual congregation's control – how else can we explain the fact that most congregations in Britain were growing in the 1950s, but declining by the 1970s (other than by the implausible hypothesis that they all changed their behaviour in the same way at the same time?). However, even the most extreme 'contextualist' would be unlikely to claim that congregations are powerless to do anything to alter their fate, for they have the ability to take account of their wider contexts, and respond in more or less appropriate ways. This certainly does not mean that they must always 'go with the flow', for it may be more appropriate in some circumstances to resist. But it does mean that an awareness of contextual factors, perhaps mediated by congregational studies, may be of interest to congregational members as well as to those who study them.

The fact that the congregational domain in the UK has been declining steeply since the 1960s poses a – if not the – major challenge for congregational studies. A unique opportunity currently exists to study the disappearance of institutions that have been central to the religious and social landscape for many generations. Because it is always easier to study what is still there rather than what has disappeared, the natural course for congregational studies is to concentrate upon congregations that are faring relatively well – and it is certainly important to ascertain how some congregations have managed to buck the wider trend. But another option is to study a dying congregation, and to try to explain its failure (in terms of local, national or cultural factors). In order to understand congregational decline more fully it is also important to conduct research among those who have ceased to attend church, not to mention those who have never attended and have no wish to do so. As Richter and Francis' (1998) study of church leavers in the UK indicates, such study moves beyond the boundaries of congregational studies in a strict sense since it moves outside the congregational domain in order to contact those who have turned their backs on it. However, the study of 'disaffiliates' still begins with congregations – in order to track down those who have left them – and it undoubtedly makes a key contribution to congregational studies in the broadest sense.

Practical Ways of Studying the Context of the Local Church

1 Taking account of the local context

The first step is to determine what counts as the 'local' context of a congregation or congregations: guidance can be found above. It is then useful to mark out the boundaries with which one is going to operate on a detailed map of the area. Relevant socio-demographic data for the area can normally be obtained by contacting the local council. It interesting to compare this with the national picture to see how representative the area is – information is available at *www. statistics.gov.uk.*

Statistical information can be combined with 'thicker' information about the area obtained by observation and interview. It is a good idea to walk or cycle around the local area, and note down the key characteristics. Description should be narrowed down to the key pieces of information that a stranger would need to form a realistic impression of the area. Vivid examples such as graffiti on a wall, winner of the 'best kept village 2003', etc. all tell a story. It can be helpful to interview a few representative local people to try to find out what they think of the local area; it is often good to talk to those who have lived there a long time as well as more recent arrivals.

It is also interesting to consider the whole 'religious marketplace' of a local or wider area. With which other forms of sacred association – Christian, non-Christian and post-Christian – is a congregation in 'competition'? It may be useful to mark these on the map too.

Tip: It's easy to get carried away! The only point of studying the local area is as potentially important *context* for the congregation that is to be studied – not for its own sake. If there are good reasons for thinking this context is not terribly important, then it is better to take more account of contexts that *are* important.

2 Taking account of the national context

The first question is: How does the congregation that is being studied relate to the national context? The next question is: Which national context are we talking about – political, economic, social, cultural, religious, etc.?

For many studies, including studies that take account of congregational decline and growth, the national religious context may be the most salient. As mentioned above, Peter Brierley's detailed statistical surveys of churchgoing in England, Scotland and Wales are a particularly useful source of information on the national picture (see *www.christian-research.org.uk*). It is very interesting to try to build up a picture of how the numbers of Sunday attendances in a congregation have changed over time – particularly the last few decades. Some congregations keep their own records, others lodge their records in the local records' office, and others keep no records at all.

If a congregational study is concentrating on some particular angle of congregational life it may be helpful to relate *that* to the national picture. If, for example, a study is concerned with the political leanings and activities of a particular congregation, it may be illuminating to relate findings to political trends at the national level. It is helpful to consult scholarly literature that can help build up a picture of the particular national context being investigated.

3 Taking account of the cultural context

Here the question is: What is going on in the wider context and how may this be relevant to the congregation being studied?

One way of beginning to answer this question is by looking at studies of contemporary western culture, and then considering how the trends they observe may or may not be relevant to the congregation being studied. Ronald Inglehart's work has already been mentioned in this context.

Another approach is to look at the congregation itself to try to discern what cultural forces it may be reacting to. For example, if sermons and literature attack 'New Age religion', this is a clue that this particular cultural development (or the way in which it is perceived) is important in some way. To take another example, if the congregation is giving increased attention and effort to some area or activity (for example, healing ministry or counselling), it is worth considering how this relates to wider trends in the culture – for example, to the growth of activities concerned with personal wellbeing and quality of life.

Tip: Congregations may be (a) reacting against, (b) accommodating to, or (c) ignoring wider cultural trends. It is important to establish which, or which combination of these, applies to a particular congregation – and what the effect is.

4 Taking account of the global context

As explained above, the first task is to ascertain whether or not a global context is relevant for a particular congregation, and if so which one. Is the subject of study a charismatic or Pentecostal congregation that is part of a global charismatic movement? Is it an evangelical church that borrows ideas and initiatives from sources in the USA? Perhaps it is a Roman Catholic congregation that is closely connected to other aspects of this global church – e.g. to Lourdes and Rome. Does the congregation have a mission outreach to some other part of the world? Have concerns about the (global) environment had an impact on congregational life? If so – how important is the global dimension of congregational life and what impact does it have on theology and self-understanding?

Case study

In the year 2000 I joined a team of four other researchers and academics to look at associational forms of sacred activity in the town of Kendal in Cumbria. We found 25 congregations in Kendal, and selected four for in-depth study by way of participant observation, interview (around 25 formal interviews per congregation plus many informal conversations), and the administration of a questionnaire (at the end of the research project). The research took two years to plan, two years to complete, and another two years to analyse and write up.

Although we considered the relevance of local and national contexts, we found that the most important context shaping the fate of the congregations in Kendal (one of decline) was cultural. As explained above, we came to believe it was the growing cultural concern with personal and relational quality of life that was shaping the fate of the congregational domain in Kendal. We found that most of the congregations we studied were much more concerned with affirming God-given roles and rules than with helping individuals to find the sacred by way of their own unique experiences and life-paths. We concluded that this 'mismatch' with widespread cultural expectations is a major factor in congregational disaffiliation and decline.

Further reading

Guest, M., K. Tusting and L. Woodhead (eds) (2004) *Congregational Studies in the UK: Christianity in a Post-Christian Context*, Aldershot: Ashgate.

Considers the history, types and methods of congregational study in the UK (comparing them with study in the USA), and offers several recent case studies.

Heelas, P. and L. Woodhead with B. Szerszynski, B. Seel and K. Tusting (2005) *The Spiritual Revolution: Why Religion Is Giving Way to Spirituality*, Oxford: Blackwell.

Looks at congregations in the English town of Kendal, and relates their fortunes to what is happening in western culture more generally.

Warner, S. (1992) *New Wine in Old Wineskins: Evangelicals and Liberals in a Small-Town Church*, Berkeley and Los Angeles: University of California Press.

A classic study of a congregation in California which relates its life to wider trends in American religion. An example of congregational study in national context.

Organizational Studies Strand – Context

Helen Cameron and Stephen Pattison

Introduction

This section attempts to set the local church in its organizational context in four ways. First, by considering the form local churches take as organizations. Second, by outlining how changing ideas on organizations and management may affect the local church. Third, by observing the local church in its network of relationships (local, national and global) that both constrain and further its purposes. Fourth, by understanding the local church as set in time – having a relationship with past, present and future which may be woven into the stories it tells about itself. There is little empirical research that addresses these concerns and so reading that chimes with the authors' own experience will be referred to.

Summary of Key Concepts

These definitions are designed to provide a way into any material in this section that may be unfamiliar.

- *Form*

Denomination – the separate traditions within Christianity – most but not all local churches belong to a denominational structure or grouping of congregations.

Organizational form – the legal form or constitution of an organization.

Polity – the structures and processes by which authority is exercised. This varies between denominations often for historical and theological reasons.

Stakeholders – the different groups that have an interest in the success of an organization.

• *Ideas*
Authority – the legitimate power to get people to do things but within the boundaries set by the organization. Authority only really works if those subject to it accept the basis upon which it is exercised, for example rational rules, traditions, strong personalities.
Managerialism – an overoptimistic ideological belief in and commitment to, management ideas and practices as a total solution for all organizational and social problems.
Organizational spirituality – the idea that organizations have an internal as well as an external reality that needs to be nurtured and developed.
Rationality – a belief that organizational life unfolds as a result of rational decisions and processes.

• *Relationships*
Ecumenism – the name for collaborative working between churches of different denominations and the ideal of unity that underpins it.
Networks – the links between organizations and/or people by which information and resources may be exchanged.

• *Time*
Change – can come from within an organization or be triggered by its environment.
Stability – those points of continuity in organizational life that make it recognizably the same even though change has taken place.
Story – organizations have narratives that link past events and people to the present and often exemplify the character of the organization.
Tradition – the accumulation of behaviour, teaching and reflection on the Christian faith which has different emphases in different denominations.

Form

The work an organization can do is both enabled and constrained by its legal form or constitution. There is no single organizational form that local churches follow – the legal and formal rules they follow will be affected by their theological ideas and by any denominational structures to which they belong. The day-to-day operation of local churches is often highly informal and so it can be difficult to uncover formal and legal requirements (see also Organizational Studies Strand 3.4). It tends to be when big decisions need to be made that the expertise of those who understand the formalities is valued.

Definition of organizational form

The legal form an organization takes can affect the way in which:

- work is co-ordinated and managed;
- governance structures and decision-making processes render an account to stakeholders;
- the organization can secure resources;
- the assets of the organization are protected and managed;
- the organization can allocate its resources to pursue its mission;
- the organization can establish its legitimacy in the eyes of its users.

Most, but not all, local churches belong to wider church structures that are usually called denominations. The largest denominations in the UK are the Church of England, the Roman Catholic Church, the Methodist Church, the Baptist Union and the United Reformed Church. There are many other smaller groupings. The countries of Wales, Scotland and Northern Ireland have some churches and denominations that exist within their national borders as with the Church of Scotland.

Each church or denomination grouping was formed, often by breaking from another, as a result of wanting to emphasize particular theological truths and sometimes for political reasons. This is often reflected in the way in which their local branches are organized and authority exercised. The sociologist, Max Weber (Weber, 1947/1964, p. 52) observed that authority can be legitimated by tradition, charisma (personality) or rationality. However, it is also fair to say that many members of local churches place little importance on denominational differences and seek to join a local church that meets their spiritual and practical needs. Many denominations produce booklets setting out the legal rules which clergy and lay leaders are expected to follow, for example, Dudley (2002) and The Methodist Church (2003).

In seeking to undertake an organizational study of a local church, it may be difficult to get answers to the question, 'Why do you do it this way?' Indeed, more than one answer may be offered drawing on secular and/or theological ideas.

Ideas

An important part of the organizational context of any local church are the ideas about organizing that those involved hold. Some ideas are likely to be drawn from the secular world of management where clergy and congregants bring ideas of 'how to manage things' from other organizations they have worked in or belonged to (Higginson, 1996). Other ideas may be drawn from the theological beliefs of the congregation, particularly ideas about how decisions are to be made and who has the authority to ask people to do things. Because there has been little academic dialogue between management or organizational studies and theology, there are no ready models for relating these two sources of ideas. This lack of dialogue may be played out in tensions in the local church between a pragmatic concern for 'what works' and a more theological concern for 'the way we ought to work together'. Chater (1999) argues that theology can helpfully challenge management ideas by seeking to reflect upon the context of the local church and its tradition before deciding upon action. It can also challenge assumptions about what constitutes good management and offer insights about the perception and reality of success and failure.

Section 2.1 set out the different approaches that co-exist within organizational studies as an academic discipline. Ideas about management have become part of everyday culture and language, both globally and nationally. For many people, management is just the pragmatic use of a series of techniques and practices to do what needs to be done. For some, management is wholly positive and becomes an uncritical guiding ideology for the way in which they work – this is termed managerialism. For others, management is associated with unwarranted control of how people work and live and is seen as ignoring the emotional and spiritual aspects of people's lives – this is referred to as the debate about rationality in organizations. The tension between these ways of thinking can be played out in the lives of local churches.

Pattison (1997, p. 161) has produced a sustained theological critique of managerialism. He suggests that there are implicit beliefs underlying management as a system and that these beliefs need to be questioned.

Here are just a few of the fundamental beliefs and doctrines that seem to lie within much managerial practice:

- The world and other people exist for the benefit of organizational survival, exploitation and expansion.

- Human beings can control the world and create a better future if they use the right techniques.
- Individuals must be subordinate to greater goals decided by their superiors.
- Relationships are fundamentally hierarchical and require clear lines of upward accountability and downward responsibility.
- The nature and condition of work should be such as to extract the maximum from the employee.
- Everything worth doing can in some way be measured.
- The future can be planned and colonized.

Management practices cannot be treated as value-neutral for, like all practices, they are theory-laden and carry beliefs and values whether or not these are explicitly recognized as Richard Roberts (2002, chapter 2) has argued. The criticism is that management writing represents an overoptimistic understanding of human agency and ignores the constraints that frame human action. Furthermore, it implicitly supports values of maximization and exploitation without considering their long-term consequences on human flourishing and environmental sustainability.

The history of the twentieth century has illustrated the great cruelty and perversity that can be enacted in the name of formal rationality. Some would see the closing decades of the century marking an increasing reluctance to co-operate with rational-legal authority – whether signalled in the break-up of large bureaucratic employers or declining interest in political and voluntary associations. This decline in co-operation with formal rationality can be characterized in two ways.

First, what former Prime Minister Edward Heath called 'the death of deference' when responding to the satire of the political system in the television show *That Was the Week that Was* in the early 1960s. A sense that even though a politician had been elected by agreed laws, their authority could still be questioned and even ridiculed. Second, the blurring of the public–private divide that underpins the modern organization. This critique has been developed by feminist writers who noted that the modern organization was based on the premise that the male worker would be free to concentrate on the public world of work, because the private world of reproduction and household chores was being handled by women. With the entry of women into the workplace this clear divide between private and public life has been challenged although certainly not eliminated (Acker, 1992).

Some would see the 'death of deference' (Albrow, 1997), and the blurring of the private–public divide as signals of a move from a modern era, governed by a belief in rationality that would lead to an improved future, to the postmodern condition in which any overarching narrative of society is impossible. This way of thinking can be particularly challenging for those local churches that do wish to see the Christian tradition as an overarching narrative and see their role as offering hope for a better future.

The tension between different ways of thinking can often be most apparent in discussions about how the local church is to exercise authority and in particular the role of any clergy. Some may feel that clergy are professionals who are bringing their theological expertise to bear on the leading of worship and the care of church members. Others may feel that the clergy need to be good managers, ensuring that the local church is successful and growing. Still others may be seeking to move beyond these rationally based concepts and be talking more generally of leadership – relying more on the personality and ideas flowing from the leader to set the direction. Another trend is for clergy to form teams with lay people sharing the tasks involved in running the local church (Greenwood, 2000). The interaction between these ways of thinking will be shaped by the ideas about organizing that key participants contribute.

Relationships

Like most organizations, local churches have networks of relationships with other organizations. These networks are likely to be related to the different types of activity undertaken, and so it may be useful to have a typology of activities when seeking to uncover and study networks as in the following box.

This typology was developed from a study of five local churches in an English city.

Worship activity Each congregation has a pattern of worship that is expressed as its primary purpose. Without a pattern of regular meetings for worship it is impossible to describe the organization as a congregation.

Governance activities Each congregation has its own pattern of meetings and groups that undertake the governance function. In addition to this, all the congregations participate in denominational governance groups. These activities have distinctive features derived from the religious tradition to which the congregation belongs.

Core activities These are activities that seem to derive their goals directly from worship. They include: religious education; religious fellowship; lifecycle rituals (baptisms, weddings, funerals) and pastoral care. There is a high expectation that each congregation will undertake these activities.

Maintenance activities These activities tend to be the taken-for-granted activities that are necessary for the smooth running of the congregation. They include fundraising, administration, support activities for worship including the choir and arranging flowers, building maintenance, catering, communication and transport. Those activities which support worship are seen as particularly important.

Optional activities are those not found in every congregation but which some congregations have derived from their values as legitimate goals to pursue. The range of these activities is extensive but includes: public witness, youth work, social action, campaigning, mutual leisure, fundraising other than for the church, volunteering other than for the church, organized socializing and community use of premises. These activities usually depend upon congregants with a particular enthusiasm for organizing them. They tend to be secular in orientation and bring the congregation into contact with non-members. In addition, clergy or lay leaders may get involved in chaplaincy at a local institution (school, hospital, shopping centre) or represent the church on the governing body of a local voluntary organization or school (Cameron, 1998).

Each of the areas of activity mentioned above might involve interaction with local, national or global networks. Worship might be shared on special occasions with other local churches; at other times worship might be shaped by themes or lectionary set by the denomination; some churches may draw on global networks for ideas and resources they can use in worship. Even routine tasks, such as serving coffee after the service, may involve debates about using Fair Trade products and so about the relationship of the local church to global issues. Some local churches may have a sense of being part of the local voluntary sector – particularly those that engage in optional activities that involve working with other local groups. They may share concerns about availability of funding and volunteers and be interested in the actions of local policy-makers and politicians. Some local churches may see themselves as part of ecumenical networks in which different types of church co-operate for mutually agreed purposes. In some parts of the country this may extend to interfaith networks which bring together adherents of different religions for mutual understanding and shared action.

The range and complexity of networks described above may not be fully realized by the local church, but it can be a great strength in enabling them to gather and disseminate information, to influence and be influenced by their context. Often clergy act as 'boundary spanners' keeping the networks active and reflecting on the implications of the information they gain for the work of the local church. The value of these relationships and networks in the task of urban regeneration is increasingly being realized by policy-makers. It can also be unclear which of these relationships holds rights of accountability. The informality of much of church life means that there is often little sense of the organization being accountable for certain objectives – this fluidity can be a strength but it can leave partner organizations unsure of how to pin down the contribution of the local church (see also 3.2 Organizational Studies Strand).

Time

Local churches are organizations that have strongly articulated relationships with time. They transmit the Christian tradition and so have a relationship with the past. They seek to interpret the past in a way that is productive for present practice. However they are not free to abandon central elements of the tradition because they feel like it. Local churches usually have a solid commitment to the future, to being around to serve future generations and to educate the young in their faith tradition. Tensions arise when commitments to past and future seem to require different actions in the present. Local churches are some of the oldest organizations in many neighbourhoods. They have a commitment to a continuous identity and practice in one place that may not be a factor for other organizations.

This relationship with time is often expressed by stories and by statements about the character or identity of the congregation. Hopewell (1987) suggested that the stories congregations tell about themselves draw together key people and incidents into a coherent narrative that both expresses and forms the congregation's character. This links with the importance that Gabriel (2000) attaches to organizational myths as means by which organizational participants negotiate the significance of past events for the present culture of the organization. Davies has also considered how Christians evaluate and divide up time (Davies, 2002, pp. 187–92).

There is a growing awareness of the idea of organizational spirituality and the need to respect and nurture the internal identity and values of an organization so that it is a humane place to work (Pattison, 2000). It is not just individuals who may have an inner aspect to their bodily and material existence, but also organizations. People talk about there being a good spirit or atmosphere in some organizations. It might, therefore, follow that organizations corporately have spiritual characters and needs that require nurture and care if they are to flourish.

Change is an important concept in writing about organizations (Collins, 1998). Much of that writing contains managerialist assumptions that change is always a good thing, that a strong manager can bring about change and that the environment in which an organization operates can be conquered. Local churches can exhibit more ambivalent attitudes to change. For some participants the church may be valued precisely because it is a point of stability in an otherwise turbulent life. Many participants may regret the decline in church life and attribute this to changes in society or changes in the church they feel are for the worse. The Christian tradition contains different views of change (Pattison, 2004). It can be seen as an inevitable if regrettable decay, as a positive response to a divine imperative or as a feature of human existence which is transcended by God. Christian ideas about the future (eschatology) are based upon their understanding of past traditions and may give them a present commitment to survival and continuity as they seek to be faithful until 'the end of the age'.

Ways of Studying the Organizational Context of the Local Church

Observing worship and meetings of church committees can be an important way of picking up assumptions about how things should be organized. Mapping networks and relationships between the local church and other organizations may need to be done on several occasions using different informants before it is complete. Because whole activities are often delegated to sub-groups of the local church, important links may only be known or used by particular people.

For those using this handbook to study their own church, it may be helpful to involve someone from outside when trying to uncover ways of thinking. Palmer (1997) has noted that the construction of a timeline or story for the congregation by its members can be a powerful trigger for expressing hopes about the future.

What questions can be asked?

The questions that follow are an attempt to stimulate thinking about research questions – in the end, however, each researcher must identify questions that fit their purposes.

- What sort of organization is this?
- What ideas and practices (theological and secular) affect the way in which it thinks about and shapes itself as an organization?
- What relationships does it have with other organizations at local, national or global level and what does it give and receive from these relationships?
- What stories does this local church tell about its past and future?
- What limits (structural, physical, intellectual, theological, financial, etc.) permit or restrict the self-conception and possibilities for action of this local church?
- In what ways does the polity of the denomination affect the way in which the local church is organized?
- What links with the wider world does this local church have and how are they maintained?
- What hopes for the future does this local church have and how does it link them to present and past?

Case study – Graham Dover

Willow Creek Community Church was formed by Bill Hybels in 1975 in suburban Chicago with a vision to create a 'seeker-sensitive, biblically functioning (Acts 2) community'. In 2004, over 20,000 attend weekend church services and a new auditorium is being built to deal with the continued growth.

In 1992 the Willow Creek Association was created as a global network to share Willow Creek's vision, values and resources with local church leaders around the world. In 2004 there were 13 country 'affiliates', Willow Creek-managed organizations, with 9,500 member churches from over 90 denominations. The UK Association has over 700 church members and has doubled in the last four years.

So why do local UK churches continue to sign up to and stay in membership with an organization thousands of miles away which doesn't appear to look anything like them? The answers lie in the perceived benefits of being part of the global network. In a recent internal survey (2004) commissioned by Willow Creek over 40 per cent of member churches in the UK surveyed (approximately one third of UK membership) 'directly associate their numerical growth due to Willow Creek materials and training. Over 60% believe they have a renewed passion to reach lost people as well as building community in their churches and over 75% believe they have a stronger sense of vision for their ministry'.

The Association also acts as an independent facilitator building bridges between like-minded leaders regardless of denomination and providing a forum for exchanging ideas. The network, acting as an alternative source of authority to denominations, derives its strength from the example of Willow Creek: allowing members to associate themselves with and learn lessons from a perceived 'success story'.

Replicas of Willow Creek won't be found in the UK as the network encourages churches to adapt its ideas to local contexts and is therefore best understood in terms of value transmission, the aim of which is long-lasting growth.

Further reading

Collins, D. (1998) *Organizational Change: Sociological Perspectives*, London: Routledge.
A critical analysis of writing on organizational change.

Gabriel, Y. (2000) *Storytelling in Organizations: Facts, Fictions and Fantasies*, Oxford: Oxford University Press.
Sets out different ways of thinking about organizational storytelling.

Greenwood, R. (2000). *The Ministry Team Handbook*, London: SPCK.
A practitioner handbook conveying a model of teamworking in Anglican ministry

Hopewell, J. F. (1987) *Congregation: Stories and Structures*, London: SCM Press.
A classic in congregational studies showing how literary metaphors can be used to interpret congregations.

Pattison, S. (1997) *The Faith of the Managers: When Management Becomes Religion*, London: Cassell.
An analysis of the impact of management that compares managerialism to a religion.

Theological Strand – Context

Chris Baker

Introduction

This section discusses different understandings of the evolving relation-ship between the global and local, a defining feature of postmodernity and a useful background for understanding the concept of the 'local church'. A key theological term for this exploration is *catholicity*.

> The term *catholicity* was first used by Ignatius of Antioch in the early second century to embrace both the universality of the Christian church and its orthodoxy. It was reinforced geographically by the spread of Christianity throughout the Roman empire following the conversion of Constantine in the fourth century, and the growth of the See of Rome as the epicentre of this new global faith. After the Reformation in the sixteenth century, the concept was reinforced to describe uniformity and obedience to the creeds of the Roman Catholic Church. In Refor-mation and Orthodox traditions, the word also carries connotations of a mystical sense of a perfect church order which will only be manifested at the end of time, but which infuses the direction and impetus of the earthly church.

The notions of universality, homogeneity and conformity implied in the concept of *catholicity* have fragmented since the 1960s by proces-ses of globalization and economic migration, causing the emergence of increased plurality and diversity in local communities, especially urban ones. Combined with the emerging voices of indigenous peoples in post-colonial societies, this has led to the emergence of 'local' pres-sure on the traditional concept of catholicity to allow hybrid forms of worship and theological expression to emerge (i.e. a mixture of local and global, old and new; for examples see Ward's references to *hybrid-ity* in the Theological Strand of Section 3.4).

Issues of power between dominant and subordinate groups in churches remain problematic, but nevertheless a *new theological understanding of catholicity* is emerging which describes the ability to hold disparate identities together in tension with one another; a new 'wholeness' (Schreiter, 1997) based not on homogenization, but exchange and communication leading to a unity founded on diversity.

In this reading, the local church bears the 'mark' or stamp of catholicity in a way that is postmodern. It reflects local conditions and contexts (i.e. contextual) while at the same time still being seen as part of wider whole (i.e. the global church).

The diversity and plurality of contextualized churches within a 'tentative wholeness' is a very different understanding from traditional interpretations of the word 'catholic'. The *new catholicity* foregrounds postmodernity's stress on the importance of the experience of local and contextual as the basis for theological reflection. It does not attempt to fit human experience into universalized and pre-given theological categories. It is closely linked with the *praxis* model identified by Ward elsewhere in Section 2.2.

With this theological perspective of the new catholicity I will explore in more detail what constitutes *local theology*, and offer four typologies of local church, which have emerged as a response to postmodern shifts in physical space and social behaviour. From this I draw some conclusions about the role and identity of local church and how it might best engage with changing urban, cultural and social realities occurring at the local level (Eastman, 2004). Before defining postmodernity, however, something must be said about *modernity*.

What Is Modernity?

Many commentators agree that the idea of *modernity* emerges at the cusp of the seventeenth century. Descartes, for example, epitomized the idea of modernism in his insistence that the new basis for knowledge and advancement of the human race rested on human rationality alone. He declared 'the Independence of Man' (Kumar, 1995) from Christian philosophy and the knowledge of the Ancients. Bacon meanwhile saw the modern age as characterized by 'mechanical arts and merchandise', forces shaping the world with 'greater power and influence on human affairs' than any 'empire, sect or star' (Kumar, 1995).

Although the seventeenth and eighteenth centuries saw revivals in apocalyptic and millenarian thinking, the idea of modern 'truth' became enshrined in linear, evolutionary views of history (rather than cyclical or apocalyptic), in scientific and technical achievement, and a human rationality unhampered by what Kant called the 'moral terrorism' of Christianity (Kumar, 1995) with its threat of world annihilation at the Last Judgement.

Key political and industrial events throughout the second half of the eighteenth century reinforced these philosophical themes under the guise of *modernization* (seen as the outcome of modernity). Social revolutions in the American colonies in 1776, and France in 1789, with their tenets of equality, brotherhood and liberty, appeared to represent the final victory of secularism over religion, and also birthed notions of urban democracy as an alternative to 'monarchical city-states and colonial empires' (Soja, 2000). Meanwhile the birth of the Industrial Revolution in the 1750s in Britain culminated in the growth of Manchester, the first city produced by the social-spatial processes of industrial capitalism. Industrial urbanization was born, a decisive shift from the rural to urban. By 1900, Britain was more than 80 per cent urban.

The economic and technological superiority contained in industrial cities like Manchester could not have happened without the creation of global demand for manufactured products. Nations like Britain used their empire links to create and control demand for products. These processes continued to the latter half of the twentieth century where common perceptions of modernity were closely linked with images of industrialization, urbanization, technological innovation and social change evident in New York and Chicago's skyscrapers, supersonic travel and space technology. So, too, with developments in heart transplants, human embryology, the Pill and liberal social policy in countries like the UK that decriminalized homosexuality and abortion. Kumar offers a sweeping generalization of the achievements of modernism which is helpful in its identification of its main themes: 'History and Progress; Truth and Freedom; Reason and Revolution; Science and Industrialism: These are the main terms of the 'grand narratives' of modernity that the post-modernists wish to consign to the dustbin of history' (Kumar, 1995).

What Is Postmodernity?

Having identified some processes and philosophies associated with modernity, we now turn to *postmodernity*. Throughout the modern period, major critiques also emerged, challenging the dominance of scientific progress and human enlightenment. Within the Marxist tradition, Engels exposed the exploitation inherent in processes of industrial capitalism during his time in 1840s Manchester, calling it 'Hypocritical City' because of the polarities of poverty and wealth he saw there. The philosophy of Rousseau and Voltaire and the poetry of the Romantics expressed an acute sense of the persistence of the cycles of death and decay within the rhetoric of human progress, and a passionate railing against the spiritual and creative impoverishment of human imagination in the relentless quest for progress and efficiency.

Postmodernity (as a formally constructed development of modernity) emerged at the latter end of the twentieth century, inspired by sudden and traumatic changes to most aspects of human society. The list might include:

- the Vietnam War, the Paris riots, Watergate;
- collapse of many industrial economies and the macro-economic consensus that had maintained state control over economic forces;
- intensified global immigration of different ethnic groups to add to those already in Europe and North America;
- fragmentation of the nuclear family;
- rebellion against modern architectural movements such as Functionalism and Brutalism by the postmodernist movement towards playful pastiche and irony;
- emergence of diversity and plurality within cities and the mixing and hybridization of popular culture in food, music, fashion.

Paradoxically, the intensified flows of people mentioned above, precipitated by globalization, also created places of greater local polarization along economic, religious and ethnic lines. Sandercock is one of a number of commentators to identify the fear of 'the Other' as the major pastoral problem affecting urban communities within multiethnic cities of the twenty-first century which politicians, planners and faith groups must address:

> The multicultural city/region is perceived . . . as more of a threat than an opportunity. The threats are multiple: psychological, economic, religious, cultural. It is a complicated experiencing of fear of 'the Other' alongside fear of losing one's job, fear of a whole way of life being eroded, fear of change itself. (Sandercock, 2004)

The sense of threat and alienation is a 'down-side' to postmodernity, and along with a growing crisis of trust in 'the expert', erodes the modern belief that human rationality can lead to salvation.

So What Is the Local Within the Postmodern?

I want now to define the series of values and realities now referred to by the word 'local', and to do so, I will use the socio-economic theories of Manuel Castells and Zygmunt Bauman. Castells, for example, describes one of the results of global capitalism as a shift from conceiving of *space as place* to *space as flows*.

In economic terms, *space as flows* describes how capital investment, the new service economy and advanced technology connect in ways which no longer 'depend on the characteristics of any specific locale for the fulfilment of their fundamental goals' (Castells, 1996). The advanced services which now dominate the wealth-creating agenda of globalization require 'the dynamics of information-generating units, while connecting their different functions to disparate spaces assigned to each task to be performed' (Castells, 1989). In other words, once a product has been designed, its various stages of production can be established anywhere in the world wherever market costs are cheapest, causing increased migratory activity as both middle-managers and workers follow the flows of this investment. Castells notes some of the *social* and *spatial* consequences of his theory:

> The new professional managerial class colonizes exclusive spatial segments that connect with one another across the city, the country and the world; they isolate themselves from the fragments of local societies, which in consequence become destructured in the process of selective reorganization of work and residence. (Castells, 1989)

The rest of the local space not connected to the flows of wealth (populated by the largely unskilled workforce required to engage in routine assembly or auxiliary operations) is subject either to increased segregation and chronic poverty or gentrification, whereby pockets of wealth co-exist, or at least are well-defended, within larger areas of poverty. This leads Castells to suggest that local space can become sites of resistance for those excluded from the new flows of wealth and knowledge.

The communes of resistance defend their spaces, their places, against the placeless logic of the space of flows, characterizing social domination in the Information Age. They claim their historic memory and/or affirm the permanence of their values against the dissolution of history in timeless time, and the celebration of the ephemeral in the culture of real virtuality (Castells, 1997).

A counterbalance to Castells' antagonistic view is provided by the more nuanced perspective of Roland Robertson's theory of *glocalization* (Robertson, 1995). He describes the symbiotic way in which local and global interact with each other as time and space boundaries collapse with advanced telecommunications and cheap air travel. Globalization need not only be seen solely as a threat to local space if the two-way dynamic is recognized where the local shapes the global and benefits from the global in turn. However a more pessimistic view again emerges from Bauman's idea of neo-tribalism. Here the constant fluidity between local and national identities caused by flows of migration leads to disorientation, fear and insecurity. Traditional, locally based communities (with strict membership regulations of inclusion and exclusion) have been largely destroyed. *Neo*-tribes emerge instead to meet the need for distinctive belonging based on ethnic, religious or political affiliations, but also on desire and fear. The crucial difference is that neo-tribalism relies on individual acts of self-identification and choice. It results in 'concepts' of community, rather than 'integrated social bodies' (Bauman, 1995) and reflects identities created by fashion, leisure, lifestyle or ethnic-religious origin within diasporic or global networks. Bauman's terminology suggests that far from creating greater tolerance and diversity, the processes of postmodern globalization create situations of polarity and segregation.

The Identity and Mission of the Church in the Postmodern World

We now look at four emerging typologies of local church, which in their own ways engage with the dynamics of postmodernity, of 'local' and 'global' outlined above.

Church as Idealized Moral Community

This understanding of the church has a long theological pedigree, but has re-emerged with renewed vigour in recent years. It belongs to a tradition which stresses the christocentric nature of divine revelation and Christian ethics as expressed in the person of Jesus Christ and the biblical tradition. The word of God stands in sharp contradiction and judges 'worldly' sources of revelation based on natural law or human rationality. The church is therefore central as the preferred locus of moral discourse and behaviour.

The tradition has been strongly expressed in recent times by the influential American theologian Stanley Hauerwas. In the 1980s, he constructed a church typology based on a community whose main task is to reflect practically and theologically on its own narrative. *Praxis* is expressed precisely in the shared communal life at the local level: 'the first task of the church is not to supply theories of governmental legitimacy or even to supply strategies for social betterment. The first task of the church is to exhibit in our common life the kind of community where trust, not fear, rules our lives' (Hauerwas, 1981).

A similar self-sufficient Christian response to the wider world is reinforced by the radical orthodoxy writers emerging in the 1990s. John Milbank, for example, argues that Christian revelation undergirds social theory and as such is fundamentally incompatible with 'truth claims and conceptions of morality'. In other words, within a postmodern context of fragmented narratives, the Christian narrative out-narrates other narratives. As Milbank says, 'There is no independently available "real world" against which we must test our Christian convictions, because these convictions are then the most final and at the same time, most basic seeing of what the world is' (Milbank, 1997). Of great importance to him is the way the Christian church embodies this principle of ethical reflection rooted in cross and resurrection. The church is an 'ideal type' in which local members exemplify a life lived in peace and trust, and where alternative economics based on free gift exchange can be practised, both as a response to, and a symbol of, the ultimate reality of God's grace.

This idealized picture of church life can be criticized for its lack of serious dialogue or engagement with the everyday reality of all human beings (including Christians) who struggle with the ambiguities of life this side of the cross. It can also ignore the gap between idealized model and actual reality in churches which can be far from the community of trust and peace envisaged by Hauerwas and Milbank.

Scenario 1

While this idealized church type can be a fantasy easily dismissed, there are some churches that manage to combine a strong ethic based on christocentric revelation with an inclusive engagement with the wider community. The Eden project in Openshaw, Manchester is one of many youth-based projects started in the late 1990s in areas of UK deprivation. The overt evangelism at the heart of Eden's identity, with its stress on discipleship and personal decision-making was controversial in the early days, and is still viewed with suspicion by some local residents and existing community development agencies. But the project in Openshaw has learned from experience and appears more at ease working with a wide variety of partners, both secular and religious, including other churches that have a more liberal approach. They have gained respect for their work with hard-to-reach groups and the sensitivity, openness and accountability with which they engage with vulnerable groups. Its ethos locates it in this church type, but what is new with the Eden project is its willingness to engage with a wide variety of partners. In its alliances, it hints at a new and informal expression of ecumenism that sits lightly to denominational identity (i.e. post-denominational).

Liberation theology model

This typology is modelled on the methodology of liberation theology in South America. It makes the experience of the poor and marginalized the given starting point for theological reflection and mission. Paulo Freire's work was important in fostering and raising people's levels of awareness through adult education, especially within peer-groups. This was a prerequisite for social and political transformation. Its greatest strength is its commitment to the social analysis of the wider context in which the church community is placed, an openness to the many influences and power structures that shape cities at both local and global level combined with a firm commitment to be a genuinely local church community incarnated within a local setting.

Usually this model will seek to express this commitment by gathering in local (often eucharistic) worship, which is unconditionally inclusive. This worship setting, sometimes replicated by cell groups meeting in peoples' homes provides the opportunity for the narratives of peoples' experience to engage with both biblical and symbolic frameworks. In this way, faith comes alive and gives emotional and spiritual resources by which to live a life of dignity in situations that may seem hopeless. Sometimes, the church will also choose to become involved in issues of local concern, joining with other organizations to create better conditions on behalf of the wider community along the lines of Castells' 'communes of resistance' referred to earlier.

The weakness of this model is that, with the analysis of issues facing local communities, can come a pro-poor rhetoric which tends not to do justice to the multicausal nature of poverty and wealth in postmodern communities. There is also evidence to show that both the nature of

the poor and the role of the local church can be idealized and romanti-
cized by a nostalgia for a lost narrative of church and community that
supposedly existed in perfect harmony (Baker, 2002).

The local/institutional model

The traditional model of church that still exists in most areas, though it
is tending to decline in poorer communities, represents at a local level
a national institutional church (especially within Anglican and Roman
Catholic ecclesiologies). Its strengths are long-term identification with
local communities, and a strong association with family histories and
local events. The institutional church can be the place where the 'local'
community gathers to mark some national event of grief or joy. The
sense of being rooted in a local space and carrying its narratives is
symbolized by the physical building, often an important local land-
mark within communities undergoing rapid physical change. Whether
in decline numerically or experiencing growth, the institutional type
can be the nexus for sets of local relationships which form part of the
invisible network of community cohesion. However, there does appear
to be a growing trend for successful churches to become less and less
'local' in the geographical sense, as increasing numbers of members
come from people travelling from outside the locality.

Scenario 2

A local institutional church in its public worship and rites of passage
offers what one East Manchester vicar calls 'the value of a different
rhythm and a sense of a quiet, healing space and long-term sustainability'. East Manchester is in the throes of massive regeneration, led by
the arrival of the Commonwealth Games stadium and an Asda-Walmart
hypermarket. These are expected to attract large numbers of professional singles and couples to settle in the area. His description of what
the institutional model of church offers partly relates to the regeneration
approach that is concerned with short-term turnarounds and targets,
but also speaks to a growing consumerism and freneticism that much
investment-led regeneration presupposes: state-of-the-art fitness
suites, 24-hour café and dance-club cultures and apartments designed
for home-working.

The institutional/local model can be slow to react to rapid change
because of its long traditions. This in turn can lead to insularity, and its

institutional character can make it harder to introduce the flexibility of worship and approach now required to connect with new patterns of lifestyle and identity.

Network model

The network model is a form that Castells would recognize. It emerges from the 'space as flows' concept and mimics more fluid forms of civil society. The traditional sectors of civil society, welfare associations and charities, the family, churches, political organizations and trade unions are in decline because of, for example, the breaking up of the traditional family structure, the growth of suburban sprawl and the growth in electronic entertainment (Putnam, 2000). Some of these sectors are also becoming more professionalized, thus alienating those people who have traditionally volunteered for its own sake (Centre for Research and Innovation in Social Policy and Practice, 2003). Growth in civil society is in the non-institutional sectors; broad-based organizations (i.e. networks or coalitions of disparate groups formed around single issues such as a living wage), or direct action campaigns focusing on large public demonstrations to change government policy or global trends (for example, Stop the War, Jubilee 2000, The Countryside Alliance).

The identity and role of network church (as far as it has emerged in the few case studies currently available – e.g. Community Pride in Manchester, IMPACT in Sheffield, and TELCO in East London) has mirrored some key characteristics of non-institutional civil society. Individual church members often take the initiative in forming networks of transformation in order to address local or national issues, becoming key members of these networks, and thus accessing more powerful networks and institutions (for example, local councils, national government). As a result of their expertise and grassroots support, these individuals become engaged at the cutting edge issues of process and change.

Scenario 3

Community Pride Initiative is an organization created by the churches, which operates with the network model in Salford and Manchester. It has been at the forefront in creating a unique participatory budgeting experiment with Salford Council, as well as setting up a wide range of networks across the city, designed to inform local communities of government regeneration opportunities, support grassroots responses and offer specialized support (e.g. disability and gender perspectives). It is one of the lead bodies (appointed by the Government Office North West) for the development of the Community Network for Manchester, and is closely linked to Manchester's LSP (Local Strategic Partnership). It has contributed to national evaluation of Government regeneration policy.

This type of 'church' works well with the more 'liquid' forms of civil society and governance and unlike the institutional (or more solid types of church) has a light and flexible structure that makes it able to respond swiftly to change. With no buildings to maintain, minimum bureaucratic structures and autonomy, it can act appropriately at local level.

This model allows the 'church' to interface in the most direct way with issues that affect the wider community, but questions of visibility and identity can be raised. Those engaged in partnership or network-ing with this type of 'church' may be unaware that it is a church group. Nor is it always clear what the relationship is between a 'networking' church and the more solid forms of 'institutional' church.

Conclusion

These typologies are not an exhaustive list, but indicate current prac-tice that emerges from the postmodern and local context. Some local churches react to plurality, diversity and rapid change by stressing the uniqueness of Christian revelation and seeking a form of identity that removes them from the norms and values of the wider community. Other church communities engage wholeheartedly with plurality and diversity and explore more 'liquid' forms of identity in order to 'go with the flow' of postmodern life. They may not be able to meet the spiritual needs of people for physical buildings and public liturgies at times of crisis or celebration. Within the complexity and ambiguity of postmodern life, there is no one typology that fits all. Each typology has something to offer. For example, networks complement more 'solid' organizations by helping institutions to adapt to changing con-ditions and to attract more diverse and 'boundary-spanning' contacts (Gilchrist, 2004).

The four typologies are all examples of what we called at the start of this contribution a *new theology of catholicity*. Each has a distinctive *charism* or gift which it offers to the local community, but whose gift needs to be seen not as the definitive or only response to the local context, but one aspect that needs other forms if the wholeness of the church is to be expressed in that local context.

Practical Ways of Studying 'Locality' in Local Churches

Assessing the contribution of a local church community to local civil society can be done in a variety of ways. The William Temple Foundation's approach to this in Manchester has been to start by 'mapping' selected localities to ascertain the different ways in which local communities have changed in the past five to ten years. This has included walking around the local area with people who live or walk there, noticing new buildings, key changes of land use, areas of growth and areas of decline. We have mapped the local history of these communities, as well as undertaking empirical analysis of the latest census figures which can show the extent to which exclusion (measured by such indicators as health, housing, levels of crime and air quality) now co-exists with wealth (measured in house prices and council tax bands). Global flows in local spaces can also be detected by shifts in ethnic representation and religious groupings. We have also mapped contemporary oral histories by interviewing a variety of people which reveals quite clearly the importance of memory, narrative and identity for newcomers and existing residents alike. It also shows how patterns of power shape a local area. For example, how and where decisions are taken to demolish existing landmarks or housing, and which groups feel least safe in using public space.

Our current research phase involves doing deeper interview research with church members from the neighbourhoods within our study sample to ascertain the precise nature of their input into the needs of the wider community, and, more importantly, the language they would use by which to describe what they do. Our aim is to develop a theological discourse on local regeneration and renewal that will complement and deepen the more target-driven approach adopted by government.

Further reading

Castells, M. (1996) *The Rise of the Network Society*, Oxford: Black-
    well.
    This is still a highly influential summary of the social and urban
    consequences of late capitalism's ability to harness new information
    and knowledge-based technology to create a global market of flows
    that increasingly marginalize local and poor communities.
Kumar, K. (1995) *From Post-Industrial to Post-Modern Society,*
    Oxford: Blackwell.
    An accessible introduction to the key intellectual and historical
    events that shaped the transition from modernity to postmodernity,
    and is well-suited as an aid to both sociological and theological
    analysis.
*Mission-Shaped Church: Church Planting and Fresh Expressions of
    Church in a Changing Context* (2004), London: Church House
    Publishing.
    A report (chaired by Graham Cray) produced by the Church of
    England's Mission and Public Affairs Council. It offers a historical
    Anglican perspective on new patterns of church that have emerged
    in the UK since the 1970s, as well as a list of current expressions of
    church within the UK, which demonstrate well the features of the
    liquid versus solid spectrum of church and community explored in
    this book. It is a complementary commentary to Peter Ward's book.
Regenerating Communities – A Theological and Strategic Critique,
    (Forthcoming), Manchester: William Temple Foundation.
    A three-volume research document by the William Temple Founda-
    tion which will be completed 2005/6. It represents the results of
    a three-year, geographically based piece of theological reflection
    into the nature of postmodern urban space and emerging shapes of
    church and civil society in a representative English northern core
    city, Manchester (see *www.wtf.org.uk* for full details).
Schreiter, R. (1997) *New Catholicity – Theology Between one Global
    and the Local* Maryknoll: Orbis Books.
    A short but highly condensed overview of the impact of globaliza-
    tion on the way theo-logy is evolving to meet the challenges of post-
    modern 'glocal' world without losing sight of the justice agenda.
Ward, P. (2002) *Liquid Church*, Carlisle: Paternoster Press.
    This is a short, readable and provocative foray into postmodern
    sociology and western consumerism that asks many pertinent ques-
    tions about the new forms of church that will need to evolve in the
    early twenty-first century.

3.2 The Worship and Action of the Local Church

When the word 'church' is used, some people immediately think just of a special building. But that church would be a redundant shell were it not a location or focus for a wide range of activities expressing the worship, caring, educational and social life which members and adherents of the congregation share. At the heart of most churches' activity is some form of worship, expressing the basis of Christian community in transcendent, metaphysical terms. In this section, we will be considering what our four disciplines have already discovered about the worship and activity of local churches and indicating the various practical ways they offer for studying these dimensions of local churches.

Anthropological Strand – Worship and Action

Martin Stringer

Introduction

In looking at what anthropology can offer the study of worship in the local church I want to highlight two strands that go back to the beginnings of the discipline. Although these may, initially, appear contradictory I hope to show that it is the tension between them that pinpoints a crucial aspect of how an anthropological approach may illuminate a study of Christian congregations.

The first emerges from the work of Bronislaw Malinowski (1948/1974) and concerns ethnography – which became the principal method within anthropology. It can be explained by seeing just what Malinowski did when, during the First World War, this Polish national found himself on an island off the coast of New Guinea where he spent many months observing the life and culture of the inhabitants. He realized the value of the extended period of study for his ability to get inside and gain a deep understanding of the life of these people. Such an extended venture, living with and among those being studied, is what anthropologists refer to as 'participant observation'.

Writing about his experience, Malinowski developed a number of reasons why such extended study is preferable to shorter, survey-based work of the kind that had preceded his own work. These included the ability to gain a holistic understanding of the society, an ability to learn the language in depth and, most important from our point of view, the ability to see life from, as he put it, 'the native's point of view'. This has been an important aim of anthropology from Malinowski onwards, the attempt to see what the world looks like from different perspectives, to understand a community or society in their own terms. As we will see below, some recent anthropology has raised methodological and ethical questions concerning this aim, but the aim itself still stands because, at the heart of all anthropological analysis, lies the goal of putting the people being studied first, and understanding the world from their point of view.

The second strand is very different and focuses specifically on the anthropological tradition of the study of religion. In the 1850s William Robertson Smith delivered a series of lectures at Edinburgh University on the 'Religion of the Semites' (Smith, 1889/1927). Though he was a biblical scholar, in these lectures he went beyond the strictly biblical evidence to draw on comparative material from the Semitic world to try and gain a much broader and more detailed study of the religious traditions of Semitic peoples. He reached a very startling conclusion: that all the Semitic peoples, from North Africa and across the Middle East, placed sacrificial rituals at the heart of their religions. The killing of animals for sacred purposes was practically universal. What changed, from place to place and across time, were the reasons that people gave for engaging in sacrifice. The action, the ritual, remained the same, but the justification, the beliefs, changed. He concluded from this observation that, in order to understand the rituals of other peoples, we had to focus entirely on what was done and not on the justifications that people gave for doing it. Of course, this is probably taking the principle to extreme lengths – why people think they are performing a ritual is also an important element in understanding that ritual within that particular context. Robertson Smith's legacy, however, within the anthropology of religion has been to encourage a focus on what was done in ritual, rather than on what people said about it.

We can now see the contradiction that easily arises within anthropology. At a methodological level, like Malinowski, anthropologists are interested in investigating the 'native's point of view' while, within the specific study of religion, like Smith, they tend to focus on what people actually do in ritual and not on what they say about what they do. It seems to me that we cannot attempt both these tasks at the same time, yet, for many years anthropologists have tried to do this. The most common justification for that approach can be seen in Victor Turner's work (Turner, 1969). He was interested in rituals among the

Ndembu people of Zambia. Like Malinowski he spent a great deal of time listening to ritual specialists and ordinary people talking about the rituals. However, he still came to the conclusion that there were aspects of the ritual that could not be seen and understood by the people themselves. Indeed, that there were things about the ritual the people could never have fully expressed verbally. This view assumes that there is something about ritual that the 'natives' cannot perceive or understand and that it takes an outsider, an anthropologist, to point this out to them.

In attempting to get to grips with this fundamental contradiction some anthropologists have approached the study of Christian worship using anthropological methods. I will now highlight three such attempts and comment on the kind of conclusion they have reached. The first approach is the most recent and concentrates on the study of charismatic worship, the second takes Kieran Flanagan's study of Roman Catholic worship. He argues for a limited value of ethnographic study in gaining a clear picture of the congregation's own understanding of worship. Finally I take my own work on the worship of four different Christian congregations in Manchester.

The Ethnographic Study of Charismatic Ritual

One of the most fruitful areas for the anthropological study of worship in recent years has been in the field of charismatic worship. One of the most significant reasons for this is the relationship between text and action in charismatic worship. In most Christian worship since the fourth century texts have held a central place, so much so that the traditional study of Christian worship or liturgy has been seen almost exclusively as a study of texts. To a certain extent the Reformation allowed Christians to move away from the fixity of texts, but there is no question that the vast majority of Reformed worship is still essentially textual. Although this emphasis on texts passed through to the mainstream evangelicals, the emergence of Pentecostal worship at the beginning of the twentieth century caused a very dramatic change precisely because this new worship was based primarily on experience and action. While hymns, sermons, scripture, prophecies and other textual elements of the worship continued to be central, it was actions, the internalizing of the worship and the expression of that worship through bodily movement, that distinguished this worship from what had gone before. Speaking in tongues came to typify and characterize

Pentecostal worship and this was, very obviously, a typical non-textual activity.

In the 1960s and 1970s Pentecostal traditions of worship moved into the mainstream with the growth of the charismatic movement and Pentecostalism itself spread throughout the world. It has now been claimed that charismatic or Pentecostal styles of worship are the most commonly practised form of worship in the world today. This worship, however, cannot be studied using the traditional, textually based, liturgical methods. Anthropological fieldwork, participant observation and the study of ritual therefore offered an interesting alternative. It became clear that in order to understand the worship of a charismatic or Pentecostal congregation the scholar actually had to be there. There was no text to study and even video representations cannot provide the sense of the experience of this worship, an experience that is absolutely essential to its understanding. So, in different parts of the academic community, practically independent of each other, the anthropological study of charismatic worship began.

As with the wider anthropological study of ritual, on which this scholarship is based, the questions investigated by the scholars have revolved around what is actually done within the worship. The question of meaning, or what the worshippers think is happening, has been left to one side. Or, to be more accurate, the question of the worshipper's own understanding has been assumed by these scholars. One study, that of Csordas (1997), has been undertaken by an established scholar in the anthropology of religion who is not himself a member of the Catholic charismatic tradition he is studying. He makes practically no attempt to discover the congregation's own thoughts about the worship. Rather, he engages in a rhetorical analysis of the texts used within the worship, most specifically those of prophecy. He explores how prophetic utterances establish their own authority within the context of the worship and how they are positioned at the top of a hierarchy of authoritative utterances including testimonies and sharing within confessional partnerships. It is the internal structure of these texts that forms the basis for his study and, as such, his work is perhaps closer to the traditional liturgical analysis of worship, especially in its contemporary form, than that of less anthropologically trained colleagues.

Other scholars working in this Pentecostal field are themselves members of the churches or traditions they are studying and so claim to have an insider's knowledge of what the congregation thinks is going on, rather than trying in any serious way to understand the 'native's point of view'. Albrecht (1999), for example, undertakes a much more traditional study of Pentecostal worship drawing on what has come to be called 'ritual studies' for his methodology. He undertook fieldwork in three Pentecostal congregations in Sea City on the Californian coast. His primary interest is in the actions of the worship and the way in which these actions communicate the meanings of the people. His work is grounded in the approach of Victor Turner, but as adapted through that of Grimes (1982), in 'ritual studies'.

Albrecht's main point is to stress the fact of performance or the performative nature of charismatic ritual. This highlights what is done, and done deliberately, a conscious action, performed for a purpose. In this sense the worship is participatory, it is not something that is watched or listened to, it is something that is experienced. Through this experience the worship communicates to the worshippers values and principles that are at the heart of Pentecostal life. Albrecht does show how the different congregations communicate subtly different messages, primarily through the use of space and dress, but the messages themselves are those assumed to be present by Albrecht and this analysis is not backed up by any real attempt to discover the native's point of view.

Another study, that of James Steven (2002) on charismatic congregations in the Church of England takes the same kind of analysis but develops it a little further. Steven, like Csordas and Albrecht, picks up the performative nature of charismatic worship and stresses the importance of experience. This is the root of his analysis and comes out of a detailed study of participant observation in six Anglican congregations. Again there are clear differences between these congregations but the aim of Steven's work is to try and discover common features rather than those things that distinguish or divide. Ultimately Steven is interested in drawing theological conclusions from his analysis and the anthropology is merely a means to an end rather than an end in itself. The theology provides an overarching explanation or a metatext over and above the actual worship or the analysis of that worship. As such it is some distance from any attempt to discover what the congregations themselves believe is happening, or the meanings they are deriving from it.

All three of these attempts to use anthropological method for the study of charismatic worship generate interesting and worthwhile studies. They draw our attention to things about the worship that may not be obvious to the participants and which deserve further study. In no case could this have been done if the method of participant observation had not been used. In all three cases, however, the scholars come down on the Robertson Smith side of the contradiction as mentioned earlier. They all focus primarily on what was happening in the worship with the implied assumption that we cannot really get at what the people think, or more specifically, that we can see what the ritual itself is saying by ritual or theological analysis without really bothering to ask whether this is what the congregation itself understands from the ritual. This makes all these studies typical examples of anthropological ritual analysis. However, the conundrum I began with still stands. Is it possible to ever get at the 'native's point of view' in relation to the study of Christian worship? The other two studies I wish to focus on both address this issue head on and both take clearly opposing stances in the argument.

The Sociology of Liturgy

The first of these is Kieran Flanagan's study, *Sociology and Liturgy* (1991). Although primarily sociological in method it is included in this anthropological section because sometimes the overlap between the perspectives can only be separated in an artificial fashion. He aims to provide a sociological study of Roman Catholic worship, yet begins by claiming it is impossible for sociologists ever to undertake ethnographic study of worship. Participant observation is simply not possible in the context of Christian worship. More precisely, he argues we can never fully know what people make of worship because we cannot begin to experience or understand the worship as they do themselves. This touches on several arguments. The first relates to the broad philosophical problem about how far it is ever possible to experience the world as others do. Experience is so personal and subjective that no two people could ever claim to experience something in exactly the same way. It is not only the inability to experience as another does, but also the impossibility of truly expressing that experience to another that makes 'experience' something beyond the study of the anthropologist, or, in Flanagan's case, the sociologist. The second argument relates more to meaning than to experience. Flanagan wants to argue that there is something about the meaning of the rite that can never be fully grasped by those who take part. In taking this stance Flanagan is following Turner and, behind him, Robertson Smith, in arguing that it is impossible, or irrelevant, to discover the native's point of view.

As a solution to these problems Flanagan chooses to undertake a study of what might be called the logic of the rite itself. This leads him to focus on the importance of truth and the necessity, within the context of the ritual, of getting things right. This leads on to a sophisticated analysis of the various theories of play that see the liturgy as some kind of game. There is a great deal to be learnt from this and his work takes the element of ritual studies, based on the Robertson Smith heritage, through to highly sophisticated levels. Nevertheless, it leaves us asking Malinowski's question: What do the people really make of this? Does this kind of sophistication actually touch the native point of view in anything but the most tangential of ways?

The Perception of Worship

In my own book, *On the Perception of Worship* (Stringer, 1999), I chose to reject this stance and tried to do what Flanagan claims to be impossible, that is, to discover what it is that the people actually understand about the worship they use. I studied four Christian congregations in Manchester spending six months with each, attending and worshipping alongside people while also attending a wide range of other church activities. I listened to what people said about their worship in ordinary conversation, if anything. I also engaged in interviews to tease out what was going on behind the language that was used. It was in this combination of the personal experience of attending the worship, a participant observation of a very intense kind, and the words of those whose worship it was, that I began to tease out the nature of meaning in relation to this worship.

In one way, I came to agree with Flanagan in rejecting the possibility of ever knowing in any kind of detail exactly what any one individual actually understands of worship either in relation to a specific act of worship or more widely. This highly subjective response is beyond the scope of the anthropological investigator. Along with the reasons that are offered by Flanagan, the subjectivity of experience and the lack of real knowledge on the part of the worshipper, I argue that the meaning or understanding of worship is something that the individual worshipper could never actually put into words. To ask worshippers to express what worship means to them in words is to ask them to respond and react to worship in a way that is entirely alien. Beyond this is the possibility that so many different factors in an individual's life come into play in the perception of worship that we could never ever express this fully within an academic text. This stance, however, while similar to that taken by Flanagan, does not lead me to give up the search. Rather, I change the focus. Unlike Flanagan who sets out to find meaning in the internal logic and performance of the rite, I set out to discover how the individual and unknowable meanings of the rite are derived. I ask how the rite begins to generate meaning for the individual, not what that meaning might be.

This kind of analysis leads me to focus on four specific features of all Christian worship: repetition, significance, experience and memory. It is in the interaction between these features that meaning is generated. However, as my book shows, the way in which these features interact will inevitably be different for different kinds of Christian worship and in different contexts. In my final chapter I set out a process by which a cyclical pattern of repetition, experience and significance works within each of the congregations. Memory, I argue, forms the missing link, the driving force for this cyclical movement. However, memory is always flawed and leads to a gap on each cycle of the revolution, and this provides a space for meaning or, what I call 'the Other'. It is, I argue, the constant repetition of worship that gives it such power and meaning in an individual's life.

Conclusion

Through these various studies we can see the two fundamental elements of anthropological thought being played out. It is in trying to understand the relationship between the action of ritual and the meaning generated by the people who use that ritual, the 'native point of view', that anthropological studies of religion can contribute most to the study of Christian worship. We may never arrive at a definitive answer as to what that worship means or how it should be performed. We will rather come to appreciate the diversity of approaches, the importance of the specific congregation in a specific place, and the way in which each and every congregation comes to interact with their own specific worship.

Case Study

In my book, *On the Perception of Worship*, I recounted the experience of trying to study the understanding of worship in a Baptist congregation in Manchester. The congregation consisted of about 70 members and defined itself as theologically 'liberal'. Many of the members worked at the university in Manchester and discussion on issues of contemporary interest were a regular part of the life of the congregation. My interest was in the way in which the congregation understood and talked about their worship. I was with the congregation for six months and chose to spend the first three months simply listening to what members of the congregation said spontaneously about their worship in different contexts. As it turned out they hardly ever discussed the worship and after three months I had no real data of any kind.

This meant I had to find another way of gaining the information and began to interview most of the members of the congregation, asking them in turn what worship meant to them. At the end of the six months I was invited to present back to the congregation the findings of this research. I went through the interviews, collected together a series of quotes, and put this into an academic framework and then presented the information back to the congregation. The members of the Baptist church listened to what I had to say and then came back saying 'no', that was not how they saw worship at all: I had 'got it all wrong'.

I then had to go back to the interviews and look closely at what was said, and more importantly what was not said, and to rethink my whole approach. I realized that people were always cautious about saying anything about their worship and always hedged their statements with qualifications. In most cases the members of the congregation had said nothing directly but had told me a story about an act of worship that had meant a great deal to them. This led me to explore the nature of the story and the way in which people communicate something they could never put into words – an experience, a significant event, a time of worship. I learnt that things are never quite what they seem, but without the experience of feeding back what I thought I had learnt, I would never have begun to explore the material in more depth (Arweck and Stringer, 2002).

Further reading

Albrecht, Daniel E. (1999) *Rites in the Spirit: A Ritual Approach to Pentecostal/Charismatic Spirituality*, Sheffield: Sheffield Academic Press.
An account of the historical background to Pentecostal and charismatic religion bringing anthropological dimensions to theological concerns.

Csordas, Thomas J. (1997) *Language, Charisma and Creativity: Ritual Life in the Catholic Charismatic Renewal*, Berkeley: University of California Press.

An ethnographic study of a Roman Catholic charismatic group set in the USA and including analyses of organizational factors and worldviews related to acts of charismatic performance.

James, Wendy and Douglas H. Johnson, eds (1988) *Vernacular Christianity*, Oxford: JASO.

An interesting collection of studies and practical cases of popular Christianity from across the world.

Stringer, Martin D. (1999) *On the Perception of Worship*, Birmingham: Birmingham University Press.

See discussion above.

Sociological Strand – Worship and Action

Mathew Guest

Introduction

Here we draw from the discipline of sociology in addressing the worship and social action of local churches, focusing on three related questions: What are the social functions of worship – that is, what function does worship have for those who take part? How does worship and ritual relate to the culture of participants? And how do local churches contribute to this culture through projects of regeneration that aim to enhance the welfare of society and its members?

The Social Function of Worship

Many early social scientific studies of myth and ritual focused on questions of function, addressing what it is rituals actually do that accounts for their importance within a social group. This approach assumes that theological explanations alone are insufficient, and that social factors need to be taken into account. Moreover, these are factors about which ritual participants may be unaware. While individuals might say they attend a church service merely in order to worship God this activity also has latent functions – perhaps the consolidation of friendship networks, or the generation of feelings of personal empowerment – which are just as, if not more, important as factors in explaining why those who attend participate as they do (McGrail, 2004). This approach is central to the school of functionalist sociology, most famously developed by Talcott Parsons, but ultimately grounded in the work of the French sociologist Emile Durkheim (1858–1917).

According to Durkheim, when people gather together to perform rituals, they generate a 'collective effervescence', a sense of shared power that reinforces the shared ideas and sentiments of their social group. Individuals both learn these ideas and sentiments, and have them regularly reaffirmed, by participating in corporate ritual acts that thereby infuse reality with a sense of order and meaning. In this way, ritual and religious worship are at the centre of the process through which humans find meaning in the world. Within the context of Christian tradition, it is by taking part in corporate acts of worship that Christians are exposed to the texts, teachings and symbols that are then used to fund a developing Christian identity. Using the language of the sociology of knowledge, rituals function as 'plausibility structures'; that is, they reinforce the worldview shared among members of a religious group.

However, for Durkheim, worship and ritual do not merely produce meaning; these corporate acts also bind humans together, by gathering them around a common set of symbols – at the most basic level around what Durkheim calls the totem. He takes this idea from the culture of Australian aborigines, which forms the empirical focus of his seminal text *The Elementary Forms of the Religious Life* (Durkheim, 1915/1995). The totem is the symbolic centre of the aboriginal tribe; it determines tribal allegiances – as well as enmities – and elicits a commitment to the group that fosters cohesion among its members. This insight has obvious applications to Christian worship, which often fosters feelings of togetherness and community among those taking part. Congregations express their collective identity in worship, and through this process members reinforce their sense of inclusion within a particular group. In this respect worship reinforces community.

Durkheim argues that all ritual symbols may function in this way, and are essential to the cohesion of both the religious group and the society in which it is situated. In this respect ritual and worship are understood to have a function that extends far beyond the religious traditions that lay claim to them. They function as a centre of meanings whose influence radiates out into the 'secular' domain. Moreover, if ritual symbols begin to lose their power, then there is a risk of what

Durkheim calls *anomie*, or normlessness. In simple terms, the break-down of effective social rituals triggers a shift from order into chaos, from meaning to meaninglessness. Ritual and worship are in this respect integral to the preservation of order in the social world.

Durkheim's legacy raises interesting questions about the relation-ship between the religious and the secular. His definition of religion focused on how a body of beliefs and practices unites its adherents into a 'moral community' (Durkheim, 1915/1995). This allows him to attribute the functions we might associate with sacred rituals to what are conventionally understood to be secular activities. This has led some scholars to treat popular corporate events such as pop concerts and football matches as essentially like, some would argue surrogates for, occasions of Christian worship. Both unite participants through shared bonds of allegiance, which are expressed and celebrated at a special communal assembly. Both unite affiliates around a central sym-bolic totem, be it a winning team, pop group or sacred icon. And both express a set of values and meanings that bestow orderliness upon a complex social world.

While Durkheim presents ritual as an effective source of social order, some scholars have appropriated his work in more critical analyses of how power is distributed and maintained in religious groups. Worship events are often key contexts in which relations of power are negoti-ated, as they bring church communities together in a public space. At such events, norms of authority and hierarchy are often implicit in the very structure of devotional practice. For example, in her illuminat-ing study of Roman Catholic charismatic groups, Meredith McGuire (1982) draws a distinction between 'open' and 'closed' prayer meet-ings. 'Open' meetings are more inclusive in their membership, incor-porate fewer specialized roles, and permit all participants to actively contribute to the proceedings, offering prayers, prophecies and wit-nessing about their spiritual experiences. By contrast, 'closed' meetings are more structured, have a more exclusive approach to member-ship, and place strong limitations on who may speak and when dur-ing prayer meetings. Indeed, new members are instructed about these rules before their first meeting, and those who break established rules of conduct are faced with sanctions imposed by leaders, unrelenting members being asked to leave. McGuire shows how what appear to be spontaneous acts of expressive worship are actually subject to strict mechanisms of control. 'Genuine' spontaneity is treated as a threat to the order of the group, and ultimately, as a threat to the authority of group leaders.

In this analysis, while worship is used as a means of maintaining social order, this order includes the retention of existing inequalities of power. McGuire explores this issue by asking questions like, Who is permitted to speak? Who has the power to control the order of meetings? Who has the power to limit the speech of others? These are sociological questions, and are useful tools in unveiling social processes that often lie beneath Christian worship and ritual practice. Moreover, these insights highlight the need for worship to be studied in terms of local practice, observed in process. Only in this way may we begin to understand the differentiation of roles and nuances of behaviour that characterize worship and ritual events.

The Meaning and Culture of Worship

Sociological approaches that emphasize the question of social function have often been criticized for overlooking questions of meaning. What does it mean to take part in an act of worship, given the experiences surrounding an event? This question opens up a whole new set of issues. For example, working within a sociological frame of reference, it is not enough to merely describe the meanings participants ascribe to their actions; it is also important to explore how these meanings are constructed, and to trace the resources participants draw from in this meaning-making exercise. Moreover, it is important to be critically aware of the processes we use to access these meanings.

In one sense, the question of meaning is tied to the question of culture. It is possible to argue that worship events communicate the common culture of those taking part, i.e. the values, beliefs and behavioural norms that together make up their identity as a social collective. However, it is important to remember that while congregations do express their own identities, they are also made up of numerous individuals, and that each member will have a unique experience of each worship event. Any attempt to capture the collective identity of the congregation as it is expressed in worship will inevitably paper over these differences. At the same time we would do well to take heed of Hopewell's (1987) helpful reminder that each congregation has its own story, and that this story is shaped by the social demographics of the congregation, its history, and its location within wider social forces. This is where issues of gender, age and ethnic difference are important factors, as they can point to differentials of power and priority which influence the questions congregations ask of themselves, and influence which worship practices are judged most appropriate. So while congregations are composed of individuals, these individuals share a common pool of experiences and participate in what might be called a common discourse. It is through this discourse that the meaning of worship is constructed, expressed and affirmed in local contexts.

But how might we access these meanings, and understand the mechanisms through which they are generated? Three approaches are discernible in the literature, distinguishable by different assumptions about the bases of meaning. First, there is the approach that conceives meaning as something to be decoded on the basis of an observation of the structure and content of the worship event itself. This may be called the objectivist approach, and distinguished many early liturgical studies, which located the meaning of worship events solely in the texts that were used within them. For example, some early liturgists sought to discuss the 'meaning' of the Anglican Eucharist simply in terms of the words enunciated by the celebrant and the liturgical responses offered by the congregation. This clearly ignores many important aspects of the worship experience, not least the different social identities of those taking part. However, the objectivist approach is not to be ruled out altogether. For example, it is clear that theological elements of church tradition – shaped by denominational identity – are embedded in the structure of the worship event and may be read from it. For example, consider the differences between a Protestant charismatic service and a Roman Catholic Mass. The charismatic service may be characterized as 'interactive': it is built around a participatory model that encourages congregational members to have an active role in shaping the service. This manifests itself in shared leadership roles; impromptu outbursts of prayer, glossolalia or prophecy; expressive sung worship accompanied by dancing or improvised bodily movement. By contrast, at the Roman Catholic Mass, the congregation do not respond as individuals, but as a united group, all taking part in the rite according to a formalized order. Behaviour in this respect is not spontaneous and active, but solemn, controlled and comparatively passive. It is also scripted, with the authorized liturgy dictating the measured participation of the congregation, as well as the order of the service as a whole. In both cases, the theological values of each tradition are embedded in the worship event: for the charismatics, a clear affirmation of the 'priesthood of all believers' (emphasized in their participatory model), and of the genuine presence of the Holy Spirit in and through the congregation; for the Catholics, a sense of conformity to an established liturgical paradigm that reflects the importance attached to being a part of the worldwide apostolic church.

Thus, the structure and form of worship events are vehicles of theological tradition, expressing key values and beliefs through ceremonial order, style of sung worship and the differentiation of roles. In addition to this we might add conventions of dress, which highlight differences in status, or architectural features of churches, which reinforce the shared worldview through the definition of sacred space. However, in addition to embodying theological traditions – meanings associated with the 'official' canons of teaching that the church uses to express its beliefs – worship and ritual also embody other meanings. Indeed, worship events taken as a whole can communicate a lot about the social and religious identities of those who take part in them that does not directly refer to the religious tradition invoked. In broad terms, they transmit messages which fall into two main categories: the canonical, embodying the teachings of religious tradition, and the indexical (see the Anthropological Strand of the Global and Local Context, Section 3.1 above), which convey an individual's status within their social system (Rappaport, 1979). A focus on the 'indexical' in worship can reveal congregational peculiarities in terms of social and family backgrounds, of education, affluence and corresponding cultural identity, as well as of theological persuasion. In this respect worship is the vehicle of social as well as theological meaning. Indeed, in so far as the two are fused, worship can be seen as a means of sacralizing a shared worldview, or at least lending legitimacy to ideas that have infiltrated the event not through tradition, but through the social identities of its participants.

The second approach is based on a critique of the objectivist model, grounded in the argument that to simply decode meaning from observation is to ignore the actual experiences and perceptions of social actors. To talk about the meaning of worship while ignoring the perceptions of worshippers is to unjustly impose upon them an alien meaning framework. This critique proceeds from a broader argument about sociological method, and refers back to the work of Max Weber (1864–1920). Weber argued that sociology should not try to study social action from the outside like the natural sciences, but should acknowledge the meanings social actors themselves ascribe to their behaviour (Weber, 1947/1964). *Verstehen* (usually translated as 'understanding') is the method sociologists should use to access these meanings, and involves putting ourselves in the position of those whom we study. For this reason this second approach may be called the *Verstehen* approach.

The *Verstehen* approach has not merely encouraged researchers to attempt a greater empathy with those they study. It has also raised the issue of what place we give to what participants actually say about their experiences of worship. For, from a sociological perspective, it is not acceptable to speak about the experiences of social actors without attempting to engage with the empirical reality of the situation; in practical terms, to talk to those who take part. This produces a more complex 'meaning' of the worship experience, as it allows for interpersonal difference, and therefore demands careful handling. It is an approach that is particularly illuminating when investigating congregations in which there are clear differentials of power between different members. Interviews with participants may reveal that while some find their services are a source of immense personal fulfilment, others feel more alienated and marginalized. Such differences may be due to a number of factors, not least the allocation of specialist roles, tension between different parties, or the contentious innovations of a new worship leader – but these may only be discerned, and explored in depth, when the expressed views of those taking part in a worship event are taken into account.

The third approach moves beyond *Verstehen* in conceiving the meaning of the worship event as emerging out of a process of negotiation between the researcher and the researched. Again, this notion is a response to wider movements in the social sciences, particularly the argument that researchers are constituent parts of the research process, and bring their own influence to bear on the production of knowledge. This is the reflexive approach, and calls for the researcher to situate him/herself within the analysis, in order to render transparent the ways in which researcher influence shapes how acts of worship are portrayed. From this perspective, the objectivist and even the *Verstehen* approach are misguided, as they make the mistake of assuming that the researcher can detach him/herself from the object of study. Instead, the reflexive approach places the researcher at the heart of the research account, and refers back to the experience of the researcher in gaining insights into the worship event.

The reflexive approach can generate useful tools for analysis. Reflecting on how one's own behaviour and reactions are different from those of others present helps us to see what is distinctive about a particular act of worship. It highlights what is most alien and most comfortable to us, and thereby helps us paint a more subtle picture of cultural boundaries. In freeing us from the need to maintain objective distance, it also allows us to reflect on our own experience and include this in our accounts. To some critics, this is to go too far and admit subjective factors into the process, something that renders research at best impressionistic. However, as long as our own experiences are subjected to appropriate critical reflection, then personal experience can offer a fruitful and evocative resource not available to the non-reflexive researcher. Moreover, in acknowledging our own responses to a worship experience, we arguably engage in a more honest and respectful approach to research, as we place ourselves in a position of vulnerability alongside those we are seeking to understand.

Worship, Action and the Wider Social World

A study of the worship life of a particular church often exposes the ways in which it relates to its surrounding culture, for it is at occasions of worship that churches affirm their public mission and express their collective identities as congregations. A common route into this problem refers to the distinction between the parish, serving the needs of the locale, and the gathered congregation, serving the needs of its members. This distinction is often seen as echoing theological differences, with the latter type finding allegiance among those more evangelical Christians who place a premium on personal commitment as a signal of Christian identity, and the former finding support among more 'liberal' churches which emphasize Christian mission as public service to the poor and needy.

Some sociologists have argued that our consumer culture is especially favourable to the 'gathered' type of church, with individual attendees acting as 'spiritual shoppers', steering their participation according to which style of worship is most in tune with their personal taste. These individuals are presented as 'elective parochials', migrant workers who shift their allegiance and community involvement upon moving into a new locale, and many 'megachurches' on the outskirts of cities depend upon these transient worshippers as the heart of their congregational body. However, this trend is also symptomatic of a wider social problem, relating to the decline of local community and the depletion of what Robert Putnam (2000) has called 'social capital'.

Putnam's work has called attention to a set of problems acknowledged by both church and state, and is applied with particular utility in discussions about the declining levels of people willing to contribute to voluntary welfare services. Christian denominations in Britain have a longstanding commitment to social welfare, channelled through voluntary agencies such as Methodist Homes for the Aged and The Children's Society. However, the downscaling of the centralized welfare state in the 1980s triggered the emergence of provision at the local level, for example, through the Church Urban Fund which was established in 1987 to support social action projects in response to the Faith in the City Report. Since then, further projects such as the Anglican Church's 'Commission on Urban Life and Faith' and The William Temple Foundation's three-year initiative 'Regenerating Communities', have sought to address issues of poverty and community in contexts of rapid urban change. Insofar as these projects forge links between churches and society, they enhance what Putnam calls 'bridging social capital' – building valuable and mutually beneficial connections between different groups. Indeed, this process is arguably empowered by government intervention through the Faith Communities Unit, which oversees interaction between faith communities and the state.

Differences of belief can be a boundary to these developments, with more theologically conservative churches either focusing on the needs of their own members or preferring to channel their work through organizations, such as the Evangelical Alliance, that reflect their doctrinal position. Such churches often thrive on 'bonding social capital' – in-group cohesion – but sometimes at the expense of wider collaboration. However, some ecumenical initiatives suggest a more complex relationship. Indeed, projects in Northern Ireland have focused on bridging the sectarian divide between Protestant and Catholic in responding to social needs that apply to all those suffering under conditions of deprivation within particular localities (Bacon, 2003). This is a useful reminder that the relationship between theological allegiance and social action is complex, and is always mediated by the cultural context of the local church.

Practical ways of studying this aspect of local churches

Worship entails a distinctive type of activity – momentary, focused on the otherworldly, often communal, incorporating both rational and non-rational behaviour. While research needs to sustain a critical distance, it also needs to portray something of the lived and total reality of the event itself. The most appropriate method is participant observation, as this is less intrusive than questionnaire or interview methods and therefore leaves room for observation and experience of the multiple aspects of worship itself. It requires careful note-taking, either during or after the worship event. For some aspects – e.g. sermons and sung worship – tape recordings can be an invaluable resource if available. Participant observation is not, however, without its practical and ethical problems. Not least, one needs to tackle the problem of how much of a participant one is, taking care not to allow immersion to compromise the critical distance required of a sociological researcher. This may be an especially difficult problem for researchers who are committed Christians, or who are studying the worship of their own church. Members are in these circumstances likely to have expectations of the researcher that do not always sit comfortably with the needs of the research.

Non-Christians face different dilemmas, related to their self-presentation to church-members and their corresponding behaviour during church services. For example, while honesty may be the best policy, the researcher who sits apart from the congregation obtrusively taking notes may alienate or offend those present. When Steve Warner conducted his work in Mendocino (Warner, 1992), he resolved this problem by taking part in sung worship but not in holy communion, considering this to be consonant with his own identity without deceiving his research subjects.

Some researchers combine participant observation with interview techniques, working from the assumption that the meaning of a ritual event is constructed in a context wider than the event itself. 'Emic' (i.e. insider) understandings of worship may be accessed after church services, although a degree of sensitivity is required in approaching potential respondents, and questions are likely to be spur of the moment, and notes improvised. If more discursive data is required, for example on local 'theologies' of worship among a congregation, then data would be best elicited at a distance from the event itself, within the context of formal, recorded interviews.

Case study

In March 2001, as part of an ongoing period of ethnographic fieldwork, I attended a communion service held by *Visions*, an 'alternative' worship group based in York. There were 22 people present: 12 from the *Visions* core group, who were responsible for arranging and running the service, 9 visitors and peripheral members (including myself), and the curate attached to the group's parent church, who was there in the capacity of celebrant. The announced theme of the service was 'Loss and Moving On'. As always, the lights were dimmed, striking images were projected around the room, and the participants were seated on bean-bags or chairs in a circular formation, around the central communion table. Ambient trance music played at a subdued volume throughout the service.

After a period of liturgy, one of the core group took the microphone to introduce the week's prayer ritual. She referred back to the earlier Bible reading (2 Kings 2.1–12) about Elisha, who was sad because his master Elijah had been called to God and was to leave him. When Elijah was called, Elisha saw him riding to heaven on a chariot of fire, and his spirit passed from master to servant. She then invited us to write down our prayers to God, prayers about loss, bereavement, anger or grief, and place them in the small boat that was floating in a large container at the front of the room. Most of those present did this – using the paper and pens distributed – and approached the front to offer their prayers to God. Another member of the core group then ignited the boat and we all watched as the paper prayers went up in flames.

The worship of the *Visions* group must be seen in the light of the group's shared 'post-evangelical' theology: rooted in the Bible and a need for mission, but driven by the conviction that mainstream church services have little meaning for many people in a postmodern culture. They challenge evangelical conventions through their constant reinvention of worship space and ritual performance. There are no clear leaders in the service, organization and delivery are shared, and the mood is calm and unintrusive. Different prayer rituals are performed each week, and create room for ritual experimentation and spiritual exploration. But while this can be a source of meaning for those who find conventional evangelical worship constraining and unimaginative, it can be potentially alienating for those more used to mainstream symbolism. One newcomer I spoke to after the service said she found it 'difficult to focus on Jesus', she felt like she was browsing through a 'new age' shop. While worship sustains boundaries of meaning within congregations, it is sometimes used to challenge those boundaries through innovations that are liberating for some, but unsettling for others.

Further reading

McGuire, M. (1982) *Pentecostal Catholics: Power, Charisma and Order in a Religious Movement*, Philadelphia: Temple University Press.

McGuire's impressive sociological study of the charismatic movement among Roman Catholics includes two chapters on the use of ritual and language. Chapter 4 explores the way in which authority is mediated in prayer meetings, and chapter 5 offers a sociological analysis of divine communication through human agency, including a consideration of prophecy and glossolalia.

Peshkin, A. (1984) 'Odd Man Out: The Participant Observer in an Absolutist Setting', *Sociology of Education*, 57 (October), pp. 254–64.
Peshkin's research was based in a US Baptist school and church, institutions that supported a fundamentalist approach to Christian teaching. His article is an illuminating discussion of how he managed his own role as a participant observer, given his outsider status as a Jew.

Warner, R. S. (1988) *New Wine in Old Wine Skins: Evangelicals and Liberals in a Small-Town Church*, Berkeley, Los Angeles and London: University of California Press.
Warner's classic study of congregational change in California includes an illuminating chapter (pp. 66–87) on how he accessed the field and conducted his ethnographic research. This includes invaluable insights into the practicalities and ethics of participant observation.

Organizational Studies Strand – Worship and Action

Stuart Jordan

Introduction

Here we draw from the field of organizational studies to consider the work and organized activity of congregations: what they do and how they do it. Utilizing a limited number of published studies alongside practitioner experience, we indicate some of the different organizational factors affecting the way congregations operate internally and, increasingly, in partnership with others.

Forms of Congregational Activity

While there is no single set of categories to classify congregations by their activities, various organizational distinctions might help to determine the main characteristics and orientations that are found:

Formal and informal

The work of local congregations embraces a mix of formal and informal activity each requiring their own form:

- Some tasks will require clear structures of accountability and authority – characteristics, in organizational terms, of a bureaucracy. These include the need to discharge responsibilities as managing trustees of buildings, finances or public records or to implement national church policies or procedures.
- In many other respects a congregation is more like an association, focusing on the role of individual members and their participation in the common life of the congregation – through, for example, involvement in a study group or the sharing of a Harvest meal.
- Congregations also consist of sub-groups that gather around particular interests – such as the choir or the badminton club. Such groups may have little formal access to policy-making but often nonetheless exert significant informal influence.
- Occasionally a specific task requires its own resources, personnel and management – as when a drop-in for the homeless or other community initiative develops into a substantive project. These take the form of an agency, both related to, and distinct from, the wider congregation.

Such a variety of forms can often indicate the range of activity taking place. Since there is rarely a strict division of labour within congregations, however, and people are often involved in more than one activity, it is helpful, both for them and for others, to recognize that different forms are often required to operate in different modes (Billis, 1993).

Communal or associational

Grundy (1998), reflecting Tönnies (1955), draws a distinction between types of congregation on the basis of their relationship to their immediate context – the local community:

- Communal congregations deliberately relate to that context, seeing the wellbeing of the wider community as an essential part of their task and responsibility.

- For associational congregations, by contrast, the context is more incidental: they draw their members from a wider area and focus on the development and needs of the gathered group.

While a useful indicator of a congregation's main orientation, this is not a clear-cut distinction. Even self-consciously communal congregations embrace associational characteristics in serving the needs of their own members, while traditional understandings of neighbourhoods as coherent communities are undergoing revision.

As an interesting corollary, Grundy also identifies different attitudes shown by these two types to their wider denominational structures. The communal congregation, he suggests, sees the wider structure more positively as having potential for representative leadership within society, while the associational congregation is more likely to view it primarily as an administrative unit that may provide (as well as demand) resources, but also constrain the congregation's autonomy.

Four dominant congregational types

In a study of 23 American congregations Becker (1999) identifies four dominant congregational types, based, at least in part, on the main tasks that define their self understanding:

- Houses of worship – in which worship and education are not only present, as they clearly are in all congregations, but are determinative for the congregation's public identity.
- Family congregations – in which members value above all else a sense of acceptance, belonging and wellbeing.
- Community congregations – in which participation and the exploration of personal and social values predominate.
- Leader congregations – which seek to fulfil a public role, either through the profile of its minister or through its engagement with public issues.

These designations are neither exhaustive nor mutually exclusive (Becker herself also identifies mixed congregations which combine different elements). The detailed case studies from which they are derived, however, do serve to illustrate how the elevation of one particular set of tasks can shape the form, culture and process of a congregation's work, as well as its self-perception.

Goals and Purposes

Albrow (1997) reminds us that while the goal of an organization is usually expected to be specific and structured, there are many other less rational factors that are, in practice, just as decisive. This is particularly so in membership organizations, such as a congregation, where the loyalty and participation of members is more likely to depend on the 'expressive' benefits of friendship and support they derive than their interest in formal tasks (Harris, 1998).

Certainly, in common with many other voluntary organizations, congregations need to embrace a range of tasks and these are performed in a variety of modes:

- in delivering a programme of activities they have to be goal-centred;
- in including, supporting and developing individuals they are person-centred;
- in sustaining a range of interests and relationships they need to centre on the role of sub-groups.

Sometimes this variety is enriching; at other times it can create tensions – as when (goal-centred) needs to get a job done well or quickly have to be balanced against the (person-centred) needs of the person who has volunteered to do it.

This is part of a wider issue for voluntary organizations in general, and congregations in particular, that see themselves as value-led. Although Griseri (1998) introduces a necessary element of critical reality in exposing the 'myth of shared values' in organizations, congregations properly attribute normative status to the values derived from their faith. Herein lies a particular challenge, as Harris (1998) indicates, for the goals of a congregation often become most contested precisely in the attempt to seek congruence between the faith values to which they subscribe and the more pragmatic requirements of organizational life.

The question as to how congregations embody faith values in practice can be considered with regard to three particular activities.

Worship

Whatever other purposes a congregation might fulfil, the celebration of worship will be recognized as a central task and its single most significant event. It is in worship that the congregation shares in corporate activity and affirms its identity. Whereas most organizations rarely draw overt attention to their value system, in worship congregations regularly and publicly articulate the values to which they aspire and which they invite others to adopt.

This recognition of the centrality of worship and its symbolic significance invites further lines of enquiry for the student of congregations, especially an exploration of the congruence between values and practice:

- What, for example, does the preparation and leadership of worship reveal? Who determines the content? How important in weekly practice are issues of participation and inclusion?
- What views of stability and change are conveyed by the content of the worship? Are the scriptures and tradition used to resist change or to advocate it?
- What is the practical impact of the weekly rehearsal of a congregation's values? Is it always inspirational (recalling to task and renewing motivation), or can it also be oppressive (underlining any discrepancies between aspiration and reality)?

Congregational Programmes

In addition to public worship, congregations also engage in a variety of other activities to express the faith values they uphold:

- Religious activity – designed to enhance the spiritual or devotional life of existing members, often through small groups or by engaging others in faith issues through programmes of evangelism (Booker and Ireland, 2003).
- Educational activity – designed either to transmit traditions to children, young people or the newly joined, or to develop the faith and understanding of established members.
- Pastoral activity – designed to support individual members of the congregation and often, by extension, other individuals requiring care who have contact with the congregation; it may consist of

informal support offered by the minister or involve an organized network of trained lay people.
- Social activity – designed to strengthen the personal bonds within and between groups, and so to serve the associational needs of the congregation as a whole.

Community Service

In his major study of Christian Service Organizations, Jeavons (1994) indicates the extent to which faith values lead congregations to engage in community service. This happens in different dimensions, representing an expression of compassion, a deepening of spirituality and a witness to belief and values. The result is the creation of a complex relationship between values and practice.

Tensions clearly exist in such activity, especially when it develops to an extent that requires an organizational structure distinct from that of the general congregation. At that point a number of practical and ideological issues commonly arise concerning:

- questions of accountability and ownership: How is the relationship between the congregation and the specialized agency to be understood and maintained?
- potential competition for congregational resources – whether in terms of finance, space within the building, or the minister's time.
- potential conflicts of image or self-understanding if the activities of the project adopt a different understanding of mission or a different set of values from those of the congregation itself.

Meanwhile, Jeavons argues, such activity is often also in tension with secular realities. What is distinctive about community service provided by congregations are the faith values and the organizational style – often more people-centred than management-centred – to which they lead. These, however, must increasingly be reconciled with the proper demands of public accountability, professional service agreements, employment and other statutory procedures. The resultant pressure is always for the agency to assimilate to the external environment and in so doing the distinctive basis for the original activity is easily lost.

Intra-Organizational Relationships

Differentiation and integration

In order to achieve its goals an organization is often divided into sub-units, which if they are to be effective need to relate together and maintain their links with the organization as a whole. The more specialized and developed the sub-unit, the harder this task of integrating relationships within an organization becomes – as in the case of the community service project mentioned above.

In a local congregation different goals are often allocated to sub-units such as the youth club, ladies' meeting, choir, etc. These groups can often act independently, provided they have the support of the congregation as a whole. That support may be expressed in terms of general goodwill or the provision of practical resources such as recruits, meeting space and finance. Support is normally maintained by recognition of the group's contribution to the corporate goals of the congregation and by informal or formal mechanisms of reporting. The support is weakened when the activities of one sub-unit are seen to conflict with the goals of another (e.g. the youth club causes damage to which the property committee objects), or of the whole congregation. The more controversial or demanding of resources the activities of the sub-group, the more developed their means of integrating need to be.

Workflow

Difficulties in working relationships can sometimes be understood by considering the patterns of workflow between individuals or sub-units. Thompson (1967) has identified three such patterns:

- pooled workflow – where a number of sub-units draw on the same pool of resources but work independently of one another;
- sequential workflow – where each sub-unit is part of a chain of activity and dependent on all the others;
- reciprocal workflow – where sub-units work independently but feed work back and forth among themselves and so influence one another.

In a local congregation problems might arise if someone in a sequential or reciprocal workflow operates in a way which fails to consider their impact on the congregation as a whole, so affecting, or even blocking, the system. As when, for example, the editor of the weekly newsheet sets deadlines which regularly exclude essential information, or when the bookings secretary lets out all the rooms commercially without reference to the needs of church groups that can hence never find space to meet.

Inter-Organizational Relationships

Congregations often work in partnership with other bodies – and understanding the issues that arise may be helped by considering three different concepts that have been used to analyse inter-organizational relationships:

- Organizations are said to exist in an exchange relationship with their environment when they both give to and receive resources from other organizations.
- Where they find themselves less powerful than their partner, how-ever, they may exhibit resource-dependency, relying for necessary resources on others.
- In response, in order to secure their position (and the resources they need) they may attempt to meet the expectations of others and so achieve social legitimacy.

Increasingly, congregations, along with other voluntary bodies, are invited to enter into partnerships in order to qualify for public fund-ing. While the language of partnership is positive and collaborative, Billis' (1993) research into partnerships between local authorities and service providers suggests that, in practice, it subsumes a number of different models:

- subordination – where the authority controls most of an agency's funding and can therefore determine its policy and way of work-ing;
- contractual – where there has been genuine negotiation about the services required, the price to be paid, the targets to be met: the agency is free to enter the contract or not; the authority will moni-tor the outcomes;
- supporting – where the authority accepts the need for the agency's work as such and is prepared to offer financial support by way of grant to sustain it;

- partnership – where both authority and agency recognize the other's contribution and co-operate in a common task on the basis of trust.

As well as being clear and realistic about the nature of any proposed 'partnership', a congregation also needs to consider the formal demands and requirements of working with another organizational culture and set of expectations – and sometimes to ask whether the demands go beyond the resources available or involve too great a compromise with the values held.

There are, however, also issues about the way congregations work that partners need to know. Rarely, for example, will the focus for the partnership (the provision of a service or the sharing of a facility) represent the main purpose of the congregation, it may in practice become subordinated – in terms of urgency or resource allocation – to more pressing demands. Meanwhile, those deputed to liaise with the partner organization will often be volunteers used to working more informally than professional officers and constrained by different decision-making processes.

When, for example, a local congregation agreed to explore the joint redevelopment of its premises with a neighbouring GP's surgery the three-person project team appointed by the surgery was surprised when the nine members appointed by the Church Council (to represent different interest groups within the congregation) arrived for the first planning meeting. They were further bemused when told that a decision to accept the recommended architect's tender would need to be referred on to the Church Council meeting in a few weeks' time.

Collaboration with other denominations is a more established form of partnership for some congregations. This may take different forms, from the informal personal relationships of clergy through formalized ecumenical projects to fully constituted Local Ecumenical Partnerships.

While often energized by faith values and conviction, in order to minimize misunderstandings, such partnerships also need to recognize the organizational (as well as theological and ecclesiological) complexities that may be involved. Typically, these include:

- significant differences in church polity and governance;
- different understandings and loci of authority;
- a variety of culture and practice in decision-making processes;
- the legal and practical complexities of funding, owning and managing joint buildings;

- the demands of multiple representation to each of the denominational bodies involved and cross-representation within the partnership.

Planning and Policy Reviews

For many congregations the planning of a programme and activities is traditionally based on a cycle of annual re-enactment that assumes that established patterns are adequate and need only be repeated each year. Increasingly, however, that approach is being challenged by a local willingness, and need, to try new models. Meanwhile church agencies and denominations are encouraging congregations to reflect on their practice and priorities and providing tools – in the form of 'mission audits' or 'church reviews' – to help that take place (Warren, 2004).

This renewed focus on planning and policy can certainly assist congregations to be more intentional about their activity, but it is not without its complications.

- While ostensibly open-ended in their approach church review programmes often promote assumptions and techniques that imply that congregations are primarily rational and should be managed by objectives – without reference therefore to the more complex dynamics of congregational life examined above.
- Invitations to assemble a basic profile of a congregation and its context – typically by use of a 'SWOT analysis' that charts the organizational *Strengths* and *Weaknesses* along with the *Opportunities* and *Threats* of the wider environment – tend to assume the self-interpreting nature of the evidence gathered and, hence, to encourage simplistic responses. While these exercises can stimulate thought and discussion, by themselves they are often unable to inform difficult decisions.
- Any serious attempts to agree priorities are likely to expose the differences of understanding and interpretation that exist within any congregation. While this, and the potential for conflict to which it can lead, is not necessarily problematic, and can indeed be energizing, it can often be alien to congregational cultures more used to preserving unity.
- Church reviews are often prompted by the lack of resources – human or financial. In this context it is important to recognize that

attractive invitations to 'envision a new future', while intended to motivate, can equally have the opposite effect if there is felt to be no spare capacity to move forward.

• Even in the commercial context the limitations and misplaced confidence of long-term planning are becoming increasingly evident. Instead, interest is shifting towards the importance of trying to discern emergent patterns within and around an organization's core activities. This is a much more incremental process that pays attention to the quality of regular activities and as such is a development that might be particularly appropriate within a congregational setting.

In the meantime, congregations continue to engage in a wide range of activities involving their members, the wider community and partner organizations. Often over long periods of time they have developed mechanisms for consulting and taking decisions that seek to balance their faith values, their specific goals and their members' needs. A clearer understanding of these processes, and a more intentional approach to them may well make it possible for congregations to be more effective in what they aspire to do. At the same time their practice may embody insights from which other organizations could learn.

Ways of Studying the Worship and Action of the Local Church

Written material could be traced with the help of the local Church Council Secretary or equivalent. A prime source would be the minutes of the church's governing body or other formal committees; subgroups are much less likely to have written records. Policy documents in the form of a mission statement may exist and some denominations require a periodic review of the church's life, as well as its buildings. Local Ecumenical Partnerships are also subject to periodic external review and are likely to have documentation describing the formal relationships of the denominations involved.

A great deal of information about the way the congregation is organized and 'the way things are done' will not be written down but will have been internalized. Informal interviews with the minister or lay officers should help uncover this information, and may even reveal different understandings. The fact that so many practices are routinized and rarely examined, however, means that even those most involved may need to reflect and reassemble key information for themselves.

Any student of congregational worship will need to attend, and would be welcome at, public services. Many other activities are also advertised and open to anyone. Attendance at other meetings as an observer could be arranged through the minister or a lay official. Interviews with those responsible for specific projects, or with members of partner organizations, could also be a fruitful source of information and perception.

What questions can be asked?

The tasks of a congregation may already be familiar to many people. That very familiarity, however, often discourages critical reflection. The material in this section could help to answer more fully a number of questions asked from various perspectives:

- What is the purpose of the congregation as an organization?
- Who gets to do what, and why?
- How does the congregation relate to the local community?
- What factors shape the way things are done?
- What does its worship say about the congregation?
- How does the congregation prioritize issues and what kind of strategy does it need?
- How does the congregation understand its goals?
- Does the congregation work with other organizations?
- How do they co-operate and what are the issues for partners?

Case Study – Virginia Luckett

The parish is a Church of England team ministry of two churches, one of which was refurbished as a parish centre ten years ago. The parish centre is let occasionally on a commercial and community basis and is 'home' to ten projects, three of which are part of the parish's vision to offer worship, friendship and service to the local community. The community also actively uses the hall attached to the other church in the team. To support its communal approach and congregations, ensuring financial and legal control and adherence to its values and ethos, the parish has developed a complex organizational structure.

The legal and financially accountable corporate body for the parish is the Parochial Church Council (PCC). The PCC and its standing committee set policy and vision for the parish. The PCC delegates its responsibility to a total of seven sub-groups, one for each church, one for each parish project and two additional buildings committees; although all are PCC sub-groups, they have differing degrees of influence.

The parish project management committees are open to membership from the paid project worker employed by the PCC and stakeholders from outside the congregations, such as volunteers or partnership organizations.

The organizational complexity, multiple stakeholders with differing degrees of power and commitment to the parish vision and values, and the necessity to consult widely, has led to:

- clarity in the decision-making process, however, strategic and policy decisions are challenging and time-consuming to broker;
- competition for resources, including volunteers;
- complex power and accountability relationships within committees;
- organizational misunderstanding from outside agencies, such as funding bodies and potential partners, which always requires clarification;
- assurance of financial and organizational control and adherence to the parish's faith values;
- wider and deepening sense of commitment and ownership of the parish mission.

Further reading

Albrow, M. (1997) *Do Organizations Have Feelings?* London: Routledge.
A collection of sociological essays exploring the nature, principles and values and social responsibilities of organizations.

Griseri, P. (1998) *Managing Values: Ethical Change in Organizations*, London: Macmillan.
An examination of values within organizations and the complex way in which they operate.

Grundy, M. (1998) *Understanding Congregations: A New Shape for the Local Church*, London: Mowbray.
An introduction to the basics of congregations and their work in order to encourage more effective practice.

Harris, M. (1998) *Organizing God's Work: Challenges for Churches and Synagogues*, Basingstoke: Macmillan.

A detailed study of congregations as organizations, identifying a number of common issues they face.

Jeavons, T. H. (1994) *When the Bottom Line Is Faithfulness: Management of Christian Service Organizations*, Indianapolis: Indiana University Press.

An analysis of management issues faced by seven American Christian service organizations, described against their cultural context but with much wider application.

Theological Strand – Worship and Action

Jan Berry

Introduction

Here we draw on the field of theology to look at how the worship and action of the local church can be analysed to disclose the theological assumptions and models which, although often unvoiced, direct the congregation's life together.

Liturgy and Worship

Although there is a considerable body of writing about worship and liturgy, it usually takes the form of historical scholarship and doctrinal understanding, or appears as practical manuals aimed at providing resources and inspiration for the leader of worship. There is little that engages with the worshipping life of a congregation as a way into understanding and analysing that local church's life and theology. Browning (1991) writes about the black Pentecostal church and its preaching; Cartledge (2003) gives a sympathetic analysis of a charismatic service; and feminist writers have argued for the impact of liturgy on worshippers' self-understanding and its role in shaping belief (Wootton, 2000).

This is surprising given that worship could be said to be the distinctive activity of the local church. When the community of faith meets to worship, it is engaged in practices which have few secular parallels, although there are equivalent practices in other faith communities beyond the Christian church. This worshipping activity carries meanings relating to the congregation's identity, purpose and self-understanding: it is 'value-laden' (Browning, 1991) or 'disclosive practice' (Graham, 2002).

One useful way of studying the worship of a local church is to apply the praxis model described in Section 2.2 above:

Experience

Many studies of worship are action research projects, embarked upon by the minister or members within the congregation with the hope of making some change in the style or form of worship. In other instances the researcher may be looking at the worship of the congregation in order to learn more about their beliefs or identity. In either case the first stage of the process is similar, to use ethnographic methods to gain as much information as possible on how members of the congregation experience worship together.

Exploration

Exploration, the second stage of the model, requires further analysis of the liturgical pattern of the congregation, using methods described elsewhere in this volume, and drawing on insights from other disciplines such as sociology, psychology and anthropology. A good starting-point is the analytic observation of a service of worship, and helpful resources for this may be found in the appendices of Susan White's *Groundwork of Christian Worship* (1997). Other research methods may be used to uncover underlying attitudes and feelings, and check the observer's interpretations.

Here is an indication of areas that you could investigate, with suggested questions that could be helpful:

Space

Many churches have inherited buildings, designed for a different era, which they do not have the resources to alter. But looking at the care people have taken of the space, their openness to the possibilities, and the use they make of the different areas of the building gives some clues to their values and priorities. James White proposes six categories of liturgical space according to their function: gathering, movement, congregational, choir, baptismal and altar-table space (White, 1990).

- Is there a particular space where people gather, before and after the service, and how does this act as a transition to and from the act of worship?
- What movement takes place within the building, both around and during the act of worship, and what function does this serve?
- Is there a particular area that seems to be demarcated as more sacred, and if so, who has access to it?
- What kind of behaviours and conversations are acceptable within particular areas?
- What symbolic objects or banners or particular items of furniture have particular significance or associations for that church?

Time

Liturgical scholars (White, 1997) talk of *chronos* and *kairos* time. The *kairos* time is that marked by the liturgical seasons of the church, focusing on the birth, death and resurrection of Jesus (Davies, 2002, pp. 188–92). Preaching, prayers, hymns and symbols reflect this; but there are other occasions originating in social and cultural contexts. In recent years a number of Sundays have been devoted to particular themes or issues, in an attempt to increase congregational awareness.

- What is the pattern of weekly worship? Are there services with different congregations, ethos and power in decision-making?

- Are there services aimed at particular groups of people, teenagers, young families or the 'unchurched'?

- How does the church mark rites of passage? Even in a largely post-Christian society, many people still turn to the church to mark significant lifecycle events, such as birth, marriage and death. Elaine Ramshaw's work (1987) on ritual and pastoral care is useful in giving ways into understanding the pastoral needs met by ritual, and looking at a church's practice in these areas can yield invaluable information on how church members and adherents understand their faith in relation to these aspects of human life and relationship.

Structure

Every act of worship follows a certain pattern or structure, fixed by a predetermined order or by the pattern which has evolved in the local congregation.

- How is the structure of worship determined, by a fixed liturgy, or by the preacher, or leader of worship?
- How do people engage with different parts of the liturgy, what do they find meaningful, boring or challenging?
- In what ways can the congregation respond and participate, and what are the understandings of concepts of authority, freedom and spontaneity?

Symbol and imagery

I use 'imagery' in the broadest sense, to refer to the dominant metaphors and symbols shaping the life of the congregation. In an Anglican or Catholic setting much of the content will be determined by a fixed liturgy, but sermons, some prayers and the choice of hymns may reflect a particular perspective. In non-conformist congregations, much more may depend on the preacher's choice.

- What does the congregation see as the major themes of worship, and how do they understand and interpret the symbols and images used?
- How far do images and symbols include or exclude various groups, women, disabled people, black people, single people?

Reflection

At the third stage of the model, reflection, we turn to the theological tradition where practical theologians can draw on the resources of liturgical and historical theology. There is a body of research into the origins of Christian worship within Judaism, the New Testament period, and the early church (Bradshaw, 1992). Various denominational traditions trace features of their worship back to their origins, and, where appropriate, the study of the Reformation, or radical dissent in the seventeenth century, or the Wesleyan revival may be useful. In addition, there is the contemporary thinking on worship represented by the charismatic movement, the modern liturgical movement and what Teresa Berger calls the 'women's liturgical movement' (Berger, 1999). Less well-documented but significant influences on contemporary worship can be discerned in the work of Taizé, the Iona community, Greenbelt, and developments such as cell churches, seeker services, or the purpose-driven church (Croft, 2002).

In this part of the process we raise theological questions about the purpose and intention of worship. Susan White (1997) proposes six theological models of worship: service to God, the mirror of heaven, affirmation, communion, proclamation and the arena of transcendence. She stresses that these are not mutually exclusive; but different emphases reveal something of how the congregation understands the activity in which it is engaged, and the place that worship plays in faith and discipleship. Worship that is seen as service to God is motivated by a sense of gratitude and obedience, as part of what humanity owes to the creator and stresses God's 'worth-ship' and human dependence upon God. Worship seen as the mirror of heaven is the attempt to replicate in time and space the eternal worship of heaven; it is an understanding of worship often found in Orthodox and eastern churches, but may also reflect the theology of oppressed groups, whose worship attempts to create a sense of the eternal in contrast to the harsh realities of earthly life. Worship as affirmation is worship to support the Christian believer, to encourage, inspire and nurture Christian faith and discipleship. Worship as communion stresses the importance of relationship whether divine–human or within the human community, and sees that relationship expressed, embodied and recreated in the worshipping life of the congregation. Worship as proclamation stresses the communication of the essentials of Christian faith, the telling out of the good news in Christ. This may be for the encouragement and education of the congregation, or may be evangelistic in purpose. Finally, there is the model of worship as the arena of transcendence, rooted in the understanding that worship cannot be explained in terms of human activity alone, but must always allow for the inbreaking of the divine spirit. This is explicit in traditions as diverse as Pentecostalism and Quakerism, but is not wholly absent from any of the understandings of worship.

Looking at worship in this way uncovers issues, beliefs and values relating to the congregation's understanding of the nature of God, the relation of God to humanity and the created order, the nature of discipleship, witness and service, and the dynamics of power and leadership.

Action/new experience

In the final part of the process the cycle is completed, as the results of the study make their impact on the life of the congregation. In some instances this may mean that the leader of worship or members of the congregation have a better understanding of their own theology and beliefs; in other instances there may be specific changes to the congregation's practice. If the person undertaking the study has done the work collaboratively, involving the congregation at every stage, then the congregation as a whole (or a significant group within it) has been involved in a piece of corporate theological reflection.

> One researcher wanted to explore the theology of two congregations within his pastorate and designed a questionnaire asking members of the congregation to describe their favourite hymns and reasons for choosing them. He analysed the results and used the dominant images and metaphors in the hymns they had chosen to draw up a pen-portrait of each of the congregations. He turned to the theological tradition for thinking on hymnody, its development and uses, including contemporary music. At the conclusion of the project he shared some of his findings with the congregations in special services using their favourite hymns, alongside stories and information about their background (Muir, 2003).

It is possible to see that the act of worship itself is a process of corporate theological reflection, even if this is not systematic or explicit. This is clear where the exploration of the word is a shared process, through discussion or Bible study in place of the sermon. Where a traditional sermon is used, if the preacher engages seriously with the concerns and needs of the congregation, then the preaching becomes a reflection on the life of the congregation in dialogue with the word of God as read and proclaimed through scripture. Lyall talks about the pastor as a 'reflective practitioner' (Lyall, 2001), and a preacher who is immersed in the life of the congregation and community will reflect on that context in his or her preaching. Leonora Tisdale encourages what she calls 'exegeting the congregation' (Tisdale, 1997) – studying the needs, concerns and aspirations of the congregation with the same attention as one would pay to a biblical text, and taking this as the starting-point for preaching.

Either of these two approaches results in preaching which is a shared theological reflection on the corporate life of the congregation. This process, however, is not confined to the preaching or exploration of the word, for the imagery of hymns and prayers, and the congregational response to symbols and symbolic action, all provoke responses and reflections that may be more powerful for not being expressed through rational verbalization. Liturgy and worship is an ongoing process of corporate theological reflection; the kind of study we have described entails uncovering that process and articulating it in a more explicit way.

Care and Action

While the worshipping life of a congregation is significant, all local churches have other activities that enable us to learn about their values, dynamics and culture. A study of church newsletters and notice sheets will quickly give an overview of the programme of a local church, and most of the activities of the church will fall into one of the following categories: education, mission, building community, administration or decision-making, and pastoral care.

Education

This includes all those activities aimed at helping members and adherents of the church grow in their faith and understanding. A closer look at the learning activities taking place, however, reveals different theological understandings, methodologies and processes. For some church leaders teaching is deductive – a matter of receiving the revealed wisdom of God, made known in scripture and interpreted through the tradition of the church or the inspired knowledge of the leaders. Teaching often follows set themes, placing a strong emphasis on biblical knowledge. There is a concern for sound teaching and correct doctrine, and such churches often have a strong identity based on their theological understanding and conviction. Engagement with the contemporary world and society is viewed in terms of applying the truths of scripture and tradition, enabling the believer to live a Christlike and holy life.

In other instances, the approach to learning is inductive and exploratory, with an emphasis on asking questions and exploring difficulties and doubts. The agenda may arise from the contemporary situation, or groups may explore films or novels as a way of understanding theological or spiritual truth. Here the understanding is of faith and discipleship worked out in believers' own understandings and context, and the process is one of corporate theological reflection, with the theologically educated leader acting as a resource and guide.

Educational activities may be integrated with the Sunday services, often with separate groups or classes for children and young people, and many preachers assert that their sermons include an element of teaching. For many members of the congregation, this is the only opportunity for increasing their knowledge of the Bible and of faith. Many local churches, however, organize house groups, Bible study groups, discipleship courses, discussion groups or some form of training for new members. In addition, there are local ecumenical opportunities for study (e.g. Lent groups) and, for those prepared to make a greater commitment, courses run locally, ecumenically or denominationally. John Hull (1985) talks of the importance of learning and development in faith for Christian adults, and seeks to develop a theology which would support the local church as a learning community.

Mission and outreach

Many congregations have activities that involve those who are not members of the church, indeed to look at how a church defines and monitors its boundaries gives us insights into their theological self-understanding. Some churches have an implicit or overt evangelical theology that stresses the importance of individual conversion and a personal relationship with Christ in which the boundaries are drawn according to belief. Only those who have made an explicit commitment can be seen as fully belonging, although there may be a slight blurring of the boundaries, for those in the process of coming to faith. These churches are likely to focus on evangelistic activities, seeking to make new converts or draw others into the life of the church, (e.g. Alpha courses – Hunt 2004). Writers such as Warren (1995) and Cray (1992) stress the importance of the evangelistic nature of the church, and argue that the church must be a missionary church, sharing in the mission of God in the world.

Other congregations have an underlying model of service or inclusion. Such churches see their role as serving the needs of the community, with an incarnational theology that sees the presence of Christ in those the church is seeking to serve. Boundaries are more fluid with less sharp differentiation between members, attendees, and those who participate in other groups and activities. Activities that are of service to the community are offered, although sometimes the congregation's role will be limited to providing the use of the building and some input into management committees, with the organizations themselves taking over the running and decision-making. Rites of passage are freely offered, and there is a strong emphasis on welcome. Here the theological model is incarnational with a strong emphasis both on discovering and becoming part of the purpose of God in the world and on discerning the presence of Christ in others.

Other churches define themselves in terms of struggle or protest. These may be congregations which see themselves as promoting different values from the surrounding culture, for example, in taking a deliberate stand against injustice as in anti-debt campaigns, sanctuary or anti-deportation movements. Here the underlying theology often has strong links with liberation theology, and the church will see its role as a prophetic one in challenging oppression and injustice in the name of a God who sides with the poor (Sheppard, 1983).

Many congregations operate with a combination of these models, and often it is a question of the predominant emphasis at a given time in a church's life, or in relation to a particular issue or concern. Underlying many of these is an understanding of how far faith is a private or a public matter. Browning (1991, p. 19) talks about the privatization of American religion and churches, and many would see a similar trend here. On the other hand, movements such as industrial mission and urban theology have placed emphasis on the more public and prophetic demands of faith, and some local churches have been influenced by these wider developments. Urban congregations have taken up issues of poverty, debt or racial justice; and rural congregations have responded to isolation, and the economic impact of the outbreak of foot-and-mouth disease in 2001.

'Lamp Road' (a pseudonym) is a small congregation in an urban area. It has always seen itself as a welcoming and friendly church, and has actively supported anti-deportation, fair trade and anti-debt campaigns. The buildings are used extensively by community projects during the week, and the Sunday morning service takes place in a multipurpose worship area.

Recently the church embarked on a programme to declare itself an inclusive congregation. A process of corporate theological reflection took place through a series of morning services, followed by shared lunches and workshops, under the heading *Celebrating Diversity*. Ideas and phrases suggested by the congregation were gathered together in a written statement, which was formally adopted at a church meeting.

Beneath the surface of the process lie a number of stories. The congregation includes black members, and in the past there have been tensions, never entirely resolved, relating to race. There are gay members of the congregation who have lived through the church debates on homosexuality with pain and anger. At times the congregation has struggled to support members with learning disabilities, or those experiencing economic deprivation. Further research could uncover these stories and many more; and probably more ambivalent responses to the statement than have emerged in meetings. Nevertheless here is a church that understands its theology in terms of service and inclusion, but also with a sense of struggle for values of justice and acceptance against dominant understandings in society and in other parts of the church.

Building community

Some of the church's activities can be described under the general heading of 'fellowship'. This term may be used of youth groups, women's groups or groups meeting for Bible study, sharing and prayer. In many instances, there is little overt theological reflection accompanying these groups, and some function primarily as social or support groups, helping to build a sense of belonging and community. Underlying these, however, is a theology of the church as the body of Christ, a group of individual believers who are related to one another in a corporate sense through their relationship to Christ. Within such a theology, the building and strengthening of relationships becomes an important priority in building the life of the church.

Administration and decision-making

Every local church will have its formal structures for decision-making. But formal structures do not tell the whole story. Are there particular groups that hold the power, or some who control resources in such a way that decisions made by members of the congregation or their representatives can be blocked? Tracing the process by which an idea is proposed, a decision taken, and action implemented can be significant in revealing the hidden agenda and power dynamics within a congregation. It also speaks of the theological understandings of the nature of authority and leadership within the church, and the understandings of the ways in which the Holy Spirit moves and guides the life of the congregation.

Pastoral care

Underlying the activities and meetings of the church is a relational network, often sustained by the care and support given by clergy or other designated members. Most churches and clergy attach considerable importance to the care the church has for its members; but again this may be understood in a number of different ways.

There is still a strong expectation that pastoral care is primarily the role of the clergy; but many churches have attempted to devolve this, setting up pastoral care teams, or placing responsibility with lay leaders. We can recognize different understandings of pastoral care: the regular and proactive visits to members of the congregation, the response in crisis, and occasionally the provision of more specialist counselling services, either within the church, or through ecumenical co-operation. Some people place a strong emphasis on pastoral care as helping to promote the development of faith, others see it as the provision of support in illness, relationship-breakdown or other crisis. Care within the congregation is not limited to pastoral visitation, and may be expressed in many practical ways. Many congregations have informal networks of care which they themselves hardly perceive as significant, yet which play a vital role in forming bonds of friendship and concern. Compared to the secular world, pastoral care in a church has very little regulation, although there is growing awareness of child protection issues. Many clergy have no form of supervision for their pastoral work, and it is worth asking questions about how people in the church who are exercising or receiving pastoral care understand issues of responsibility and accountability.

Pastoral care is an area where assumptions and stereotypes easily remain unchallenged. It is an area of power and vulnerability, and has great potential for reflecting on issues of empowerment, mutuality and dependency.

- What are the perceived limits of the church's care (Davies, Watkins and Winter, 1991)?
- Is it seen as restricted to members, or does the church have an ethos of service in the local community?

- Does the church's vision of care include the prophetic, liberation dimension advocated by Stephen Pattison (1994)?
- How far does the church see its activity extending beyond itself to its local community or to an involvement in global issues?

The method of critical correlation (see Section 2.2 above) has been widely used by practical theologians, drawing on secular disciplines of psychology and sociology in dialogue with scriptural and doctrinal understandings of human nature and spiritual development (Lyall, 2001; Woodhead and Pattison, 2001).

Analysis and reflection on pastoral care within a congregation will suggest different theological models. The term 'pastoral' suggests a shepherding model, which has been critiqued by feminists as conveying helplessness and dependency (Bennett Moore, 2002), but has strong biblical roots and is still much used. The concept of church as the body of Christ is powerful, and has many different possible applications. The image of church as family is popular with many congregations, but can lead to an idealization of family patterns and structures, which excludes single or childless people, masks abuse and is damaging to those who have suffered within families. However, if the dysfunctional aspects of family life are kept in mind, this can still be a model with potential for exploring the negative, shadow sides of church life as well as the positive relationships and sense of belonging.

Practical theologians have suggested different functions or models of pastoral care. Lartey expands the traditional functions of healing, sustaining, guiding and reconciling to include nurturing, liberating and empowering (Lartey and Poling, 2003). Feminist theologians have explored the particular contributions of women as both givers and receivers of pastoral care (Graham and Halsey, 1993), and have used the image of the web to convey the interconnectedness of relationships and the importance of social context in pastoral care (Bennett Moore, 2002). Researchers studying local congregation may find these helpful in exploring the theological understandings embodied within a church's practice of pastoral care, or may develop their own models.

Conclusion

Members of local congregations often find it hard to articulate their theology in words, perhaps lacking confidence or being deskilled by the word theology itself with its specialist overtones. In this contribution we have seen how exploration of a church's worship, activities and relationships can uncover the implicit theological models, and strengthen corporate reflection on the beliefs and understandings that govern a congregation's life.

Practical ways of studying worship and action

Probably relatively few people will be investigating in depth all the areas discussed above – often research is focused on a particular area of congregational life or a specific aspect of worship. Simply being part of what goes on, whether in worship or personal encounters can offer valuable opportunities to observe the processes and dynamics at work. The material gained from such observations needs careful analysis and reflection, with an awareness of the researcher's own position and bias. Care should be taken over using information gained from pastoral encounters or personal conversation, as this may raise ethical issues with regard to confidentiality and appropriate boundaries. Questionnaires, group and individual interviews can all be used with profit in investigating worship and action.

Further reading

Cartledge, M. (2003) *Practical Theology: Charismatic and Empirical Perspectives*, Carlisle, Cumbria and Waynesboro, GA: Paternoster Press.
    This would be a valuable resource for anyone studying a charismatic church. It contains a charismatic perspective on research methodology and essays on specific topics.
Graham, E. L. (2002) *Transforming Practice: Pastoral Theology in an Age of Uncertainty* (2nd ed.), Eugene, Oregon: Wipf and Stock.
    Theoretical background to the development of practical theology with some important concepts underpinning congregational studies.
Lartey, E. Y. and J. N. Poling (2003) *In Living Colour: An Intercultural Approach to Pastoral Care and Counselling* (2nd ed.), London: Jessica Kingsley.
    A range of possible models and processes for reflection in the area of pastoral care.
Tisdale, L. T. (1997) *Preaching as Local Theology and Folk Art*, Minneapolis MN: Fortress.

Aims to help preachers take account of their listeners' context but also a useful resource for studying congregations, particularly chapter 3 on 'Exegeting the congregation'.

White, S. (1997) *Groundwork of Christian Worship*, Peterborough: Epworth Press.

A clear and accessible introduction to the theology and history of liturgy. Looks seriously at what we can learn about the church from its worship.

Wootton, J. H. (2000) *Introducing a Practical Feminist Theology of Worship*, Sheffield: Sheffield Academic Press.

An account of the developments in women's liturgy in the British context.

3.3 The Resources and People of the Local Church

Introduction

In this section, which uses the four perspectives to examine the resources and people of the local church, Peter Collins, from an anthropological point of view, explores how space is used by the Religious Society of Friends (Quakers) to create a sense of identity over time. The negotiated use of artefacts, and the particular performance of practice contribute to a contemporary Quaker sense of corporate self that owes much to its history. Sylvia Collins analyses current statistics on churchgoing as a sociologist. She is interested to find out what sorts of people continue to go to local churches and their reasons for doing so, and her contribution sets out some of the concepts used in sociological research. Helen Cameron, using the insights of organizational studies, looks at how people get involved in local churches in paid and unpaid ways, as individuals and in teams, and she provides a useful survey of how the resources of the local church, in terms of income and expenditure, buildings and financial assets, can be understood more fully. William Storrar uses an extended case study to explore how the space and place of the local church, embodied both as building but also as people-using-space, can be reconfigured in imaginative ways as a resource to serve the local community. He uses the critical correlation model of practical theology.

Anthropological Strand – Resources and People

Peter Collins

Introduction

Here we shall focus on the resources and people that come together to constitute the local church. Our strategy will be to present a series of concepts in cumulative fashion. Since our brief is to present a distinctly anthropological perspective we will develop an approach based on two fundamental tenets. First, although any analysis of social life is bound to be partial, our overriding objective is to understand the local church as a whole comprised of constituent parts. Second, we are likely to arrive at a better understanding of congregation 'X' if we compare it with congregation 'Y'.

The thrust of this discussion is, therefore, to prompt the reader into making comparisons. To that end we will focus on one type of congregation, the Quaker meeting for worship, in order to throw into stark relief certain possible features of all local churches. In order to participate fruitfully in the exercise, you should read the following account while holding in mind a congregation with which you are familiar, comparing and contrasting the whole time.

Here I will treat the following pairs of terms 'Religious Society of Friends' and 'Quakerism', 'Friend' and 'Quaker', as synonymous.

Space

The Religious Society of Friends (Quakers) consists, in the UK, of approximately 500 congregations or 'meetings'. The space they occupy, and have occupied in the past, is manifold. We will return to the more circumscribed space of the meeting house below. Certainly, the social, cultural, political and religious position they assumed during their genesis in the mid-seventeenth century has been woven into the contemporary fabric of the group. Most of all, they inhabit a shared space, forming a network that is both structural and effective. A newcomer is inevitably asked two questions: 'Have you been to a Quaker meeting before?' And if the answer is positive, then 'So which meeting do you belong to?'

Up until 1900 the space occupied by Quakerism was hedged about by a series of prescriptions and proscriptions. Quaker space was defined by a unique configuration of faith and practice, which clearly and sometimes notoriously set the 'us' apart from the 'them'. Quakers stood out and were relatively easy to identify: they did not attend church, not even for christenings, weddings or funerals. Early Quakers adopted a certain mode of speech, dress and social behaviour which further distinguished them from 'the world'. These symbolic screens multiplied during the eighteenth century up to the time where numbers began to decline somewhat precipitously. Church discipline pervaded every aspect of a Quaker's life, even the apparently trivial: the use of umbrellas, the cut of one's coat pockets, the width of one's gravestone. Contemporary Quakers reflect the ambient social climate, albeit a left of centre, lower middle-class climate: those from the 'caring professions' (medicine, social and community work, and teaching) are probably disproportionately represented in the majority of meetings. Quakers no longer 'stand out' – except insofar as they define themselves as Quakers.

Space/Memory

The Society of Friends has an exceptionally good memory, facilitated primarily by the coherence of church organization: each local meeting is self-consciously a piece of the national jigsaw. The past has served from the very beginning of the movement as a resource on which to draw in constructing Quaker corporate identity. For Quakers, the past is not some vague abstraction allowing an entirely free play of the contemporary imagination. Quaker discourse has taken many forms. From 1650 on, Quakers have inscribed their faith and practice in considerable detail; the 'written record' in this case is extremely fine-grained. The response of early Friends to their many critics was an earnest engagement in a veritable 'pamphlet war'. Although most critics stopped short of taking them further, plenty did not. The spoken and written diatribes issued by George Fox and others regularly brought Quakers into conflict with the law. Their absolute refusal to pay tithes, their determination to meet for worship and their deliberate eschewal of a wide range of customary behaviour led to a harsh regime of persecution which continued well into the eighteenth century.

Quakers were, for over half a century, in perpetual dispute with both state and church, both locally and nationally. One outcome of particular interest here is the plethora of written accounts recording the 'Sufferings' of Friends at that time. Quakers themselves recorded these events at the local, regional and national levels of what soon became a particularly well-organized movement. On top of this, there was a steady accumulation of documented proceedings from Magistrates' Courts, Quarter Sessions, and even, in the case of James Naylor, for instance, Parliament itself. Meeting for Sufferings was established in London in order to record, in detail, the travails of Friends.

Again, the rapid and thorough organization of the Society from the earliest years involved the establishment of meetings for church affairs in geographical tiers. Local business was conducted each month at preparative meetings; several local meetings came together monthly to discuss business at Monthly Meeting; a number of monthly meetings would send representatives to consider their business at Quarterly Meeting, and representatives from all parts of the country met annually, in London Yearly Meeting. Broadly speaking, this organizational structure has remained intact to the present day. Quarterly Meeting has been replaced with General Meeting, which now has a primarily social-cum-pedagogic function. Meeting for Sufferings, comprising representatives from all Monthly Meetings, now functions as a national executive. There will be participants in virtually all preparative (i.e. local) meetings who act as representatives at one or more these meetings. Quaker organization is, therefore, relatively non-hierarchical, in that power is largely distributed among the membership. Most of those employed by the Society are based in Friends House, in London. Local meetings may employ a warden to take care of their meeting house.

Minutes that record the transactions of every formal meeting are collected and in virtually every case have been available for scrutiny by Friends, and, in so far as they are stored in Public Records Offices, by anyone who has an interest. Typically, the minutes of early Quaker meetings include information on membership, on births, deaths and marriages, on the non-payment of tithes and sufferings resulting from conflicts with the law. By 1700, Quaker meetings, at all levels, were recording, in the form of minutes, a growing number of proscriptions and prescriptions delineating what had come to be known at 'the testimonies', each of which served to bring Quaker identity into stark relief. By 1700, those who wished to be thought of as Friends were, for example, not paying tithes, not willing to be called to military service, dressing and speaking plainly, and complying with the discipline of choosing a marriage partner from within the group. Contemporary minute books are likely to contain reports delivered by representatives to other Quaker meetings, the management of the meeting house and local activities.

Over and above the thousands of minute books which have accumulated steadily down the years, there were other influential forms of writing. The lives of 'public' (i.e. influential) Friends were recorded in the form of 'Testimonies to the Life of N'. Robert Barclay attempted to delineate a more or less systematic Quaker theology. William Penn wrote voluminously on Quaker faith and practice. Friends (and others) began by the mid-eighteenth century to produce personal histories in the form of spiritual biographies as well as histories of the group. Although Quakers are known for their largely silent liturgy, they should also be renowned for their fecundity in print! This luxuriant written record ensures that Quakerism has a long and densely meaningful memory.

Space/Memory/Identity

Crucially, the Society agreed in 1738 to produce a volume which set out, systematically, the still relevant rules and regulations. *The Book of Discipline*, as it was first known, has been revised approximately once every generation since then. The text has developed in various ways and the most recent edition was published in 1995 under the title *Quaker Faith and Practice: The Book of Christian Discipline of the Yearly Meeting of the Religious Society of Friends (Quakers)* (henceforth *QFP*). It is the quasi-canonical, congealed memory of the group and the most cogent representation of Quaker identity. The text, in its current manifestation, contains the current 'Advices and Queries', which, in the context of what proclaims itself to be a creedless church, most explicitly outlines the aspirations of individual Quakers. Further chapters outline the business structure and testimonies of the Society and, drawing on Quaker discourse from 1650 onwards, delineate the current shape of Quakerism. This delineation depends largely on past writing. In this way and through the public explication of a historical discourse, Quaker identity is rooted in the past: it is presented as a religious tradition. But, remember, the *Book of Discipline* is regularly revised, thus re-presenting a tradition that is not dead but alive, and able to recreate itself in perpetuity.

QFP is regarded as the handbook of British Quakerism. Yearly Meetings elsewhere, and particularly in the USA, have developed their

own versions of the book. It is presented as both practical and inspirational. There are sections on how to conduct Quaker marriages and
funerals, on the peace testimony, on 'openings' and on 'close relationships'. Each section of each chapter reveals a little more of what it
might mean to be a Quaker, to belong in the Society of Friends. We
use the term 'might' quite consciously, signalling an awareness that
individual Friends will identify more closely with some sections than
with others.

It is worth noting, further, that Quaker identity is nuanced at the
local level. There is an awareness that one's Local Meeting is 'the same
but different' when compared to other Local Meetings. This local (or
vernacular) identity derives from the specificities of the Local Meeting, from its geographical location, its meeting house, the events it has
staged, the people who have figured prominently in its evolution and
so forth.

Space/Identity/Memory/Artefact

Many religions revolve around the perpetual interpretation of 'The
Book' – in Christianity most often the Bible, in Islam the Qu'ran,
in Sikhism the Granth Sahib, and so on. In such cases the Book is
often placed at the centre of the congregation, both symbolically and
physically. This is certainly true in the case of the Religious Society of
Friends. *The Book of Discipline* is of central importance not only for
the ideas it contains but also as a material artefact. Let us replace it in
its proper context.

A Quaker meeting house is structurally homogeneous, regardless of
its size, location or period of construction. It is possible to interpret
the Quaker meeting for worship as an opportunity to pay homage to
Quakerism both as it is and as it has been. Let us expand on this claim.
Individual participants enter the meeting room at around 10.30 a.m.
They choose a place to sit on the benches which are arranged in a hol-
low square. The benches are ancient and some people have become
accustomed to sitting in the same place for decades, possibly where
their father, mother, grandfather or grandmother were known to sit.
The meeting room will be plain. There will be little or no reference to
religious practice. Since Quakerism defined itself from its birth against
the established church, there is no Christian iconography – no depic-
tions of Christ, Mary, the saints; no crosses, candlesticks, chalice:
the room is *plain*. There is no altar, no font, no pulpit. The benches

(sometimes chairs) are arranged around a table upon which are a small vase of freshly cut flowers and a copy of *Quaker Faith and Practice*. The attention of worshippers wanders – there is the sound of a black-bird singing, the drone of cars speeding along a distant motorway; the occasional passer-by drifts in and then out of view; someone rustles their coat as they search for a handkerchief. The predominant sound, however, is silence, the predominant movement, stillness. The gaze of the meeting returns time and time again to the table, to the flowers, and to the *Book of Discipline*: the tradition made sensible.

As we have said, Quaker memory is secured in an extraordinarily rich array of written texts. But, if we agree to broaden the definition of text to include material culture, then the Quaker memory is also sedimented in the meeting house and its artefacts. The building will have the lives of Quakers written into it, in the form of furniture donated, decorating completed, woodwork polished, pictures painted and hung, books gifted and so on and so forth. The storied memories of individual Friends and families of Friends will continue in the fabric of the meeting house. Some meeting houses adjoin the local Quaker burial ground – in such cases the very gravestones, typically plain, ensure that past Friends are not forgotten. Artefacts multiply memory, conflating past and present, dramatizing the sense of continuity. In such ways Friends who are in one sense absent are not only remembered but brought to mind; we might say brought to meeting and, in that sense, made present.

Space/Identity/Memory/Artefact/Performance

Each meeting comprises individuals who come together for worship each week but also in various combinations as committees slightly less regularly. Committees exist to manage the running of the meeting house premises, to co-ordinate peace and other activities deriving explicitly from the testimonies, to organize specific events such as retreats and concerts, and so on. There are many ways in which a person may become 'wrapped up' in meeting, many different ways to 'belong'.

Each Quaker meeting is necessarily different, given that each has a unique historical trajectory. Having said that, the vast majority of Quaker meetings for worship are held on Sunday morning, last for an hour and take place in a building owned or rented by the local meeting. Those present might number from one person to 200, though an average meeting would probably number around 25–50. Typically then, worship is, for the most part, a matter of sitting still and in silence. Every now and then, an individual might stand and say a few words, sometimes partly prepared beforehand but generally extempore, drawing regularly on everyday experiences, together with religious texts. Traditionally, Quakers believe that they gather in silence, waiting for God to speak through them. It should be added, however, that not all Quakers believe that vocal ministry is quite so simply understood. A great many variations on traditional belief may exist within any contemporary Quaker meeting: there are Christian Quakers, but also Buddhist, Muslim and Humanist Quakers, the beliefs of each partially overlapping with the beliefs of others. So although Quakers appear to be doing the same thing in worship their understanding of what they are doing is likely to be quite heterogeneous. Or, putting it another way: practice precedes belief.

In any case, the meeting for worship is a performance in so far as it is a shared public act. The worshipping space includes a stage, props, performers, costume and, to complete the metaphor, a script. The stage is generally level – no actor is raised above or set apart from any other – reflecting the levelling tendency which characterized the early phases of the movement. Although men and women generally sat apart until well into the twentieth century, both women and men were given the same opportunity for vocal ministry. Until 1923, the Society did nominate ministers, 'Recorded Ministers' whose ability to speak in meeting was officially noted. Such men and women were expected to speak in meeting for worship, an expectation which tended to stifle the potential in others. Contemporary Quakerism takes the levelling tendency of the founding mothers and fathers rather more literally and the congregation does indeed now constitute a 'priesthood of all believers'.

Occasionally Friends comment to one another, after worship, on the performance in which they have just participated. It is not so unusual for the hour of worship to pass without any spoken contribution. This may be interpreted as particularly sublime or oppressively arid. More than seven contributions may be glossed as 'popcorn ministry'. The canon states that all ministry should be accepted without criticism in so far as it is likely to 'speak to the condition' of someone present. This does not prevent participants from commenting unfavourably on ministry that is rambling, incoherent, mumbled or quaint (sometimes labelled 'daffodil ministry'). Furthermore, a performance (of worship) might be considered poor were someone to minister twice, or to explicitly support a cause which bluntly contradicts one of the testimonies. A 'good' performance might comprise an hour of quiet calm into which three or four participants contributed 'acceptable' ministry each developing a single thread. At the end of an hour two elders overtly shake hands, following which participants shake hands with those sitting near them. Children are likely to sit with the adults for 10 or 15 minutes or so either at the beginning or towards the end of meeting. For the rest of the hour they will spend the time together with adult helpers, volunteers from within the meeting. Activities undertaken in 'children's class' vary considerably, both in form and content.

Quaker liturgy might be presented (and, we would argue, is presented by Friends) as 'anti-ritual' (Dandelion, 2004). It lacks much of the ritual elaboration which characterizes, for instance, a Roman Catholic Mass. Then again, there is much about it that can be described as ritualistic. The silence and stillness of meeting for worship itself is framed, as it were, by the noise and animation of arrival and departure. As participants arrive they meet and mingle, exchange news and gossip, arrange committee meetings, avoid the helter-skelter of children. As they funnel into the meeting room, their behaviour is reversed, they sit in stillness and silence. At the end of an hour, they shake hands and listen as the clerk of the meeting reads out the obligatory notices, during which a certain amount of shuffling and whispering is acceptable. Following notices, participants are invited to stay for tea and biscuits. The formal order of the liturgy disintegrates into a melée of noise and activity, mirroring the earlier period of arrival. Anthropologists have long discussed ritual in terms of this tripartite structure: a liminal period (of worship) flanked as it were, by a preliminary period of transition from 'world' to worship, and a postliminal period of transition back to 'world' from worship.

Quaker liturgy has undergone relatively few changes during the past 350 years or so. While Quaker beliefs have shifted steadily away from the christocentric and towards the universalistic, the practice of worship has remained largely unchanged. However, a major objective of the anthropological method is to dwell at length, in order better to understand the subtle correspondences, tensions and lacunae between beliefs and practices. The accumulated wisdom of anthropology is that the taken-for-granted, the what-goes-without-saying, the 'commonsensical', is rarely as straightforward as it first appears.

Vicarious Religion

In her account of religion in Europe, Grace Davie (2002), drawing on the vast literature on vicarious atonement, introduced the interesting notion of 'vicarious religion', understood as religion performed by an active minority but on behalf of the majority, who both understand and approve of what the minority is doing. There is an extent to which this concept applies to all who attend Christian worship. Quakers might be considered, along with participating Anglicans, Methodists, Baptists and Roman Catholics, to be a part of the 'minority' in this sense. It is rather more difficult, in the absence of empirical data, to be sure that this is the way Quakers understand what they are doing. One might hazard a guess that Quakers, both in their local and national protests, against war and the proliferation of nuclear weapons, environmental degradation, human rights abuses, understand themselves to be performing a 'conscience of the nation' function. The question of whether those actively participating ('belonging', in Davie's terms) in congregational life, understand themselves to be 'doing the religious' on behalf of others requires considerable further research.

Practical Ways of Studying the People and Resources of the Local Church

I offer here ten 'golden rules' for researching the local church within this anthropological strand:

- Spend as long a time with the congregation as possible – at least six months.
- Always carry a small notebook – write down whatever catches your eye.
- Speak with as many participants as possible.
- Carry out as many taped interviews with participants as you can. Ask them to describe and account for the artefacts around the place; ask them to recall how the place was when they first arrived and how it has changed since then; ask them how they imagine the congregation will develop in the future.
- Take photographs of the people, the place, the locale, events.
- Make sketches of what goes on where, and when.
- Collect as much printed material from the place of worship as you

can. Depending on the congregation there may be other things you can collect, including tapes, videos, pictures, posters, etc.

- Organize one or more focus groups. This method of collecting data can be very useful when dealing with matters which are not obviously objective, such as the way things were.

- Involve members of the congregation in constructing a large, publicly available time line including events which participants find most memorable. You might include younger participants in this and other similar ventures.

- Do not ignore or discount written records that might be available to you. While some will have extraordinarily detailed records which go back centuries, many congregations will have usable records of some description.

Case Study

Dibdenshaw (a pseudonym) is a Quaker congregation in Northern England, which meets for corporate worship on Sunday morning. Participants also meet regularly during the week to transact church business as well as for discussion, worship-sharing, retreats, parties and so forth. Broadly speaking, the congregation is white and middle-class, women slightly outnumber men and there is a small group who are under 16. The congregation occupies its own modern, custom-built premises in the centre of town. While participants share a sense of belonging and common identity based on a certain unity of faith and practice, congregational life is not all plain-sailing: issues arise which are contentious and which involve careful negotiation. Like all congregations, Dibdenshaw comprises autonomous individuals whose views on various aspects of congregational life differ. For instance, most members of the congregation are local people, while others have recently moved into the area from elsewhere. The place in which they worship is full of artefacts the congregation has accumulated down the years and which are a part of the stored memory of the group and, therefore, important and meaningful. This includes the building itself, furniture and fittings, library, gardens and the pictures on the walls.

An issue arose around first one and then two of these pictures. A group began to lobby to remove a large, bold, colourful picture painted by a South American artist, depicting scenes from the New Testament, purchased from a local charity shop. Much discussion ensued both in formal and informal gatherings. Eventually, someone suggested that if the large picture should be removed then so should one other, a portrait of a strikingly Caucasian Jesus Christ surrounded by children.

Eventually both pictures were taken down. The issue was symptomatic of an ongoing narrative about congregational identity. The pictures enabled many different concerns to be aired, and functioned to remind the congregation of its identity.

Further reading

Cohen, A. P. (1985) *The Symbolic Construction of Community*, London: Routledge and Kegan Paul.
Cohen's concise account has been immensely influential among anthropologists and others in their attempts to tease out the subtle relationships between community, identity and belonging.

Stringer, M. (1999) *On the Perception of Worship*, Birmingham: Birmingham University Press.
There have been relatively few attempts to describe, compare and contrast a number of congregations in one volume and Stringer's subtle analysis of four worshipping groups in Manchester is certainly one of the best.

Toulis, N. (1997) *Believing Identity: Pentecostalism and the Mediation of Jamaican Ethnicity and Gender in England*, Oxford: Berg.
In this book Toulis has produced a model ethnography of a black Pentecostal church focusing on the interplay of religion, ethnicity and gender in the formation of members' identities.

Sociological Strand – Resources and People

Sylvia Collins

Key Concepts

The key concepts that we will be considering include: demography, church attendance and membership, personal and social attributes of the congregations (in particular gender, age and ethnic differences), factors influencing church joining and leaving, group membership, boundary maintenance and marginalization, and human and social capital.

Introduction

The number of people who attend church is in decline. England, for example, has seen a fall from 11.7 per cent of the population attending church on an 'average Sunday' in 1979 to 7.5 per cent in 1998 (Brierley, 2000, p. 27; Atherton, 2003). Sociologists usually talk about these falling figures in connection with the idea of secularization, the apparent decline in the social significance of the religion in modern western society (Wilson, 1982; Bruce, 1996). This is not to say that people have stopped believing or necessarily want to disassociate themselves from the church, the 2001 Census for England and Wales recorded a figure of around 42 million people, 71.6 per cent of the population, who still identified themselves as Christian (National Statistics Online), but it is clear that the trend is away from weekly institutional religious practice. Given these figures it is of sociological interest to find out what sorts of people buck the trend and continue to go to local churches and their reasons for doing so. This contribution sets out some of the concepts used in sociological research to explore these questions.

Demography

Who goes to church is a question of the church's demography: the size and structure of the church population and its development over time.

Size

The size of a church's population is determined by attendance and/or membership. The 1998 English Church Attendance Survey is an example of measuring size according to people's physical presence in church at a given time. The count for this survey comes from an estimate by church leaders of the number of people in their church on 'an average Saturday/Sunday in September 1998' (Saturdays are included in this count because some churches, particularly Roman Catholic ones, hold services on Saturday evenings as Sunday is reckoned to start at nightfall/evening the previous day). The figures in Table 1 relate to those attending church on an average Sunday, but only counting once those who attended twice. It shows a comparison of congregation sizes over a 20-year period based on the survey.

Table 1. Average Sunday church attendance by denomination 1979–98.

Denomination	1979	1989	1998
New Churches	213	163	138
Baptist	131	116	115
Pentecostal	129	121	102
Orthodox	103	108	98
United Reformed	104	89	78
Other denominations	97	78	80
Independent	75	96	72
Methodist	81	76	61
Anglican	99	77	60
Roman Catholic	542	449	326

Source: Brierley, 2000, p. 50.

Attendance figures which rely on estimates are less accurate than careful headcounts, but they may be more reliable than self-report surveys which simply ask people to say how often they go to church. In areas where church attendance is regarded as 'a good thing' people tend to overreport their frequency of churchgoing (Hadaway, Marler et al., 1993), and where churchgoing is seen negatively, people may underreport their attendance (Kay and Francis, 1996).

The English Church Attendance Survey is an independent survey, but churches often keep their own records of attendance for different services (midweek as well as weekend services). These may be used in submissions for denominational official statistics (see, for example, Church of England Gazette, 2002), although the accuracy of such figures is sometimes queried.

Whether the survey is independent or in-house, it is important to distinguish between attendances and attenders. Weekly attendance figures can appear higher than attender figures if attenders go to services twice or more on the days of counting and are included in the count each time.

Official membership is another way to gauge church size. The definition of membership depends on denomination, and its significance in people's lives can vary. Membership of the wider church is usually indicated by passing through a rite of passage such as baptism. Membership of a specific congregation, however, may be linked to administrative criteria as well, for example, signing up to an electoral roll. Membership and participation in the local church do not always go together. Bruce (1996) queries the significance to local churches of nominal members who rarely attend and yet retain official membership status. Equally, however, it is important not to underestimate the significance of the point of connection with the church which nominal membership affords individuals at times of crisis or during significant life events, particularly births, marriages and deaths.

Social structure of the church

The demographic structure of the church is concerned with the personal and social variables that characterize the population. Key personal variables include sex, age and ethnicity.

Despite the traditional male dominance of church leadership, women still tend to be more religious than men, both in terms of holding traditional beliefs and churchgoing practices. In this respect, some studies indicate that women hold different ideas of God than men. For women, God is often associated with 'love, comfort and forgiveness', whereas men focus on a 'God of power, planning and control' (Davie, 1994, pp. 119–20). See Davie (1994), Aune (2004) or Walter (1990) for suggested explanations of the gender differences, and Brown (2001) for a historical view of gender as an influence on the Church in England.

Religious practice varies in terms of age (see Figure 1). Pre-teenage children and older adults are the most likely people to go to church. Children are often taken to church by a parent as part of their moral, as well as religious, education. Boys then usually leave around the age of 11 and girls around 14 (Levitt, 1996). Practice picks up again when these children grow up and have families of their own. Older adults tend to go to church more often than younger adults possibly because ageing raises questions about faith, but also because retirement can afford individuals more time for institutional engagement and because churches are often an accessible local meeting place. As might be expected, church attendance tends to decline among the very elderly as health problems start to limit mobility.

Figure 1. Comparing church attenders with the UK population.

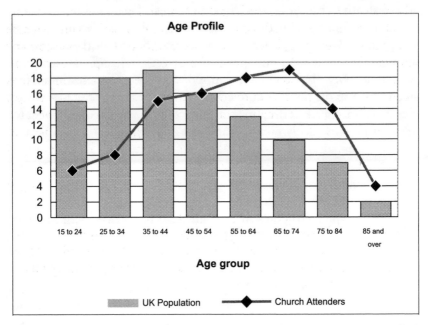

Age Profile

Source: Churches Information for Mission, 2001.

The age profile of local churches therefore reflects a lifecycle pattern. Studies also indicate a generational effect in that fewer people are now attending church as children to be socialized into the Christian faith in the first place. Consequently the churchgoing habit declines as year on year the churchgoing population of each age group becomes smaller. Generational studies see this as part of broader changes in social attitudes that have occurred since the 1960s. The 'Baby Boomer' generation (born 1945–60) were a part of major social reforms in the 1960s and 1970s that challenged the legitimacy and authority of many traditional social institutions, including the church. The Boomers' sceptical attitude meant that large numbers of young people did not return to the church when they had children themselves and so failed to bring up the next generation, 'Generation X' (born between 1961 and 1980), within the faith. Generation X has, therefore, lost some of the Christian memory that shaped much of British identity, and in turn has failed to introduce its children (the Millennial Generation) as well. Hilborn and Bird (2002) provide an extensive analysis of generational change as applied to the church. Gordon Lynch (2002) gives an interesting account of the religiosity of Generation X.

In terms of ethnicity, minority groups in England tend to practise their religion to a greater extent than the majority white population (Brierley, 2000). Indeed, the local church can have an important role to play in maintaining ethnic identity. Places of worship can be a safe and familiar setting for people who have migrated from one country to another, and it is not uncommon for extended immigrant communities to develop around churches, providing newcomers with social, as well as spiritual, support in turn. However, churches have not always been very accommodating in this respect. In the 1950s and 1960s, for example, Black African and Caribbean immigrants were subject to racism and marginalization in many white churches. This encouraged the development of separate black-led churches in England (Parsons, 1993, p. 253), which is where the majority of the black Christian population now worship.

Other variables that can be usefully profiled in studies of the local church include class, marital status, educational attainment, income, employment and retirement levels. These social factors influence the identity, confidence and resources of the local church in its ability to maintain itself and minister to local needs.

Joining and Leaving

Populations are rarely static in the modern world and people move into and out of churches as their personal circumstances, preferences, life and faith-stage change. Mapping these changes is another task for the sociologist. How long do people stay? What are the patterns of movement? Some churches, such as those in university towns, for example, are subject to a high turnover and seasonal variation as they fill up during academic terms and empty over the holidays.

Interesting work has been done on why people join and leave churches. Reasons for joining and staying with a particular congregation include a mixture of faith-based reasons (for example, wanting to be a part of a worshipping community, a place to pray and receive teaching in the faith), a sense of tradition and familiarity, and more socially orientated motivations (enjoying singing in the choir, meeting friendly people, using the church as an inroad to a local church school). Finney's (1992, p. 79) study of people's spiritual journeys toward making a public confession of faith found that the main reason new Christians chose their particular church was the recommendation of friends. Other reasons included knowing the minister, the locality of the church, the style of worship and a sense of being led by God.

Just as there are a range of reasons why people join churches, so too are there various reasons for leaving them. Richter and Francis' (1998) study of church leaving found the following: church life was too demanding; people lost or outgrew the faith as presented by their church; the church was seen to lack authenticity or credibility; people moved location and failed to join somewhere else. Divorce left some people feeling alienated from the church; illness and/or the effects of ageing made churchgoing too difficult; the church failed to live up to expectations; some people lacked a sense of belonging and ended up feeling isolated in the church. All of these reasons caused people to leave churches. However, many leavers in Richter and Francis' study did not rule out the possibility of returning to church sometime in the future and church leaving certainly does not always mean a loss of faith (Jamieson, 2002) and people may 'believe without belonging' (Davie, 1994).

Local Context

Churches vary in the extent to which they draw their population from the local area. Traditionally people attended the church of their denomination nearest to where they were living as in the model of the parish church. Belonging to the church was a communal activity and indeed churches which continue to draw people primarily from the local area and which are concerned with the people in the local neighbourhood are sometimes referred to as 'communal' churches (Eccleston, 1988, p. 7). However, with good transport, people's sense of 'local', particularly in urban areas, has altered. It is now quite common for people to adopt a consumerist mentality in their churchgoing and travel some distance to go to the church they like. Churches with many such commuters ('associational churches') generally have a high degree of internal social affinity (like-minded people of the same social class, theological persuasion, etc.) but may have little in common with the local neighbourhood population.

Boundaries and Marginalization

To attend a congregation is only a small part of what it is to be a member of a local church. What people do, how they interact, what is expected of them, are also important factors which define who belongs to the group and who does not.

Social networks

One way to explore patterns of interaction is to consider the social networks that exist within the congregation, and between the congregation and local people. Formally organized sub-groups within the church might include home groups, prayer groups, women's fellowship, leadership and pastoral teams, and, indeed, attenders at different worship services can form very distinct groups themselves. Sociologists are interested in how these sub-groups relate to the wider congregation, whether they are representative of the church as whole, how long people have been in them, whether there is any special status or influence attached to them. More informal social networks can also be observed: who sits with whom in the congregation, who stays after services for a coffee, whether or not there are any dominant families, and so on.

Beyond the church itself, but still within the wider church, congregations may have links with parachurch groups, such as missionary societies and ecumenical projects, which extend congregational boundaries. What is the extent of networks of this kind and what level of involvement do church members have with them? Finally, there are the church's connections with the local neighbourhood and the secular world, which includes the wider social networks to which individuals belong in their leisure and at work. To what extent are church leaders and members active in the local neighbourhood as individuals and as a church, and how does the local neighbourhood respond? The public presentation of the church is important here. For example, the church increasingly has to consider its self-presentation through literature, internet sites, and the news media (see Mitchell and Marriage, 2003 for more on the relationship between the media, religion and culture).

It is not just the quantity of social connections that is of interest. The quality is also important. The quality of relationships determines whether a social network is simply a loose collection of people or a real community. Bauman describes the nature of community as identity and 'togetherness' (Bauman, 2000, p. 99). In other words, people living as community have a sense of belonging to a group of 'people like us', who share basic values and ideals, engage in meaningful encounters, dialogue and interaction, and support one another. This sense of togetherness can benefit members by providing a form of 'social capital' (see below). However, if it becomes too strong it can lead to an inward focus that is defensive or even sectarian in nature.

Sects are exclusive groups where membership is hard won. Strong boundaries are maintained between the sect and the wider world, and indeed suspicion and disapproval tend to characterize the relationship between sect members and those outside the group. Ties with the outside world may therefore be hampered or cut to defend the sect against unfavourable influences or contradictory ideas. Sects tend to have a strong sense of doctrinal purity and their theology and social organization are often conservative. The demands on members are usually high in terms of the time, money and energy people are expected to give to church activities. (For more details see Troeltsch (1931), Niebuhr (1957), Bruce (1996) and Aldridge (2000).)

Whatever form the local church takes, there will always be some social pressure to conform to its norms and internal rules. As people become established in the church they are socialized into its ways of being. They may adopt certain styles of dress, characteristic forms of expressing themselves in worship, and particular forms of language and discourse. Conformity to these patterns of behaviour signifies group membership. They are identity markers or 'group-membership badges' (Watts, Nye et al., 2002, p. 209). Individuals who fail properly to display group membership, or who feel uncomfortable acting in the way of the group, may be fringe or marginal members who feel they do not belong.

Marginalization processes happen in direct and indirect ways. Direct ways include overt policies and official responses to current debates that prevent certain people from taking up particular roles or activities in the church (for example, the exclusion of women and gay people from some areas of leadership). Indirect marginalization includes the subtle messages that are inherent in some of the assumptions congregations hold. For example, many churches assume a happily married family ideal for members' home life. Services are labelled 'family services', sermons make reference to family life; in-house courses are held on parenting. All of these practices, though helpful in many ways, can marginalize single people (Aune, 2003) or childless couples. In considering social networks it is therefore worth looking at who is not included as well as who is, and in particular who is involved in the decision-making processes (Atherton, 2003).

Resources

An analysis of a church's newsheets, notice-board or internet site will reveal a range of activities that are undertaken on a weekly or periodic basis. Some of these activities are necessary for the day-to-day functioning and maintenance of the church (cleaning and prayer rotas, administrative jobs, etc). Other activities are part of the church's mission and outreach (mother and toddlers groups, church fêtes, pastoral visiting, etc.). All of these activities need the resources of the local church and sometimes of the local neighbourhood as well. Resources include physical or material capital (buildings, finance, etc.), and human and social capital (people). Sociologists are particularly concerned with the latter two.

Human capital

Human capital refers to people's individual qualities that contribute to getting a task done. The demographic profile of the church gives some indication of the types of human capital within a congregation in terms of people's ability to contribute manual labour, practical and intellectual skills, time and personality. Indeed, sometimes churches make an inventory of the sorts of 'gifts' people identify in themselves (ability to cook, do odd jobs, pastoral skills, musical ability, teaching and financial skills, etc.). Human capital may also be drawn from outside the congregation to deal with specific tasks. These volunteers may be members of neighbouring congregations, or people from the neighbourhood who are willing help the church from a sense of communal responsibility. For example, a local church may draw on outside help to run a club for children during school holidays. Any study of a church's human capital needs to take these outside volunteers into account as well as members.

Social capital

Social capital refers to the networks of reciprocity and trustworthiness (Putnam, 2000, p. 19; Morisy, 2004, pp. 45–65; Office of National Statistics, 2001) that exist between people and help them make their way in the world. Churches are usually good at establishing social capital (see Francis, 2003, on potential denominational differences), not least because religion is a powerful motivator and much religious teaching is concerned with social and moral responsibility. People in churches with a high degree of social capital are prepared to help one another without looking for immediate reward (apart, perhaps, from the knowledge that they are doing God's will). They are, however, likely to benefit from reciprocal help later on. Putnam refers to the type of social capital that operates within a group as 'bonding' social capital since it helps keep people together. Churchgoers, particularly in communal churches, are also likely to look beyond their borders and engage with people in the local area. This Putnam calls 'bridging' social capital as it binds one group of people to another, generating good will between the two (Putnam, 2000, p. 22). Writing about the United States, Putnam highlights the importance of religious organizations in the generation of social capital, 'Faith communities in which people worship together are arguably the single most important repository of social capital in America . . .'

Churches provide an important incubator for civic skills, civic norms, community interests and civic recruitment. Religiously active men and women learn to give speeches, run meetings, manage disagreements, and bear administrative responsibility. They also befriend others who are in turn likely to recruit them into other forms of community activity. In part, for these reasons, churchgoers are substantially more likely to be involved in secular organizations, to vote and participate politically in other ways, and to have deeper informal social connections (Putnam, 2000, p. 66).

An analysis of local church life and its relationship to the neighbourhood needs to have a good understanding of the physical, human and social capital available to it. This will include an understanding of the social processes that encourage effective resource mobilization such as appropriate leadership, good communication, clear goals, a shared ideology, and the social and political opportunities that make an action appropriate at a given time.

Practical ways of studying this aspect of the local church

Sociologists draw on a range of methods to study local churches and their social context. Census data (readily accessible via the National Statistics Online website *www.statistics.gov.uk/*) provides useful data on the population of the local neighbourhood (employment rates, car and home ownership, etc.), as do other published sources. For example, local health authorities may provide information on the Jarman Index score, which provides a measure of deprivation in a geographical area (DPHE, 1999). A walk around the local area will reveal the sorts of social services available to residents and give an impression of the quality of housing people are living in. This information can be compared with observations and possibly surveys of the local church to assess the degree to which the congregation is representative of the local neighbourhood population.

A content analysis of church documents (newsheets, electoral rolls, baptism and marriage registers, visitors books, notice-boards, accounts, plaques on walls, internet site, etc.) will provide evidence on the church's identity and mission. These documents can also reveal individuals' level of involvement within the church.

Self-completion questionnaires and face-to-face interviews are helpful methods to gather information on attitudes, beliefs and behaviour within a congregation and the wider community.

Spending time with people, getting to know them by participating in church and neighbourhood activities is also time well spent. Participation is a means of building up rapport with people and an opportunity to observe and monitor life as it is really lived.

Case study

The sociological analysis of a church and its context can by illustrated by Elizabeth Clark's (1996) study of a church on a housing estate in Surrey. The research was undertaken to review the life of the church and its mission to the local community.

The church was a 'communal' church with social and spiritual responsibilities for the people living and working in its neighbourhood. Through a careful analysis of life on the estate and within the church using census data, church documents and statutory reports, forums and surveys of local people, statutory agency professionals, voluntary workers and congregation members, and by spending time participating in daily life on the estate and in the church, Clark was able to identify how the church made a contribution to the people of area. She found the church was respected and appreciated for how it supported life on the estate. However, few of the local people who benefited from church activities made any connection between faith and action. They used the church on a 'take-away' basis, coming to it for what they wanted (social activities, health care clinics, baptisms, social support, etc.) but going away again afterwards. Clark's analysis also revealed the struggles and fears church members faced in meeting their mission to serve the community and spread the gospel. They lacked physical, human and social capital, as they were few in number and elderly with little energy and some had mental and physical health problems. They lacked confidence and material wealth and there was little group co-ordination.

Clark recommended actions that would provide support for the congregation in its mission and generally empower both the church and the wider community. These were implemented during the course of the research, so the effects could be assessed and monitored by those involved and actions adjusted accordingly. This process in itself empowered people and follows a tradition of research known as 'action research' (Blaxter, Hughes et al., 2001).

Further reading

Aldridge, A. (2000) *Religion in the Contemporary World: A Sociological Introduction*, Cambridge: Polity Press.

Aldridge's text is a thorough overview of the sociology of religion. It discusses classic and contemporary theories and is particularly helpful for readers who want a clear academic text.

Avis, P. (ed.) (2003) *Public Faith?: The State of Religious Belief and Practice in Britain*, London: SPCK.

A collection of essays which together give both an interesting account of religion in Britain and a commentary on different methodological approaches to studying religion.

Davie, G. (1994) *Religion in Britain since 1945: Believing Without Belonging*, Oxford: Blackwell Publishers.

Davie's book is now something of a classic text on postwar religion in Britain. It covers areas such as the social context of religious change, the nature of religious constituencies, the beliefs and practices of British people, and the relationship between church and state.

Richter, P. and L. J. Francis (1998) *Gone but not Forgotten: Church Leaving and Returning*, London: Darton, Longman and Todd Ltd.

The results of a large survey of church-leavers in Britain. It is comprehensive in its analysis and introduces the reader to a range of theories and perspectives in its commentary.

Watts, F., R. Nye, and S. Savage (2002) *Psychology for Christian Ministry*, London: Routledge.

Good accounts of the micro-social processes of church life as revealed through cognitive and social psychology.

Zuckerman, P. (2003) *Invitation to the Sociology of Religion*, New York, NY: Routledge.

This is an accessible introduction to the sociology of religion for anybody coming to the field for the first time. Zuckerman discusses the questions and approaches sociologists take to the study of religion and in so doing highlights some of the tensions that may be felt by people of faith who shine a sociological light on their beliefs and practices.

Organizational Studies Strand – Resources and People

Helen Cameron

Introduction

In organizational terms, local churches have two main resources: their people and their assets, both financial and physical. Here we look at how these particular resources are brought into the church and how they are used. Other strands will pick up the way in which beliefs and tradition are a resource. There is very little literature of direct relevance to this topic and so I will draw upon ideas and models that have arisen in my work as a consultant with churches. There is further material relevant to people in Section 3.2 (Organizational Strand) on the work of the church.

Summary of the concepts covered in this contribution

People

- Engagement – the different ways in which people get involved in local churches.
- Activism – ways of thinking about the unpaid work that people contribute.
- Unpaid roles – the expectations of people doing unpaid work.
- Paid staff – the issues that arise for a church when it has paid staff.
- Teams and leaders – how the different roles relate to each other.

Resources

- Income generation – the ways in which money comes into the local church.
- Analysing income and expenditure – matching the use of resources with the mission of the church.

- Buildings – identifying the purpose of church buildings.
- Financial assets – policies on the management of assets.

People

Engagement

Local churches are unusual as voluntary organizations in offering a wide range of ways in which people can engage. These include:

- Member – someone who has formally joined the church; many churches have different types of membership and some have no formal membership.
- Regular attender – someone who attends worship and other activities of the church on a regular basis; local churches will vary in their definition of what counts as 'regular' attendance. Some people will attend without taking the step of becoming a member.
- Occasional attender – someone who attends worship or other church activities less frequently. This lack of regular participation may be for a wide range of reasons (for example, ill health, old age, family circumstances, travel difficulties, not feeling the need for regular attendance), so it is important not to make assumptions about the level of attachment occasional attenders feel towards the church. Someone who attends an activity of the church but doesn't attend its worship is likely to be perceived as less 'attached' or involved than someone who attends worship.
- Volunteer – many local churches run activities that aim to serve their local community (for example, social care services, educational programmes, youth work, arts, leisure activities). Sometimes people will volunteer to help with these activities while having no other association with the church.
- Employee – for many congregations their clergy are their only employees and often they are not employed directly but via their denomination. Other local churches will have no clergy. It is increasingly common for local churches to have paid employees undertaking work such as administration, co-ordination of church projects and youth work. Sometimes these employees will be members or attenders of the church, but for others their employment may be their only contact with the church.

- Service user – where a church is offering services to its local community someone might only have contact as a service user.
- Lifecycle rituals – for some people their only contact with the local church is for baptisms, weddings, funerals or special family times such as Christmas or Harvest (see chapter 11 by Davies in Guest et al., 2004). Thomas (2003) argues that the churches have underestimated the significance of these links and need to reorganize what they offer to make it more accessible and attractive to this group.
- Networks – Ward (2002) argues that the formality of membership is off-putting to people and that they want looser networks to engage with as they feel necessary.

In studying the people of the local church it is important to bear in mind this variety of engagement, to be clear about the basis upon which the study is conducted and to clarify 'local' definitions of the different categories. Changes in clergy are recognized as significant transitions for local churches although there is variation in how these changes are made.

Activism

Most of the work done in local churches is done on an unpaid basis and so it is necessary to understand activism. It is a feature of the voluntary nature of local churches that expectations cannot be enforced by an employment contract and so the psychological expectations and norms of the group assume a greater importance.

Fichter (1953), an American sociologist, tried to explain why Catholics varied their commitment to the parish church. He had noted a general decline in commitment from the days of primary immigration when the church was the most important institution for Catholics. He proposed a fourfold typology of church members' participation: nuclear, modal, marginal, dormant.

- Nuclear members – those involved in parish activities; adopting Christian behaviour; holding religious values; and fulfilling the sacramental requirements of the church.
- Modal members – who fulfil the sacramental requirements of the church by their regular attendance at Mass.
- Marginal members – who attend occasionally on the major festivals.

- Dormant members – who were baptized as an infant; got married in church; and have had their children baptized but don't otherwise attend.

Dhooghe (1968) is concerned with member commitment to the local church but he offers a different typology. Two dimensions are proposed: conformity–contestation and passivity-activity. Members are classified into four quadrants, as below.

	Active	Passive
Conforming		
Contesting		

He defines each box of the quadrant as follows:

- Active conformity – the activist members who run the church, but who may have to give way to others who have technical skills or knowledge they do not possess.
- Passive conformity – the modal members, inevitable in a large church, who will readily allow activists to represent them.
- Passive contestation – latent disagreement with the expectations of membership which can cause withdrawal from the church if the problem is not articulated.
- Active contestation – involves contesting the legitimacy of values or their interpretation.

Most churches aim to turn passive members into active ones. Dhooghe's model implies that this depends upon how contesting behaviour is handled.

Unpaid roles

The word 'role' comes from the French for 'script', and suggests that we learn what is expected of us in an organization, including how to fit in with others. Employees often have job descriptions to help them learn their role, but expectations for unpaid roles in the local church can be more difficult to uncover. Little is known about how these roles are learned. In some denominations there are people with the full status of clergy who work without pay.

Although not much research has been done on this topic, the following are some of the differences between members and volunteers that have been suggested from research on congregations (Cameron, 1999; Harris, 1996).

- Members are more committed to organizational values than volunteers, which can lead them to do too much and so suffer from burnout.
- Members have greater expectations than volunteers that their views will be taken into account.
- Members have religious expectations of clergy which give clergy an added dimension to their authority over the work of members as opposed to volunteers.
- Members have a greater sense of reciprocity in their work than volunteers. This may be direct reciprocity, in the expectation of a short-term return for help offered; it may be serial reciprocity, helping because one has been helped in the past or an expectation that one will be helped in the future; or a more indirect reciprocity, where work for the congregation is seen to strengthen an institution upon which the member depends. This is not to suggest that volunteers do not benefit from the work they undertake, but that there is often an indirect link between the kinds of help they offer and the kind of help they receive.
- Members develop a stronger overview of how the work they are doing fits into the congregation as a whole. Members have a sense of ownership of the organization as well as of the task.
- Members of congregations do not seem to see much of a divide between the public and private worlds in the work they do. They may be donating their time for a particular purpose but they expect that their emotional, physical and spiritual needs will be taken into account. This holistic approach often involves family interconnections as the context within which the member operates.

These differences are more a matter of degree than polarities.

Paid staff

With a paid member of staff a congregation assumes the responsibilities of an employer and has the livelihood of an individual and his/her family in their hands (Peacock, 2000). Not having sufficient money to pay the worker's wages is likely to cause them feelings of stress and insecurity. Before it had employees, the organization fluctuated according to the time volunteers had available, now it must accommodate itself to the working hours that the worker finds acceptable. Before, the objectives of the organization were determined purely by the members of the management committee; now the worker has a better overview of what is going on than the committee and could make proposals that shape what the organization does. Unsurprisingly those proposals may contain elements to make the worker's job more congenial and which do not merely serve the purposes of the organization. The paid worker may need to formalize certain processes to make best use of their time, which may clash with the idiosyncratic preferences of members and volunteers.

It is common for a voluntary organization to recruit its first paid employee when it is under stress, often because it is successful and expanding and the volunteers can't cope. This set of circumstances creates the feeling that all will be well once the worker arrives, and when they do arrive there are a lot of unexplained and unresolved issues, leading, possibly, to an early breakdown in the employing relationship.

Another scenario is when short-term funding to employ someone has been secured and volunteers fear that once the paid person is gone they will be expected to cope with all the extra work that has been generated.

Teams and leaders – the relationship between roles

The work of the local church depends not only on the roles people play but the ways in which those roles relate to each other. Different Christian traditions have different models for those relationships. Some use hierarchies, some democratic procedures and others consensus. At present there is interest in getting clergy and lay leaders to work in teams (Belbin, 1993; Greenwood, 2000; Widdicombe, 2000). It can be difficult to graft the more egalitarian model of a team onto a local church that has a hierarchical tradition.

There is a huge literature on leadership but little of it adopts a critical view of human power. Some useful secular exceptions include: Block (1993); Chrislip (2002) and Grint (1997). Jamieson (1997) provides an autobiographical account of being a woman and Christian leader.

Resources

Income generation

Many voluntary organizations begin life as member-funded. As they acquire and have to maintain assets (such as a building) or commit themselves to providing services to non-members their need for income often exceeds what members alone can provide. They usually seek to diversify the sources of income available to them or become dependent upon one or more major external funders. A few will acquire some capital and use the interest from that capital to sustain their work.

There can be an assumption that churches are funded purely by member income but that is decreasingly the case and in some denominations has never been the case. A range of other activities may bring in money:

- Tax relief on member giving – how does the church ensure this is maximized?
- Donations from the public or members on special occasions.
- Grants from other local charities for particular activities.
- Subsidies from the denomination or other local churches.
- Trading income from running bookstalls or coffee shops or letting the buildings to other users.
- Fundraising events ranging from simple coffee mornings to elaborate fêtes.
- Capital appeals which are instigated when a substantial sum is needed, most often in connection with the church building.

Grieve (1999) and Durran (2003) have produced useful guides to fundraising for churches.

In my consultancy work, I have identified four main ways of thinking about income which are summarized in the box below. Each model carries assumptions about what the church should be doing to secure the resources it needs. When those assumptions are challenged uncomfortable conversations often follow.

Models of local church income

Donative – most income from member giving or fundraising between members.

Mixed – income from a number of sources such as giving, letting, fundraising, trading, grants.

Endowment – dependence upon interest from trust/deposit accounts or legacies to balance the books.

Contract – long-term relationships with public or voluntary agencies that bring in income.

Analysing income and expenditure

Analysis of income and expenditure into different categories can indicate what the main dependencies and priorities are. Overdependency on a single source can make a church vulnerable to changes in that source (e.g. declining membership). On the other hand multiple sources of income can require different methods of accountability which can be time-consuming (e.g. reports to funders).

Four Es

In the wider voluntary sector it is common to have explicit discussions about the criteria for judging the organization's use of its resources; these often include 'the four Es':

- Economy – Is waste of resources avoided? Are wise purchasing decisions made? For example, shopping around for utility suppliers.
- Efficiency – Is the most value obtained for the resources consumed? For example, reclaiming tax on donated income.
- Effectiveness – Are resources being used in a way that best meets the mission of the church?
- Equity – Are the resources being allocated in a way that is fair and in keeping with the church's understanding of stewardship? For example, contributions to the denomination or to churches overseas.

Voluntary organizations are increasingly encouraged to have numerical indicators of their performance or to conduct evaluations of their work (Paton, 2003). There is rarely the same impetus in the local church, which can make it difficult to judge how resources are being used or to make comparisons with other churches. Here are some examples of indicators that could be collected.

Indicators

People: Members per clergy person
People: Attenders at worship   (5-year trend)
People: Members   (5-year trend)

Property: Hours church building open per week
Property: Seats per attender in the main worship area

Income: Tax refund as percentage of giving
Income: Giving as percentage of total income

Assets: Total church funds held per attender
Assets: Value of capital assets per attender

The value of indicators is not so much what they measure but the discussions they can generate about the priorities of the church.

Buildings

For some churches, it will be the need to review their buildings that prompts them to study themselves or to seek help with such a study. To examine issues about the building can be an unsettling experience as questions arise about the purpose of the church, its relationship with its locality and the proportion of its resources which it wishes to allocate to its building. It also generates non-routine decisions which in turn can lead people to question how 'big' decisions are made.

Gill (2003) has helpfully set such questions in a historical context. He points out that all denominations, apart from Roman Catholics, have built more churches than they need, and the fact that so many local churches struggle to maintain buildings and survive numerically is, in part, a legacy of this overbuilding.

Finneron and Dinham (2002) note that the buildings of faith groups can be a positive resource for local communities, particularly in areas of deprivation where other facilities may be limited. They urge the thoughtful reordering of buildings to meet local needs. Giles (1999) suggests practical strategies, linked to the church's understanding of worship, by which this can be done.

The box below suggests different views about the purpose of church buildings. Where members can agree about their building, a way forward is easier to develop.

Purpose of church buildings

House of worship – the building is seen as a beautiful place that enhances the worship of God. It needs no further usage to justify its maintenance.

Family meeting place – the building is a place where people can get together and support each other. Relationships are the main focus and the building is a means to that end.

Mission base – stewardship demands that the building is used as much as possible for the mission of the church. Activities, even those not run by the church, have to serve local needs.

Community resource – the primary function of the building is worship, but if it is available for community purposes, the letting income can be used to maintain the building.

The box below proposes a series of options (which can be taken solely or in any combination) open to all major denominations as they deal with the issue of what to do with buildings, when members alone cannot finance their running costs and upkeep.

The church building as a:

- venue for delivery of statutory or voluntary services by other agencies but adding a 'human face' because of church involvement;
- venue for small businesses or intermediate labour market contributing to economic regeneration of the locality;
- redeveloped site, e.g. housing, retail, office space with church becoming 'minor user' thereby retaining assets and a presence;
- heritage site supported by secular 'friends';
- place of sufficient social action to generate grant and trading income;
- disposal of building, but using the money to enhance and then rent space in a community building/shared church/LEP.

In some of these options there will be the question of why the church does this, rather than a secular voluntary agency or local authority; possible questions about legality within the church's charitable purposes; or questions of where the expertise and energy is to come from.

Financial assets

While buildings are often the main assets of a local church, they are not the only ones. Indeed some churches consciously decide not to own buildings but to rent or meet in people's homes so they have lower running costs and greater flexibility.

Some churches have investments or deposits that need to be managed. Sometimes there is a policy for what reserves should be held, for how the assets should be managed and on the ethical basis for any investment decisions. In other cases these decisions are in the hands of a committee and follow custom and practice. Developments in the regulation of charities encourage greater transparency about the management of assets so that stakeholders can be aware of the true potential of the organization.

Ways of studying the resources of the local church

Local churches vary in the records they keep of their people. Most keep some record of members and have a system for updating, others will have ways of recording those who have a loose association and of staying in touch with them. Sometimes sub-groups or activities will have records of their participants. This variety of definitions and record-keeping also makes it difficult to do comparative studies of local churches particularly when they are from different denominations. Nevertheless much can be learned from the analysis of membership rolls with an informed insider to help.

For those without formal financial training, there can be nervousness about studying the finances of the local church. However, even a simple approach can yield useful information. Many church accounts are kept by people without professional training and so consist of a simple statement of annual income and expenditure and a summary of the assets held by the church. Some denominations provide pro formas for churches to set out this information. Where church finances are conducted in a more sophisticated way, the person concerned will usually be willing, with appropriate safeguards regarding confidentiality, to provide the information required.

There can be a tendency to study the resources of the local church in isolation from its mission. This area of church life can be seen as 'technical' and best left to the experts, and so theological reflection is put to one side. But where a local church is considering major changes to its buildings, this is best done in the context of a study that embraces all four strands of the handbook. It can be particularly helpful to work with a consultant who will ensure that difficult questions are not overlooked.

In studying people and resources, it can be useful to mix quantitative and qualitative methods. There are facts that can analysed, but attitudes and values play a significant part in how resources are handled.

What questions can be asked?

Here are some research questions you could explore using this contribution:

- What types of people and resources are used by the local church? Are they increasing or decreasing?
- How do the people and resources in the local church compare with other types of organizations in this locality?
- Does the use of people and resources reflect the stated priorities or mission of the local church?
- How has the church managed the process of hiring and supervising any paid employees?
- What are the expectations of people involved in the work of the church?
- What do the people who attend this church expect to get from their participation?
- What proportion of the resources is spent on running and maintaining the building?
- What capacity does this church have to provide services to its local community?

Case Study
Rivertown Methodist Circuit – Ian D. Johnson

In March 2004 I was invited to act as consultant to the Rivertown Circuit Strategy Group (a pseudonym) to assist them in addressing a question which had arisen in the course of previous staffing policy discussions: 'Do we use our buildings to their full potential for the circuit and for mission in the community?' The circuit is based in a market town with two churches, Bethesda and Wesley. The remaining four churches are in village locations.

With a lack of any policy direction and the limited amount of information about the circuit churches and the usage of the church premises, I requested a set of information which is summarized in the following tables:

Church	People Members 2003 (5 yr % change)	People Attenders 2003 (5 yr % change)	Seats per Attender	Annual Offering per member £ per annum	Income Tax received as % of offerings	Assets per member	Fund Raising per member	Assessment per member at 31/08/03
Newton	13 (-41%)	8 (-60%) pm	7.5	226	19%	481	130	198
Bethesda	13 (-19%)	11 (-21%) pm	14.5	256	14.5%	193	6	188
Westerley	31 (-24%)	30 (0%) am	6.66	212	15.4%	537	537	170
Oldtown	16 (+78%, Meth. only) 35 joint	24 (-43%) am (is this all attenders?)	5	228 (joint)	16.25%	281	281	137
Wesley	272 (+7%)	230 (+28%) 22 am (-12%) pm	1.74 18	138	18.07%	255	255	138
Southover	38 (+2%)	25 (+67%) am	3.2	128	22.26%	301	31	128
Total	360	328 (main serv)	38.6					
Average	60	54.7	6.43	189 (adj)	17.58%	293 (adj)	52.63 (adj)	152.59 (adj)

Table B Property

Church	Church Use		Community Use			Income from Lets	Mainte-nance Costs per member p.a.	Insured Value
	Hrs p.w.	Total Nos p.w.	Hrs p.w.	Total Nos p.w.	No. of Groups			
Newton	4	20	-	-	-	50	79	182,757
Bethesda	2	11	6.5	60	3	990	148	?
Westerley	7.25	84	13.75	Not Known	10	3534	105	605,162
Oldtown	6.5	89	7	85	3	100	34	207,912
Wesley	50.5	1085	11.25	216	8	3831	51	2,619,786
Southover	3	36	5.5	56	3	884	33.50	251,200

As a result, my report to the Strategy Committee included these questions:

- What strengths and weaknesses do these facts and figures help us to identify?
- What are the aspirations for mission in each of the churches? What might realistically be attempted?
- Could the struggle to keep all our churches open be the very reason why they may feel threatened with closure?
- Where does the circuit believe the possible growth points are?
- Where would you judge community use of the premises in the circuit to be appropriate Christian mission?
- How could you best identify the criteria necessary to make major decisions about the buildings in the circuit?

Further reading

Giles, R. (1999) *Re-Pitching the Tent: Reordering Church Building for Worship and Mission*, Norwich: Canterbury Press.
This suggests ways in which church buildings can be adapted in sympathy with the worship and values of the church.

Gill, R. (2003) *The 'Empty' Church Revisited*, Aldershot, Hants: Ashgate.
Second edition of a book that provides a historical perspective on the decline of the churches, in particular the overbuilding of churches.

Paton, R. (2003) *Managing and Measuring Social Enterprises*, London: Sage.
A valuable critique of the different methods of measuring the work of voluntary organizations – helpful in making sense of requirements from external funders.

Widdicombe, C. (2000) *Meetings that Work: A Practical Guide to Teamworking in Groups*, Cambridge: Lutterworth.
Detailed guidance on improving the effectiveness of all types of meetings.

Theological Strand – Resources and People

William Storrar

Introduction

When we consider the people and resources of the congregation, we typically think of them in terms of the ordained and the organized; finances, property; and so on. Churches themselves typically understand their own spiritual vitality in terms of the growth and decline in these factors measured over time. This statistical perspective is a valid but limited and potentially limiting one. The question is whether it helps us to think *theologically* about the congregation; in terms of God's activity in the world and the church's faithfulness to the gospel. In this section, we shall study the people and resources of the local church from the alternative perspective of space and place. This spatial perspective on the church is not unfamiliar: at Christmas the church sings of God in a stable; during Easter it remembers an upper room and celebrates an empty tomb. After Pentecost, it finds itself in the street, moving to the ends of the earth. Its story begins in a garden and ends in a city. To locate the congregation's people and resources in space may prove a fruitful way forward.

If we are to use the concepts of space and place, we must first define these terms and distinguish between them. John Inge, in his recent study of *A Christian Theology of Place,* offers this:

> What begins as undifferentiated space becomes place as we get to know it better and endow it with value . . . The two terms might be thought of as tending towards opposite ends of a spectrum which has the local at one end [place] and the infinite [space] at the other. Spaces are what are filled with places. (Inge, 2003, pp. 1, 2)

Unbounded space turns into meaningful place when people imaginatively make it their own, by bodily movement in and through it; by deliberately naming, making or using it. Thinking about churches in spatial terms has traditionally been the preserve of those interested in church architecture, liturgy and art. However, these related concepts can help us to see the life of the congregation as *space* that expresses its self-understanding in the way it creates and inhabits the *places* within its buildings and locality. This spatial perspective on the local church offers us theological insights, as in the example of the case study below.

The Case Study and the Research Method

The significance of the concepts of space and place for a theological reading of congregational life occurred to me as I worked with an urban parish church in a poor community over three years as a practical theology teacher on an annual fieldwork visit with students, and latterly as a researcher. On the first two annual visits, I interpreted the innovative work being done at Millhill Church (a pseudonym) by congregation and minister in terms of existing models of local church and good practice in ministry, with relevant community involvement and reflective leadership. On the third visit something new emerged in my thinking. The ministry and mission initiated in that period all took place within the church building itself, with new uses for existing spaces within its walls. This was a deliberate decision by the ministry team and significant for them. It made sense to think of the people and resources of the church by mapping their configuration in space and place, rather than by assessing their programmed activities over time.

On further reflection, I tried to correlate the experience of the changes to the Millhill building with other normative, informative and imaginative sources (the Bible and Christian tradition, social sciences, contemporary culture, literature) to reflect on the religious and social significance of space and place. Doing theology like this emerged out of my experience at the church. It did not start with an existing theology or theory, but was prompted by the disruption of my own theological assumptions. It led me to adopt a spatial approach to doing theology in congregational studies. The reader will realize that this is an account of how I used the 'critical correlation' model (see above, Section 2.2). However, my approach to the case study also has elements of the praxis method, which often starts with that same disruptive experience, and as I reflected with the church, also with the model of corporate theological reflection.

A description of Millhill Church follows in the text box. I then offer a further correlation of my thinking on space and place with biblical, anthropological, theological and literary perspectives, in order to show the relevance of spatial concepts within this model of critical correlation in congregational studies. I then make suggestions on how these concepts and this model can be used in the practical theological study of congregations, before ending the contribution with an annotated bibliography for further reading.

Millhill Church

When Lynn, the present minister, came to Millhill Parish Church in the late 1990s, local people thought that the church building was closed. Windows were boarded and the roof leaked. It was built in the 1930s, part of a new public housing scheme on the edge of the city for miners, brewery workers and their families. As these industries declined, this working community experienced the multiple problems of long-term unemployment, but retained a resilient community spirit. The once-active congregation declined with the local economy, and with the wider secularization of society. An able minister in the 1960s tried and failed to motivate the leadership and membership to embrace new patterns of mission. By the late 1990s the dwindling, ageing church members were struggling to survive.

Lynn responded to the social and pastoral needs of the community by redeveloping the dilapidated church building and halls for new forms of ministry, including a food co-operative and second-hand goods store. In partnership with church members, especially Jean, a local woman who became a church project worker and fundraiser, Lynn opened a community café. They developed the cruciform sanctuary into a place of pastoral support for the bereaved. One side aisle became a chapel of remembrance where the local people could honour their dead on the leaves of a sculpted bronze tree. At one end of the sanctuary, they established a professional counselling centre for bereaved local children who have lost parents to death or addiction. Built with internal windows, the children and staff can look into the place of worship. Church membership remains small but the church building has been transformed into an open, welcoming place where local people belong and find hope for their lives and community.

The Congregation as Space and Place

How are we to interpret the particularities of this story theologically? When Lynn arrived, Millhill Church was failing on every statistical measurement as an active membership organization. Little has changed from that perspective: it remains a small, frail and ageing congregation. But is that the only way to think? Theological reflection began when I visited the new counselling centre for bereaved children. Lynn and Jean pointed to the windows into the sanctuary. As we shall read below, everything they did to create the new places within Millhill Church – the community café, the memorial chapel, the counselling centre – found its meaning in the worship of the sanctuary. Each place was designed to lead people into the space of worship, so that the ways in which place was inhabited spoke of who they were as church.

An arresting biblical image suggested itself after I conducted a semi-structured interview with Lynn and Jean and read the transcript: this local church was becoming a *temple-like* place. As Lynn said, they have given up trying to meet the denomination's expectations of a parish church or ministry, with its organizations, congregational visiting and constant hunt for office-bearers. There are not the resources. Instead, Lynn typically spends her day in the church building in a ministry of presence and encounter with the café clientele or mourners in the sanctuary. Church members more willingly serve in these new forms of ministry than on committees. All are in the process of becoming something, or rather, someplace different. New people and resources are involved: through the active participation of the local community and through partnership with external funding bodies. In one of the poorest communities in Britain, the gospel is inhabited and walked, rather than measured. I would have missed the theological significance of this had I not begun to think in spatial rather than statistical terms. What further theological insights can we gain by correlating this case study with various spatial perspectives on the local church? I start with the biblical image of the temple.

Temple: A Biblical Correlation

God's people inhabit many spatial sites in the Bible: wilderness and holy mountain, tabernacle, temple, synagogue and household, promised land and foreign land. Each image suggests ways of thinking spatially about the local church. Why the temple-image in this particular case study? In the temple in Jerusalem that features prominently in the history of Israel and the ministry of Jesus, there were outer and inner courtyards, leading to the inner sanctuary. The primary purpose is the worship of God, although many ancillary activities are pursued within its walls (as the gospel story of Jesus driving out the moneychangers reminds us). Over three years, Lynn and Jean never used temple imagery; this was my own selected image as a researcher. However, they did speak of what they were doing in ways that later prompted such an interpretation. Jean described their plan to site the counselling centre within the church sanctuary itself like this:

> We designed it so because we feel that everything that goes on should really be part of the church as opposed to something that the church is doing away from the church because it is the place where we want to be.

Lynn echoed that remark. It was the building that declared the Christian identity of the congregation:

> There is a theory about doing things off the premises and starting up say a shop or something in the community, particularly in communities like this. People have gone into the idea of house churches and moving away from buildings. I think if you scrape the surface of most of the people in the church, they still feel that it should be around the church . . . and I feel it should be in the church. Not because I want the gathering in here but because I think it is important to make that connection, to be honest about it and say, 'This is who we are', and that the project will be run by people who, it doesn't matter if they have faith or not, we need them to do this job for the children, but there is something about linking it in to the memorial chapel and the tree and the services of remembrance we have had there for children as well as adults.

For both Lynn and Jean the church building was important as a place to connect the Christian faith and the needs of the community. The church café, memorial chapel and counselling centre functioned like the outer and inner courtyards of a temple, leading local people through different zones into the ritual place of worship at the heart. Nor was the worship escapist in the life and suffering of this community. As Lynn put it:

> . . . it seems to me that the importance of worship is where life is and so that's when you come back to the café, and you come back to the suffering and you come back to, how do you bring this back into the life and worship of the church?

It is not immediately obvious that the use of temple imagery is compatible with New Testament views of the temple. Jesus is seen as the new temple in his own person (John 1.14; 2.21), replacing the Jerusalem temple as the place where God dwells. There are, therefore, no longer any buildings or places that are holy or sacred for Christians (John 4.19–24). It is the bodies of Christians, rather than their places of worship, that are described by Paul in 1 Corinthians as the 'temple of the Holy Spirit' (1 Corinthians 3.17; 6.19). This has led many today to stress the church is a community of faith, the body of Christ with many members (1 Corinthians 12.12–27), and not a church building.

However, feminist theology and biblical studies also bring to our attention the embodied nature of the biblical narratives. The new temple may not be a building but it is a body in space and place: Christ's body and the body of Christ. As the Jesus of John's Gospel moves in and through space with the women disciples, for example, they create new places for the gospel: a room filled with the perfume of a woman's costly ointment, preparing Jesus' body for his death. The households of the first Christians, which included women, gentiles and slaves, embodied a gospel of reconciliation. Movement and action in space, which create theologically significant place, are integral to the life of this new temple. At the very least, Christians cannot spiritualize away the embodied life of the church. It is their bodies in space that are the temples of the indwelling Spirit and it is their embodied lives that create places of true discipleship (1 Corinthians 6.15–20).

By calling Millhill Church a temple-like place I am not thinking of it as intrinsically holy or sacred space, but rather as a socially constructed space where local people find healing and hope by their bodily movement in and through its building, reconfigured as a welcoming and worshipful set of places. Unlike the temple in Jerusalem, which excluded women, gentiles and sinners from its innermost courtyard and sanctuary, all people in this temple are encouraged to move through the different courtyards and the sanctuary itself. I am therefore calling the Millhill congregation a temple in a *double* sense: it is an *embodied spiritual temple* inhabiting a *temple-like building*, where people move, mingle and express faith in social, pastoral and liturgical practices. This is a postmodern temple where the boundaries between church and neighbourhood, member and neighbour, church or community resources and funding, are permeable and at times blurred. If we are to understand the people and resources here, then we must watch how they inhabit place and move through space, rather than simply measure formal membership and official activities over time. To explore further, we now correlate this biblical interpretation of spiritual and spatial embodiment with anthropological perspectives.

Walking: An Anthropological Correlation

In an essay on spatial taboos in the Australian Aboriginal landscape, Nancy M. Dunn argues that anthropology needs to work against 'abstracting the problem of space from that of the body and action' by co-ordinating space, time and bodily action in one paradigm of changing relations (Dunn, 2003, pp. 92–109). The need for such a paradigm also applies to congregational studies. Too often we study the congregation as an organization over time without reference to embodied action within its delineated space. For example, we could describe the Millhill counselling centre as an organized pastoral response to the number of bereaved children in the community. However, for Lynn, it is a pattern of movement within the building:

> It's hard without seeing the building but it's almost as though we've physically kind of walked up there anyway because . . . we had the memorial chapel and the things that are in it . . . We started a music room for bereaved children . . . and through that partly came [the centre]. Through working with the children and through visiting the parents we seemed to be walking toward the area at the back of the church anyway.

How are we to understand these references to walking? They echo a study of sheep farmers in the Scottish Borders by another anthropologist, John Gray. He draws on Michel de Certeau's famous interpretation of walking as a practice that creates 'places'. Pedestrians make cities their own place not by following the cartographer's map but in the improvised act of window-shopping or strolling. Gray interprets the life of a hill-farming community through observing this non-verbal practice of walking: 'My aim is . . . to analyze how, in going around the hill, shepherds make a variety of places to which they become attached as a matter of their identity as hill sheep people and Borderers' (Gray, 2003, pp. 226–8). Through walking around the hills, this human action in space creates places of 'human significance and emotional attachment' for the shepherds.

Similarly, by paying attention to the non-verbal practices of movement around the church building we can see how a congregation and its neighbours create similar 'places' to which they also become attached in terms of their spiritual identity. Through such anthropological insights into space and place, we realize that these are not only metaphors for congregational life but also a constitutive part of it, without which the local church cannot exist or be understood. Like the anthropologists, we also need a paradigm that integrates space, time and bodily action in congregational studies. Has the Christian tradition itself ever understood the local church in such spatial and bodily terms?

Fragmentary Place: Correlation with the Christian Tradition

I draw here on four examples of Christian thought on the theological significance of the church building for understanding the congregation. Each shows how we can mine the Christian tradition for rich spatial insights into the theological meaning of the local church, its people and resources. The first is taken from the ancient eastern church and the writings of St Maximus the Confessor, a seventh-century Greek theologian. In his *Mystagogia*, Maximus reflects on the physical church building and its spiritual significance for the unity of the worshipping congregation:

> For a church, although put up as one building, is partitioned in conformity with a definite plan, with one place set aside for priests and servers, which we call the sanctuary, and another open to all the faithful, which we call the nave – and yet, the Church is essentially one, and not divided in kind by the differentiation of its parts . . . the Church is one and the same in and throughout each section. (Maximus, 1982, pp. 68–9)

This way of looking at the church building found full expression in the great medieval tradition of cathedral building. As Philip Sheldrake has reminded us, the cathedral was a sacred place where worshippers could enter into a different world:

> To enter the cathedral was to be transported into heaven on earth by the vastness of the space, by the progressive dematerialization of walls with a sea of glass and a flood of light and by the increasingly elaborate liturgies in which, sacramentally, the living church was united with the whole court of heaven . . . This was a utopian space in which an idealized harmony, to be realized only in heaven, was anticipated in the here and now. (Sheldrake, 2002, pp. 59–60)

Such theological significance in space and place was not restricted to great cathedrals. It was also discerned within the humble local church. This finds artistic expression in the work of the seventeenth-century Anglican clergyman and poet George Herbert. His collection of poetry, appropriately called *The Temple*, includes meditations on how each part of the church building taught worshippers the Christian life. He writes in *The Church-Floor*:

> Mark you the floor? That square and speckled stone
> Which looks so firm and strong,
> Is *Patience*:
> And th' other black and grave, wherewith each one
> Is checkered all along,
> *Humility*:

For Herbert the church building was a text to be read like scripture. It was also a contested space where the theological controversies of his day over design and use of the sanctuary were played out. He rebuilt his parish church of Leighton Bromswold for the same reason that he wrote *The Temple*, to create a teaching place for his ordinary congregation (see *www.shu.ac.uk/emls/iemls/pd/herbarch.html*).

Coming into the present, the legacy of Martin Luther King as an American civil rights campaigner continues to inspire congregations to oppose racism. King was above all and always a preacher, whose public dream of a racially reconciled America was a spatial extension of the most formative place in his young life, the sanctuary of his home church, Ebenezer Baptist Church in Atlanta. As one theologian has written of King's life:

> In the ordered environment of the African Baptist Church, King discovered his vocation and the strength to carry it out. The architecture of the sanctuary symbolized the cosmos in which King had grown up and that he never ceased to inhabit . . .The sanctuary dictated the boundaries within which [he] sorted out the relationship of suffering and hope. (Lischer, 1995, pp. 16–17)

This is a rich Christian tradition to help us to understand the Millhill congregation as theologically freighted space. With Maximus we see that the café and sanctuary, though differentiated places, still constitute one church community, where inhabitants see themselves as 'belonging to the church', whether formal members or not. With the medieval cathedral worshippers, those who enter Millhill's walls are also entering a utopian space where the lifting high of the poor is anticipated in place after place. With Herbert, the symbols of the Millhill memorial chapel and its mourning rituals teach its worshippers the Christian gospel. And, with King, the bereavement counselling centre enables staff and children to understand the relationship of suffering and hope in the wider world, through its window into the sanctuary.

These historic voices do not have the final word in this conversation, however. All four had a coherent Christian worldview (Orthodox, Catholic, Anglican, African-American Baptist) of the sanctuary. How can the inhabitants of Millhill Church see the Christian meaning of their lives in the temple courtyards? It is glimpsed only in fragments, perhaps, as when some local drug addicts get into a lively competition with the minister to remember all ten commandments over lunch in the café; or when an employed cook in its kitchen insists that this makes her a church member; or when a local boy wants to plan and conduct his own mother's funeral in the memorial chapel. To address that fragmentation of life and meaning we can correlate the Millhill experience with contemporary theological and poetic interpretations of place.

Spatial Encounter: A Theological Correlation

The mystical, pedagogical, liturgical and political theologies of secure and fixed 'sacred space' that we find in Maximus, Gothic cathedrals, George Herbert and Martin Luther King do not fully address the twenty-first century problem of fragmentation of faith and life. For that we need to engage in a more contemporary and contextual theological reflection on space and place. A theologian like Timothy Gorringe helps us to do that by making the case for seeing all space as potentially sacred, even a dilapidated church building. In his book, *A Theology of the Built Environment*, Gorringe's understanding of sacred space draws on Karl Barth's analogy for understanding the Bible. Just as scripture is not the word of God but becomes it, 'as the water of the pool of Bethesda healed when the angel stirred it', so:

> ... all space is *potentially* sacred, waiting for the moment of encounter in which it mediates God ... If that is the case, *then sacred space is bound up with event, with community, and with memory.* What we conventionally understand as sacred spaces have a sacramental

significance with regard to all other space: they are a reminder of the potential for epiphany of all other spaces. (Gorringe, 2002, p. 40)

On Lynn's arrival, Millhill Parish Church was only a sacred space for the local community in the memory and associations of the older church families. It became so again only as the relentless events of untimely death in the local community were brought into the memorial chapel and counselling centre. Jean returned, having long felt alienated from Millhill's membership demands and assuming that the church was closed, when she encountered God in the quality of Lynn's pastoral and liturgical care at her son's funeral. She then committed herself to help Lynn renew the building as a place of similar encounter for her community. For Gorringe, the God who is glimpsed in such an eventful, communal and mindful built environment is the triune and crucified God who turns bad places into good and frees their inhabitants. Christian worship structures all the spaces and practices of Millhill Church and offers encounter with God's creative, reconciling and redemptive action in the world. This spatial good news is best seen in stark relief against the artist's imaginative depiction of such broken-down places as Millhill's local community.

Mapping: A Literary Correlation

In her collection of poems, *An Atlas of the Difficult World,* Adrienne Rich writes memorable lines of spatial imagination about her own land of America that could as easily describe the places within Millhill Church and its locality:

These are the suburbs of acquiescence
silence rising fume like from the streets
This is the capital of money and dolor whose spires
flare up through air inversions whose bridges are crumbling
whose children are drifting blind alleys pent
between coiled rolls of razor wire
I promised to show you a map you say but this is a mural
then yes let it be these are small distinctions
where do we see it from is the question (Rich, 1991, p. 6)

Millhill has to be located somewhere on that kind of map, as do all local churches in poor or prosperous communities. Doing theology in congregational studies means naming the contested and suffering places of the local church and its locality through the honest window of the artist's imagination. 'Where do we see it from', and, even more, 'Where does God see it from', are indeed the theological questions to ask.

Conclusion

The critical correlation of the case study findings from Millhill Church with these five perspectives on space and place lead us to a new way of thinking about the local church, its people and resources in a secular, pluralist Britain. By understanding the congregation only in *temporal* terms as a membership body over time, we are locked into the internal problems of the decline and ageing of the church membership and its ministry *over time*. By reimagining the local church in *spatial* terms, we are open to the theological interpretation and practical renewal of the congregation as a temple-like place of divine encounter for a diverse community of neighbours as well as members. As the American journalist Gary Dorsey wrote, after spending 16 months with one such congregation, an experience that led him back to church:

> There is a church . . . that sits at the peak of a hill beside the river . . . and the light that slips across the surface of things every day inspires people to come. They spend their day in daydreams. They have visions, suffer silences, sing songs, dance, laugh, practice, and forget to hope. They curse and tell stories. They go round and round . . . It was there I found my harbor place, where people pledged to live by remembering, and over and over and over again, experienced the miracle of wonder. (Dorsey, 1995, pp. 382–3)

Doing theology in congregational studies need not be a lament for decline or a plea for growth over time. It can be about watching people and resources go round and round, over and over again, and naming the places of remembrance and wonder that they make out of such whirling space.

Practical Ways of Studying this Aspect of the Local Church

As a researcher, individually or in collaboration with a group of theologically reflective participants from the congregation in question, you
may want to follow a similar model of critical correlation, using these
methods:

- A vicinity walk. Draw an 'imaginative map' or a mural of the local
  church and its locality with your own place-names, to indicate
  the kind of space you now see it to be, answering Adrienne Rich's
  question: 'Where do we see it from is the question'.
- A time line.
- An ethnographic study, observing over a reasonable time period
  (week, month, year) where, how and why people move in the church
  building (e.g. do children race around? Are visitors restricted?
  Where does the minister encounter people?).
- An exercise in corporate theological reflection, asking a group
  about their sense of 'place' within and around the church building,
  e.g. where do they feel welcome or uncomfortable? Which of these
  places connects their faith to their life experience? How do official
  church names and uses compare and contrast with the informal
  'places' and 'place-names' people make out of these spaces (e.g.
  church youth gathering in stairwell; homeless sleeping in church
  graveyard).

Further reading

Dunn, N. M. (2003) 'Excluded Spaces: the figure in the Australian
    Aboriginal Landscape', in Setha M. Low, Denise Lawrence-Zuniga
    (eds) *The Anthropology of Space and Place: Locating Culture*,
    Oxford: Blackwell Publishing, pp. 92–109.
    A provocative essay on the need for a new paradigm of space
    and bodily action in anthropology, applicable to congregational
    studies.
Gorringe, T. (2002) *A Theology of the Built Environment: Justice,
    Empowerment, Redemption* Cambridge: Cambridge University
    Press.
    A wide-ranging interdisciplinary study of the theological signifi-
    cance of constructed places for human and planetary flourishing.

Gray, J. (2003) 'Open Spaces and Dwelling Places: Being at Home on Hill Farms in the Scottish Borders', in Setha M. Low and Denise Lawrence-Zuniga (eds) *The Anthropology of Space and Place: Locating Culture*, Oxford: Blackwell Publishing, pp. 224–44.

Insightful use of de Certeau's notion of walking as place-making to study a community's sense of place and identity, worth transposing into congregational studies.

Inge, J. (2003) *A Christian Theology of Place*, Aldershot: Ashgate.

A stimulating theology of place from a sacramental perspective.

Pahl, J. (2003) *Shopping Malls and Other Sacred Spaces: Putting God in Place*, Grand Rapids, MI: Brazos Press.

A personal account of the spatial character of American theology and popular culture, relevant to British inhabitants of that shared trans-Atlantic world.

Sheldrake, P. (2002) *Spaces for the Sacred: Place, Memory and Identity*, London: SCM Press.

A profound study of the meaning of sacred space in Christian spirituality, in conversation with other disciplinary and literary accounts of place.

3.4 Power in the Local Church

Introduction

This section offers perspectives on the local church evoked by the concept of power. Power is an important idea in the social sciences and theology. Like any other human gathering, local churches provide the opportunity to exercise and respond to power. Unlike secular organizations, they hold beliefs about the nature of divine power and the way in which it is mediated to humans. Contributors in this section link power to issues of leadership, decision-making, ritual and symbol, identity and networks.

Anthropological Strand – Power

Douglas Davies

Power, a major feature of all social life, is as evident in religious activities as in the more obvious domains of politics and economics. Power relates to the influence people have over others and accept from others. Its formal acceptance and use is called authority. In religious groups power is a complex idea because believers usually identify some power as divine and some as human in origin.

Although believers may see power as coming from God, a strictly anthropological perspective can only speak of 'religious' power as being human in origin. Anthropology describes what believers say about power and about their experiences of the divine. This contribution discusses the following key ideas: divine power, sites of power, thought and behaviour control and vigilant leadership.

Divine Power

People are unlikely to engage in religious activity unless they derive some benefit from it, not least some sense of power coming to them or arising within them. Ideas of transcendence and ecstasy attest to this. Their expression varies from those who feel overwhelmed by an encounter with something or someone greater than themselves to others who simply sense a degree of comfort in the meaningfulness of life. Churches account for such experiences through their particular theology and beliefs. Catholic traditions root power in the authority given by God to the church and expressed through the hierarchy, sacraments and the devotion of the faithful. Protestant traditions locate power in scripture and the faithful preaching and hearing of that divine 'word'. Orthodox forms of Christianity emphasize the tradition of the liturgy and doctrinal theology as the medium of power, while charismatic traditions focus on events in which the power of the Spirit is reckoned to be manifest. To understand 'power' in a church, its theology of power must be studied.

Historically, churches have often restricted access to power by their structure and organization. This can become problematic if an individual claims direct revelation, a personal power from God or otherwise challenges the established leadership. The Reformation was just such a challenge and, once the 'protestant principle' combined individual judgement and direct influence from God over interpreting scripture, the birth and rise of innumerable sects began. Sects often claim privileged access to truth, and a belief in possessing more divine authority and power than earlier or other groups. Belief in direct inspiration or in special revelation is often associated with the God-breathed dynamism that raises up a particular leader.

This issue of leadership provides a bridge from power as divine energy to power within human beings. Here, the importance of 'claims' to inspiration cannot be ignored for they pose the possibility of false claims, see for example, Bible stories of false prophets or deceitful leaders. The New Testament, with its accounts of the Holy Spirit as the life-force of earliest Christianity manifest in and through various spiritual gifts and types of leadership, soon recognized that false manifestations of the Spirit could occur. Accordingly congregations had the responsibility of 'testing the spirits', a religious formula acknowledging the problem.

Anthropology has done a great deal to show some of the intricacies of 'power' in the ordinary ritual practices of a group as well as contexts where people are said to become inspired or possessed by a spiritual power. Theology would want to make distinctions between the Holy Spirit and other possible kinds of 'spirit'. However, the significant anthropological point is that people the world over use the idea of 'a spirit' as a means of talking about experiences that make them feel different from their everyday sense of self. This can occur in and through the ordinary rituals of a church in which particular actions are repeated at regular intervals. Here it is useful to distinguish between rites of intensification and rites of passage. The former include worship services or the Eucharist in which people experience a strengthening of their belief and a reinforcement of their religious commitment. The latter involve rites in which a person's status undergoes a change, as in baptism, confirmation, marriage or a funeral. Some anthropologists talk of rites of passage as involving an encounter with the spirit power underlying a religion.

Spirit possession can occur in either form of rite. Sometimes people train to become possessed and, subsequently, gain a new status as a shaman or other kind of ritual specialist through a rite of passage and, subsequently become able, through trance states, to bring help or advice to others. During their trance they may speak in what is described as a spirit-language and reckon to take a journey into the domain of the spirit-beings. Others simply become possessed, often in special ceremonies and as a form of rite of intensification. Anthropologists often interpret such phenomena as behaviour that develops within these individuals in response to their life situation and in the hope of gaining some appropriate response from others. The interesting feature of societies in which spirit possession occurs is that it is, largely, possible to predict the status of people liable to possession (Lewis, 1986). It is often those deprived of social status and recognition that become possessed and, through that possession, gain some attention and status for a period. If men are possessed they will tend not to be the socially powerful but those deprived of status. Similarly, in many social contexts, women are deprived of appropriate recognition and, accordingly, may become possessed. This type of explanation works on a 'deprivation theory' of the human need for status and recognition and sees possession as one means of gaining it, and the power implicit in it, albeit for a limited period of time. This is a good example of how power in society at large is deeply related to religious groups.

In contemporary church life, some studies of immigrant groups show how churches may be the one arena within which individuals may gain a positive status and a sense of 'being somebody'. The need for this recognition and the means for bringing it about can take the form of religious beliefs about how the Spirit is manifest in them. Another facet of power achievable through church occurs when the group praises and prizes someone's character and quality as a person and not, for example, their level of education or wealth. In other words churches can be places of achieving a form of power not available to that person through their 'worldly' status. This is, also, an intriguing aspect of church life within strongly consumerist and competitive societies when only certain aspects of a person's character may emerge in their work context and, even if they are very successful in that domain, they may still feel the need for a different kind of affirmation and engagement with a group of people concerned with more ultimate sets of values and beliefs.

This debate about the deprivation theory shows how an anthropological analysis of the human religious condition can feed into theological concerns. So, for example, if this deprivation theory is accurate what theological responses and questions are raised? It would be easy to reject this theory out of hand and say that it is dishonouring to the very doctrine of the Holy Spirit, or that it is 'reductionist' and explains everything in terms of one thing: in this case, status and deprivation. However, many churches have come to take the idea of liberation theology, a theology of the poor or of the notion of bias to the poor seriously (Sheppard, 1983). This approach means asking just who the 'poor' are in any specific context and, if the anthropologist is right about the status of those who are candidates for 'possession', then it might be wise to think of them as in need of special care and attention. Perhaps they possess abilities of great use within the church that are not being used or recognized elsewhere. At the same time, this anthropological view would encourage caution over people who lay claim to special spiritual powers that might give them a status in a group that they do not possess elsewhere. This is especially important in groups that give precedence to those who seem much closer to spirit-power than others.

Sites of Power

The place a church holds on the social map of power often relates to these manifestations of status. The Church of England, for example, functions as a state church and, in civic services, when royalty, judges, the police and military may be present, the face of power that is seen is that of the society itself. The same church building, when hosting a healing service may reveal a different face: that of succour and help for those lacking the strength of social office. Around the corner from the highly visible Anglican church there may well be, in a back street, a Spiritualist church attended by some Anglicans when they have suffered the death of a loved one. Their need for some sense of the wellbeing of their dead brings them to a séance where a medium undergoes a kind of possession and brings a message from the dead to the living. Such a voice of comfort involves a power quite different from the civic ceremonial. In research, the nature of the ritual and its symbols could be compared and contrasted, as could the geographical location of the church buildings as expressions of social status: the 'High' Street being more important than a 'back' street.

Thought and Behaviour Control

Moving from location to the human body, we highlight one distinctive contribution made by anthropology concerning the way power is controlled in groups. The anthropologist Mary Douglas (1970) is most widely associated with this approach. She related different types of control to the way in which human behaviour became associated with the human body and the idea of embodiment. Embodiment concerns the way in which the values, expectations and beliefs of a society or group are expressed in, through and 'as' the bodies of members of that group. No society or religious group simply holds religious beliefs and values as some kind of abstract system separate from the behaviour of its members. Values come to shape the lives of people in immediate and direct ways. Values influence not only what people might wear or how they dress their hair, but also what they eat and even how they 'carry' their body. Even the forms of physical expression, how people walk, talk or smile can become an expression of, or a vehicle for, their beliefs and values. Religious leaders reflect this in their dress; the pope traditionally wore the triple crown, bishops wear mitres while 'free churches' often move entirely away from such dress, even though they often develop a uniform style of their own.

Mary Douglas approached this complex aspect of life by focusing on how a group might control, first, the physical behaviour and, second, the thoughts of its members. The element relating to physical control she called the 'group' factor and the control of ideas or belief the 'grid' factor. So some religious communities might be very concerned with what people did, but not so much with exactly what they believed. Many Jewish congregations or meetings of The Society of Friends, for example, might have strong opinions on how their members should behave while leaving them free to think whatever they like. Many Anglican congregations, by contrast, leave their members wide scope both on their belief and their actions. It is relatively rare for a religious group not to care at all about either the behaviour or belief of their members. For the purposes of research it is possible to take these grid and group concepts and ask how high or low any particular church is on each. It is also possible to take individuals and see where they might lie on a grid–group spectrum within their church.

Mary Douglas called this general idea of control the 'purity rule', arguing that the greater degree of general control a group exerted over its members the greater degree of control would be exerted by a member over his or her body. This is where the 'embodiment' element returns to our discussion. The control of one's body would be expressed in forms of dress or speech or laughter, of eating and drinking, of attitudes to sexual activity or even to types of sport. It would also be apparent in the forms of worship used in a church. In sociological terms, the more sect-like a group is the greater tends to be its degree of control over both belief and behaviour of its members. It is likely, for example, that a strongly sect-like group will hold meetings where members are tutored in the doctrine to enable them to become 'word-perfect'. Quite different would be groups in which greatly varied opinions are tolerated and, perhaps, even fostered.

During periods of social change it is to be expected that a church may contain groups of people representing a variety of kinds of control. For example, many Anglicans who attend their early 8.00 a.m. Sunday holy communion service might have much stronger views on what is 'proper' dress, behaviour, speech and music than those attending the later family service, or a much later young people's 'alternative' worship service. Where both generational and cultural change is reflected in church membership issues of 'control' become quite complex. Still, it is useful for studies of any church to consider these forms of control and responses to them, not least because they may indicate points of conflict or dissension between generations or between people with different views of life and faith. The very fact that behaviour and belief are intimately combined in subtle ways is important to bear in mind when analysing any religious group. Issues such as those of how people should move about or within a church building relate to this 'purity rule'. The considered and relatively slow movements of priest and people at a formal Mass, the very way church processions move, are quite different from the jerky and relative rapid movements that might occur in services of faith healing or of some phases of a charismatic worship event. These different movements reflect the sense of contact with divine power in different ways.

The anthropology of religion would encourage any concern over power to involve a study of the preferred rituals of a group as a means of assessing the kind of power expressed within them. Key questions would include whether all take equal part in a rite or whether there is a single leader. Are all parts of a rite equally important or are some singled out and emphasized? In Christian groups are some rites deemed more core and 'closer' to the real power of church than others? Is the prayer meeting more important than the family service? Is the sermon more important than the Eucharist? Is an evangelistic campaign more central than a quiet retreat? Indeed, even the words 'campaign' and 'retreat' indicate differing versions of power. In such analyses the anthropologist is looking for the dominant symbol in a ritual. Is it, for example, the bread and wine as Christ's symbolic body, or the priest, or the Bible and sermon, is it speaking in tongues or a healing event, is it a special kind of silence that falls over a group? Or perhaps it is something else.

The anthropologist Victor Turner analysed a symbol in terms of two 'poles', the sensory and the ideology poles (1969). The sensory pole refers to our experience, to what we see, feel, taste or smell, while the ideological pole refers to the ideas, doctrines or beliefs enshrined in a symbol. The bread at the Mass, Eucharist or Lord's Supper has a sensory pole of sight, touch and taste and an ideological pole of ideas of Christ's body sacrificed for sin. Many other experiences and ideas can 'condense' onto a symbol giving it many meanings or voices, indeed Turner spoke of symbols as multivocal and most ritual symbols can be analysed in this way.

Vigilant Leadership

With religious leadership, we encounter something of a paradox. On the one hand divine power is believed to give life to the church and yet, on the other, it must be controlled lest it fall into the wrong hands. So it is that the vigilance of leadership emerges to control abuse of power. Yet a further complexity arises in that leaders can be the very people who can so easily abuse the power that comes to them. While this is a problem for all social groups, it is a particularly difficult issue for churches precisely because of the possible conflict of 'powers' in the sense that Christian people acknowledge that there is a 'power' that comes from God, while also firmly acknowledging the nature of human 'power'. Church traditions cope with this perpetual problem in a variety of ways. Here I develop the issue through two approaches, first, the notion of *Homo religiosus* and second, the balanced notions of jural and mystical authority.

The Latin term *Homo religiosus* or 'religious man' offers a way of approaching the issue of religious power. It is an ideal-type definition, one that gives a shorthand description or cameo of the essential features of a leader. It answers the question, 'What would an ideal leader be like?' even though it is acknowledged that no single leader is ever likely to match each detail. For example, when a church writes an advertisement for its new minister what it produces is, in effect, an ideal-type definition. When studying a church it would be worth either trying to get a copy of such an account or else asking a group of people to write one. In so doing they would, in all probability, articulate their prime values and try to see what those ideals would 'look like' in a leader. Does it speak of a person who is expected to lead and take all the decisions, in other words do they think of power as a decision-making energy vested in one person? Or, perhaps it refers to one of a team who shares a sense of collective responsibility? Does it, perhaps, speak of power in terms of humility or supportive encouragement? Here it might be worth gathering further information on how a particular church uses religious language about God when framing its picture of power. Does the emphasis fall upon the 'Almighty' nature of God the Father? Or upon the nature of Jesus or of the Holy Spirit as triumphant over the devil and demons? By contrast, power may take the form of servanthood, with a stress on Jesus and believers as servants of all. The Bible itself furnishes a wide variety of notions of power and can influence a church's discourse or way of talking about things. So, too, through the ritual of a church, its liturgies and hymns, these expressions are brought to light.

A second way of exploring power in leadership starts from an analysis of the balance between two kinds of authority found in churches, the one concerning jural (or legal) and the other mystical authority (Needham, 1980). To allow such a balance is to do some justice to the complexity of 'power' in religious groups. Jural or legal power refers to the power needed to run organizations, some churches might regard this as 'worldly' power. The clergy as a professional body, for example, need jural power to control their activities and the proper scope of their duties. Within the Church of England, as a state church, for example, this aspect of power and authority becomes clear at the service introducing priests to their parish church for the first time, and it does so in the person of the diocesan registrar as the legal officer representing the church as a formal institution within society. That person will be dressed as a legal person and not as an ecclesiastical figure. In a sense the registrar focuses the more specially legal aspects of authority which, in technical terms, is also vested in the bishop who is also present. But, of course, for believers there is much more to a church than legal power. What of the presence and influence of the divine? It is here that mystical authority comes into play, an authority that somehow focuses and makes real the relationship between God and people. Often this is literally embodied in a distinctive type of individual, either with special care going into selecting those persons admitted to a 'mystical authority' office, or with just those persons possessing the appropriate qualities being identified by others as worth consulting.

In many churches there are individuals who can be pointed out as 'real saints', as 'spiritual' or 'godly' people or as 'weighty Friends' among the Quakers. They may become spiritual guides and helps to others; they may be priests, leaders or lay people. In some way these people bring the spiritual qualities of the life of faith into balance with the 'worldly' or 'rational' forms of control that institutions often develop as a necessary part of surviving over time. But, without such mystical authority present the rule-led church would lose its heart. In the Mormon Church, for example, the local bishop or area president carries the fullest 'legal' or jural power, but his work is complemented by that of the 'patriarch' whose job it is to give people a personal and individual blessing, by the laying on of hands and the speaking of a blessing believed to come by direct inspiration of the Spirit. He is the mystical agent of his church. In another kind of way the saints of Catholic and Orthodox traditions also often carry a sense of the mystical authority of God and become partners in prayer with believers for that very reason. The Virgin Mary is a good example of mystical authority and may, in some contexts, complement the more jural power of God the Father. One of the reasons for the success of the Catholic Church over such a long period of time lies precisely in the balance that has emerged between legal and mystical forms of controlling power. Indeed, it is the nature and extent of checks and balances over different types of power that enables a church to survive over time.

Case study

I began studying Mormonism in 1969 with work focused on interviewing leaders, missionaries and related families. I attended one particular Mormon congregation with occasional visits elsewhere. My Anglican background questioned why these Latter-day Saints, whose general attitude to their faith was deeply respectful, were not particularly quiet or reverential before, or even during parts of the main Sunday services. During the Sacrament Service, the Mormon holy communion, I also observed that even quite small children or infants would eat the bread and drink the water – for Mormons do not use wine. Only after years of study did I come to grasp two things. First, that the noise coming from mothers, fathers, children and siblings itself symbolized the ultimate importance of the family within this faith and expressed what the Saints really prized, namely, their family life. Second, that it was the regional temple, whose ritual really united families for eternity, and not the local congregation that really attracted what other churches might view as quiet reverence.

Different attitudes to power were also being expressed in these two locations. The local congregation was, essentially, about family life as lived from day to day and a degree of bustle was appropriate to that, indeed, teenage priests of the lower or Aaronic Priesthood conducted the Sacrament Service. The temple, however, concerned the eternal family, involving baptism for dead relatives and an eternal sealing in marriage conducted by the higher, adult, Melchizedek Priesthood. The temple rites were reported as much more solemn. In anthropological analysis, I now saw more of an equivalence between the Mormon Temple and the Eucharist of other churches than between the local Mormon Sacrament Service and the Eucharist of other churches.

Further reading

Davies, Douglas J. (2000) *The Mormon Culture of Salvation*, Aldershot: Ashgate.
This shows how local church life relates to family life and to temple rites and explores ideas of religious power expressed in different kinds of salvation.

Davies, Douglas, J. (2002) *Anthropology and Theology*, Oxford: Berg.
An introductory conversation between anthropology and theology on the major topics of embodiment and incarnation, merit and salvation, sacrifice, ritual and experience, sacrament and symbolism.

Douglas, Mary (1970) *Natural Symbols*, London: Pelican Books.
An influential study of the symbolic capacity of the human body and its relation to wider society.

Lewis, Ioan (1986) *Religion in Context*, Cambridge: Cambridge University Press.
An anthropological analysis of religious power in forms of spirit possession and witchcraft.

Turner, Victor (1969) *The Ritual Process*, London: Routledge and Kegan Paul.
An influential study of ritual in African and some other contexts. Important for rites of passage and for symbolism.

Tyson, Ruel W., James L. Peacock and Daniel Patterson (eds) (1988) *Diversities of Gifts*, Urbana and Chicago: University of Illinois Press.
An excellent set of studies on congregations, religious experience of worship, hymns and sermons in the southern states of North America.

Sociological Strand – Power

Paul Chambers

Introduction

This contribution explores various aspects of power from a sociological perspective and discusses how they might be researched within a congregational context. Key concepts include: the nature and distribution of power within the local church and its relation to organizational structures; formal and informal power; authority and resistance to authority; social control; and social cohesion. External factors and their relation to mission are also explored. These include: social networks; social capital; symbolic boundaries; human and material resources; and competition between congregations.

Sociological Perspectives on Power and Religion

Power is the ability of individuals and groups to make their interests count. Power can be said to be concerned with two areas of social life, the allocation of material (and other) resources and the legitimization of authority (Giddens, 1997, pp. 215, 338–9). In terms of legitimacy, authority is invariably linked to factors such as status, tradition or rules. The exercise of power includes the ability of certain individuals and groups to protect and advance their interests by imposing their will on the less powerful and also strategies of resistance to this in the form of compensatory (or countervailing) powers. If power both enables and constrains, it is also a finite resource. It follows that the distribution of power must of necessity be unequal; characterized by material, cultural and social inequality and in some cases conflict relating to these asymmetries of power (Lukes, 1974). Religion is no exception in this and discourses of power pervade religious systems and institutions. Although all religions advance some notion of supernatural power, it should also be stressed that sociology must necessarily remain agnostic towards such metaphysical questions (Wilson, 1982). Still, in terms of how those beliefs might inform social action, forms of organization and the distribution of power, there remains much for sociologists to say.

Right from the inception of their discipline, sociologists have placed power at the centre of their analyses of religious systems. For example, Marx (1818–83) argued that the distribution and exercise of power is largely determined by material factors. Dominant groups emerge and seek to harness and control the economic forces of any given era for their own benefit. This necessarily leads to conflicts of interests between social groups. Inasmuch as Marx focuses on religion, it is in terms of the ways that religion has historically legitimated the economic (and by extension – social and political) *status quo*. While Marx admits the possibility that religion can operate in autonomous ways, in practice it tends to reflect the prevailing views of the ruling power elite. Thus the role of religious institutions is primarily directed to legitimizing both the idea of private property and those social and political arrangements that underpin this notion. Power then is grounded in conflict and religion is essentially a conservative force whose primary role is to make the prevailing distribution of power appear natural (McLellan, 1977).

Although his approach to religion is less reductive than that of Marx, Max Weber (1864–1920) also grounds his view of power in patterns of conflict between sectional interests. The key concept here is that of meaningful social action, where subjective meanings and related social dispositions inform group behaviour. Therefore, religion is not merely the legitimizer of existing patterns of power but can act independently of these forces and even, in some cases, influence them. The exercise of power in Weber's formulation is, accordingly, an essentially contested concept that is always related in some way to values and which may not necessarily display any inherent 'logic' in its observable outcomes. In this sense, purposive action may have unintended consequences at odds with any stated intention (Weber, 1963).

Building upon Weber's insights, Michel Foucault suggests that the sociologist should be less concerned with the question of what power is and where it comes from and rather more concerned with identifying how and by what means power is exercised and what its effects are (Foucault, 1984). In contrast, Emile Durkheim (1858–1917) views religion in cosmological terms, that is, as a worldview, an integrated set of ideas constituting a collective representation (real or imagined) of the social world (Durkeim, 1915/1995). He therefore grounds religion in social consensus rather than conflict, and the power of religion and religious systems lies in their ability to produce social cohesion and a coherent worldview.

The Social Organization of Power

In terms of the local church, all the different facets of power discussed above will impact on congregational life. However, patterns of power will vary in relation to differing organizational structures and theological orientations as well as in relation to the types of external societal factors and variables discussed elsewhere in this volume by Woodhead (Section 3.1 Sociology Strand) and Collins (Section 3.3 Sociology Strand). Therefore, the initial point of departure for any sociological study of power in the local church entails some focus on the organizational characteristics of congregations. Congregations can be distinguished by a number of recurrent forms of social organization that relate to theological dispositions. In this respect, sociologists have customarily drawn from models derived from Weber and developed by Troeltsch (1931) and Niebuhr (1957) as ideal types. These encompass three organizational types – church, denomination and sect – which broadly correspond to the various ways in which power is distributed within Christian groups. Churches have a high ecclesiology, reflected in vertical top-down power structures. In terms of authority they are both hierarchical and bureaucratic. Denominations tend to have more horizontal power structures, reflecting their associational nature and a more relativized approach to authority. Sects tend to rely more on authority deriving from 'charismatic' leadership, where there is a strong emotional or affective commitment to leaders and, usually, a high degree of normative consensus which can be rigidly enforced. Bureaucracy tends to be weak and these groups are often fairly fissile.

While these typologies are useful in identifying and abstracting broad patterns of power, in practice, matters can be far less straightforward. Within the context of the United Kingdom, it is increasingly the case that most churches now operate in a practical sense as denominations and there is little other than ecclesiology to distinguish the two. Both churches and denominations increasingly tolerate diverse groupings within their boundaries while ecumenism and parachurch initiatives such as Alpha have done much to collapse previous distinctions between different groupings. Furthermore, the emergence of independent Christian fellowships as a significant strand of congregational life also needs to be considered, as they now constitute 14 per cent of all congregations (Hunt, 2003, p. 78). While it is clear that these groupings conform to some of the sociological characteristics of sects, it is also increasingly apparent that many of these 'independent' congregations have formal or informal connections with other like-minded fellowships and even informal links at the congregational level with mainline denominations. Indeed, in those cases where formal links are in place, we might view some 'new church' groupings as proto-denominations (Walker, 1985).

Clearly, sociological models of this type have their limitations, both because they are essentially abstractions and because they need to be constantly revised in the light of social and cultural change among the churches. However, for the researcher they can constitute a useful tool for initially orientating themselves towards the rather more complex nature of power within the congregational context.

Mapping Power in the Local Church

Mapping patterns of power within the local congregation is rarely straightforward. Formal organizational characteristics constitute one factor, but as with any organization there are also many human elements to be taken into account. These include such variables as: the social dynamics of relationships; the presence of informal modes of organization; and a raft of sociological factors relating to class, gender, age, ethnicity and ideology. Moreover, the subjective meanings applied by members of the congregation to these variables need to be considered and the sociologist should also be sensitive to the unequal nature and distribution of power. With this in mind, and in the light of Sylvie Collins' observations relating to the demographic imbalance between customarily male leadership and predominately female laity (Section 3.3 Sociology Strand), considerations of gender should be thoroughly explored (Aune, 2004). Furthermore, any consideration of the nature of power in the local church is deficient if it does not take into account external as well as internal factors, particularly where congregations are seeking to engage with or recruit from their surrounding social environment. In this sense power is best envisaged as resembling a double helix – encompassing populations outside and inside the congregation. However, for the purposes of analytical clarity, I propose to deal with internal and external factors separately, although the researcher on the ground will find that matters are invariably never as clear-cut as this.

The internal dynamics of power

In terms of the internal dynamics of power, the obvious place to start is with formal 'leadership'. Styles of leadership can range from the authoritarian to the egalitarian and patterns of leadership can vary from the collegiate to the single authority figure. In practice, the distribution of power in most congregations tends to fall somewhere in between these polarities. While the presence of a paid religious professional automatically implies some sense of hierarchy and, by extension, of the ordering of powers, invariably clergy are also supported in the exercise of power by various internal lay bodies. Examples would include: Parochial Church Councils, elders and the various sub-groups concerned with organizational and administrative activities relating to the life of the local church. All these groups represent in some sense a formal distribution of powers within the congregation although how this works in practice can vary widely.

For example, Parochial Church Councils often do little more than 'rubber-stamp' policy decisions predetermined by the clergy (Davies, Watkins et al., 1991; Chambers, 2004). However, this is not always the case. The potential researcher should be sensitive to the fact that lay participation in the organizational life of the congregation is invariably the province of the most active members, some of whom may have their own policy agendas, particularly where the distribution of internal resources are concerned (Jenkins, 1999). Moreover, with very few exceptions, clergy career patterns invariably entail movement between congregations and the presence of any one individual is essentially temporary. Conversely, active lay members are often able to accumulate power to themselves over many years and can represent a formidable force for a new minister. Power can become embedded in various individuals and groups and clergy must negotiate their way through this distribution of powers, not least because they are often dependent on the goodwill of active members for the smooth running of the affairs of the congregation.

In mapping patterns of power, careful attention should be paid to these sub-groups, their status, relations with other groups and the ways in which they operate and co-operate together to influence the life of the congregation. Sociologically, it is these internal networks of social relations and the customary distribution of power as much as theological dispositions that go to make up the identity of a congregation. Where this identity is threatened in some way, and this can often be the case when a new minister arrives on the scene, tensions can sometimes arise between these active members and clergy. This can result in the minister attempting to stamp his or her authority on the congregation. However, authoritarian styles of leadership are rarely successful for very long and can often point the researcher to severe underlying problems within a congregation. Moreover, there are many potential ways in which congregations can resist the perceived abuse of authority. These range from active members withdrawing their goodwill, strategies of resistance through inertia, to in the final instance, members voting with their feet (Chambers, 2004).

Not all power struggles are between clergy and laity. Both Clark (1970; 1971) and Jenkins (1999) describe the ways in which middle-class 'incomers' to traditional congregations sought to challenge customary models of power and the resulting polarization of groups within the congregation. Pagden (1968) suggests that, where this is also accompanied by rapid congregational growth, schism and the emergence of a separate congregation based on one of the competing sub-groups is also likely to occur when the congregation reaches a figure of 240 persons. While this figure might appear arbitrary, more recent research suggests that this figure is remarkably accurate and church leaderships are well aware of the leadership difficulties inherent in promoting social cohesion in large congregations and the potentially problematic nature of powerful sub-groups for internal cohesion (Chambers, 1997; 2004).

In the case of Free Churches, matters are further complicated for religious professionals by the particular models of congregational polity that they have to operate within. Where there is a diaconate (or some similar body) in place this can operate as an alternative power-base to the paid ministerial function. In principle, deacons should be elected by the congregation on an annual basis, although in practice deacons often serve for many years, accumulating considerable power in the process. Diaconates control material resources including finances, and in principle, all deacons have an equal measure of power to the paid minister. In terms of policy matters and the internal administration of the church, the minister can advise a course of action but this is then subject to a free vote by deacons, who are the formal representatives of the congregation. Here authority and power are technically administered through a collegiate and egalitarian system although in practice matters are again not so clear-cut. An authoritarian leadership style can subvert this model with the deacons adopting an acquiescent role and a culture of ministerial dependency emerging where power is concentrated in the one person. This is more likely to be the case where there is regular turnover of deacons. However, where deacons have accumulated power over the long-term, they can present something of a problem to their minister in terms of organized resistance to change. Inevitably, this can result in much politicking and in these situations ministerial authority can end up largely confined to the sphere of spiritual and pastoral matters.

In very rare cases, power can be exercised in terms of authoritarian patterns of social control that might be deemed to border on the 'abusive' (Chambers, 1997). Reports of abuses of this type tend to emphasize a congregational culture where there is a strong commitment on the part of leadership to enforcing a rigid lifestyle, the promotion of a culture of deference and submission to authority, and symbolic boundaries that delimit relations with 'outsiders'. Congregations of this type are invariably sectarian in nature, strongly patriarchal and often confrontational in terms of their relations with other congregations (Wright, 1997). However, in terms of power relationships, the researcher should be sensitive to the fact that congregations of this type are often 'self-policing' in terms of the monitoring of commitment. This is, in the main, a process of voluntary mutual reinforcement by members, rather than involuntary or unthinking submission to authority.

The external dynamics of power

Congregations do not exist in a social or cultural vacuum. In terms of power they face a number of challenges relating to the decline of churchgoing and the parallel loss of social significance of churches at the local level. In terms of mission, the churches no longer have the power to influence local morals and manners in ways that they used to and it is an exceptional congregation that has not experienced some difficulties in the recruitment and retention of members. Theologically, mission might be defined in the rather narrow terms of proselytization or in somewhat broader terms of establishing of closer relations with those individuals or families that lie within the immediate social orbit of the congregation. Sociologically, we might subsume both of these issues in terms of the impact that congregations do, or do not, make on their local community or catchment population. Key sociological factors here are the presence or absence of social networks linking congregations to these populations and the related nature of the social boundaries that characterise congregations and which delimit relations with the surrounding population.

Social networks constitute the basic building blocks for all social life and constitute the starting-point for any sociological analysis of power (Hirst, 2003). Clearly, if a congregation lacks access to the type of networks that might establish meaningful linkages with a surrounding population, then the task of mission becomes extremely difficult to get off the ground. These linkages might be forged through formal initiatives such as evangelistic projects or through the provision of community facilities, but they are more likely to be found within the mundane nets of local social relations constituted through family, friends and neighbours. Where the latter are strong, congregations tend to retain a sense of connection with their surrounding population and vice versa. Even where personal relationships are less localized and more geographically dispersed, the network principle is not necessarily negated and, as Collins notes (Section 3.3 Sociology Strand), loose associations can still build social capital. Indeed, for some congregations, particularly larger independent post-denominational churches that draw from wide geographical areas, this can be translated into successful mission outcomes (Chambers, 2004).

However, the researcher also needs to situate these patterns of social interaction within the internal context of the congregation. Key concepts here are symbolic boundaries and human and material resources. The stronger a sense of congregational identity the more likely it is to inhibit relations with those outside the congregation through the creation of symbolic boundaries that in turn delimit relations with the external environment. In some cases these boundaries can be theological in provenance (Dowie, 1997), or they may merely represent the concrete expression of a strong sense of social or cultural solidarity (Chambers, 2004). In both cases the outcomes are likely to be similar. Other key variables include levels of human and social capital, material resources (finances, buildings, etc.) and levels of competition between local churches. Where congregations are declining in numbers and the membership is ageing, it is likely that this will be accompanied by a sense of powerlessness in terms of engaging with and influencing surrounding populations. In most cases, existing (and these are usually diminishing) resources are likely to be perceived as under strain and remaining social capital tends to be orientated towards the internal needs of the congregation. In subjective terms, congregations that perceive themselves as relatively powerless inevitably respond to this by looking inwards and this inward-looking orientation invariably results in the strengthening of symbolic boundaries and the weakening of relations with the surrounding population (Chambers, 2004).

Congregations are also operating within a religious 'marketplace' and in localities where there is an overprovision of places of worship and congregational numbers are accordingly low, perceptions of decline can set in that reinforce this sense of powerlessness and lead to inertia (Gill, 2003). Conversely, where there is both an underprovision of places of worship and a deficit of social capital among the surrounding population, these conditions create potential opportunities for those congregations willing and able to engage in mission (Gill, 1994). Clearly, local conditions can both objectively impact upon congregations and affect their internal self-understandings, and any exploration of patterns of power within congregations must take account of both the internal and external dynamics of power. Moreover, it should be recognized that notwithstanding their specifically religious setting these dynamics of power always conform to the more generalized sociological principles with which we began this discussion. In this sense, power is, in the final instance, best viewed through the lens of social relations and the ways in which these relations shape patterns of power within congregations.

Practical Ways of Studying this Aspect of Local Churches

Researching congregational power relations is never straightforward. As the researcher immerses herself in the life of the congregation any initial impressions of the distribution of power invariably need to be modified in the light of fresh information. Unpacking those social relations along with which power is distributed takes time, requires sensitivity and is best accomplished through a mix of formal interviews, informal conversations and participant observation. Careful mapping of the formal and informal sites of power and the identification of in-groups and out-groups is a crucial element in this process. A diagrammatic model may be useful in this respect although this will invariably have to be modified in the light of further data. This model needs to be wideranging in scope, taking in those who occupy low level positions as well as the obvious candidates. It is always good practice to talk to older members in order to gain a longitudinal understanding of relations within the congregation and to identify key past events that might inform present understandings.

Power relations are also inherently unequal and are often the site of tensions. Therefore, the researcher also needs to pay constant attention to ethical issues relating to confidentiality and the protection of the anonymity of sources. In the same manner, the researcher must constantly strive to maintain a critical distance in his relations with members of the congregation. In my own experience, where researching power is concerned, it is all too easy to get sucked into disputes or to find yourself overidentifying with some groups within the congregation. As Guest notes (Section 3.2, Sociology Strand), it is important to strike a workable balance between a critical distance and that empathetic understanding necessary for an in-depth understanding of a congregation. This is best achieved by establishing some time-distance between fieldwork and writing up.

Case study

This case study concerns a mainstream Baptist church where the question of the exercise of power and its effects was a crucial factor in the progressive decline of this congregation (Chambers, 2004). Over the years this church had undergone a process of internal secularization where organized 'social' activities enjoyed a high profile in the life of the congregation. Power had become concentrated in the hands of a clique of long-serving deacons and they jealously guarded the privileges of the various internal 'clubs' while promoting an insular approach to relations with the surrounding community. These deacons were also officers of these clubs, successfully protecting their group interests through their control of the management of buildings and allocation of resources with the tacit support of long-term members.

A young minister had been recently appointed and he saw his immediate task as the spiritual revitalization of the congregation in order to equip them for mission. He was supported in this vision by a small minority group of more recent arrivals who were likewise dissatisfied with the spiritual health of the congregation and its insularity and who coalesced around the weekly Bible study group.

While long-serving deacons and older members were aware of many problems relating to the future direction of the church, notably declining numbers and finances, they chose to use their embedded power to resist any changes that might upset the status quo and threaten their group activities. Consequently, the minister found his power to initiate change severely curtailed, not only because of the intransigence of some deacons but also because his power-base lay within the most marginalized section of the congregation. Relatively powerless and unable to initiate meaningful change, this section of the congregation supported by the minister effectively became a 'church within a church'. The congregation continues to decline.

Further reading

Chambers, Paul (2004) *Religion, Secularization and Social Change in Wales: Congregational Studies in a Post-Christian Society*, Cardiff: University of Wales Press.

    Contains three case studies (Anglican, Baptist and Independent Evangelical) that examine all the facets of power that the researcher is likely to find within congregations.

Davies, Elwyn and A. D. Rees (eds) (1960) *Welsh Rural Communities*, Cardiff: University of Wales Press.

    Exemplifies the type of 'community studies' approach that seeks to integrate a discussion of religion within the context of the wider local community. Strong on social networks, status hierarchies and embedded power.

Davies, D., C. Watkins, M. Winter, et al. (1991) *Church and Religion in Rural England*, Edinburgh: T and T Clark.

    A useful empirical study that is particularly good on clergy–laity and church–community relations and which also covers subjects such as worship and organization.

Dowie, Alan (1997) 'Resistance to Change in a Scottish Christian Congregation', in *The Scottish Journal of Religious Studies*, 18/2, pp. 147–62.

    This study focuses on the dynamics of power within a Scottish congregation by examining such sociological variables as tradition, authority, status hierarchies and symbolic boundaries.

Hunt, S., M. Hamilton and T. Walter (eds.) (1997) *Charismatic Christianity: Sociological Perspectives*, Basingstoke: Macmillan.

    Includes two case studies of neo-Pentecostal churches and other material relating to the impact of the charismatic movement within a broad spectrum of congregational and institutional contexts.

3.4 Organizational Studies Strand – Power

Margaret Harris

Introduction: Power and Authority

Following the classical sociologist Max Weber, power within organizations can be seen as *the ability to enforce your own wishes; to get somebody to do something that you want them to do*. There is no necessary connotation here, as there is in some everyday speech, of power involving physical violence, bullying or, indeed, any other kind of 'unpleasantness'.

For those studying local churches, this organizational concept of power opens up two helpful insights.

First, 'power' can be contrasted with *authority* which (again following Max Weber) can be understood as *legitimate power*; an ability to enforce your own wishes which is sanctioned by prevailing rules, laws or customs. Churches are organizations with a rich array of such rules, laws and customs. So anybody studying local churches needs to be aware of which groups and individuals have been given organizational authority. By becoming part of a local church, people are implicitly agreeing to conform to its norms about authority.

Second, those seeking to understand what is going on in a local church, as in any other kind of organization, need to look out for manifestations of power in its daily activities and its decision-making processes. In all organizations there are people and groups who have the ability to enforce their own wishes – irrespective of whether they have the authority to do so. This is not necessarily a bad thing. Indeed many organizations only stay on the road because people with initiative and commitment get things done, even though they do not actually have the authority to do so. Such people may be seen as 'busybodies' or, equally likely, as 'the backbone of the community'.

The key point for students of the local church is to be alert to manifestations of power and not to make the mistake of assuming that *what is officially the case* according to the rules and laws, is *in practice the case*. In fact, the need to distinguish between official statements and what is happening in practice is fundamental to any kind of organizational analysis. Often people repeat official statements (laws, regulations, denominational requirements, policy aspirations) when they are asked to describe what is happening within their organizations. In local churches, particularly, people may feel ashamed or guilty when practice differs from 'theory' and they can be reluctant to admit to the discrepancy. In fact, it is an organizational truism that practice differs from official statements. Finding out who has power within a local church requires moving beyond the official statements.

Many of the problems and difficulties which arise in organizations cannot be understood fully without taking power into account. In fact, some organizational theorists have gone so far as to see power as the key explanatory factor. So when you are studying local churches you need to be 'power conscious'. That is, you need to be aware of the concept of organizational power. And you need to be alert to the possibility of power manifestations and conflicts because they are rarely overt and obvious. Indeed, in local churches there can be norms about politeness and respect which mask 'power play'.

Having looked briefly at the key organizational concepts of 'power', 'authority' and 'legitimate power', we turn in the remainder of this contribution to look at three areas of activity in local churches which can be seen, from an organizational point of view, as arenas in which power and authority are exercised.

- Governance
- Decision-making
- Conflict

Governance

The term 'governance' is used these days in voluntary sector and public policy writings to refer to two different, but related, concepts. Both have relevance to studying the local church.

A point of decision and accountability

One use of the term 'governance' is to refer to the official decision-making structures and mechanisms of the organization. In a company this would be the board and related senior management groupings. In a local authority it would be the elected council plus other groupings of senior councillors and paid staff. Voluntary organizations have a variety of structures and a variety of terms by which they refer to their governance structures, e.g. council, trustees, management committee, board. The governance structure of a local church is the *point of final accountability* for whatever happens within it.

In some local churches, clergy are the official final point of decision-making; and they have to 'carry the can' if things go wrong. In such churches there may be an array of committees and even some kind of elected board, but they are in effect support groups for the clergy. Using the terms mentioned above, committees in such churches do not have any authority although they may in practice enjoy a great deal of power. However, if something goes wrong, it will be the clergy who are called to account by the denomination and other internal and external 'stakeholders'. Clergy who are aware of being the official final point of accountability are often, understandably, reluctant to cede much decision-making to lay groupings within the church.

At the other end of the governance spectrum are local churches with a 'congregational' structure in which the official final decision-making body and point of accountability is a board (elected or appointed) of lay people. In such churches, clergy are, in effect, employees of the lay board – although they may not be treated as such on a day-to-day basis. Towards the centre of the governance spectrum are churches with an array of decision-making structures combining lay and clergy authority in some way. These are the churches which have most potential for conflict between lay people and clergy over who has the authority to issue instructions to whom.

A key factor in determining the official governance structure of a local church is the authority and decision-making structures of the denomination to which it is affiliated (this is sometimes referred to as the church's 'polity'). In this respect local churches are different from other kinds of voluntary associations in that they generally have very little choice about what kind of governance structure they adopt to run their affairs. Totally independent churches, of course, do have a choice but all those who wish to be a part of any kind of denominational or broader structure will find their choices more circumscribed.

We should emphasize here that this section has referred to *official* governance structures. The way a local church works on a day-to-day basis will not necessarily reflect the official authority statements about governance. However, should anything go seriously wrong in a local church, or should there be a major internal dispute, it will be important to turn to the final point of accountability and decision-making.

Networks and partnerships

A second use of the term 'governance' is related to the first and is also relevant to understanding the challenges faced by local churches.

Over the last 20 years, political scientists have struggled to make sense of the changing way in which the UK is governed. We have seen a proliferation of 'non-departmental public bodies' and 'quangos'; public services like the railways dependent on private finance; appointed 'trusts' which run the National Health Service; and non-profit bodies providing welfare to citizens. Devolution of powers to Scotland and Wales, the rise of administrative structures for English Regions and the impact of the EU complicate the picture further. Not only do we have a plethora of new kinds of organizations whose authority challenges our old simplistic ideas about 'representative government', but there is also a wide and growing range of systems and structures intended to draw these many bodies together so that policies and services are 'joined up'. 'Local Strategic Partnerships' and 'Inter Faith Forums' are two current examples of such attempts to establish co-ordinating 'networks' and 'partnerships' at the local level.

Analysis of the changing way in which we are running the country has led political scientists to suggest we are living now in an era of 'governance' rather than 'government' (Rhodes, 1997). In other words, they are using the term 'governance' to refer to the interlocking networks of organizations which exist at local, regional and national levels of the country and which constitute increasingly the means through which public policy is implemented and public services are delivered. The relevance of this for local churches is twofold. First, it alerts us to a new way of understanding the civic environment of the local church. Second, it offers a new way of thinking about how things are run in churches, in other organizations and in our country as a whole. We become aware that authority relationships are not necessarily best understood as linear or hierarchical. Often authority is exercised through networks of systems and forums. In the case of local churches, their governance may occur in practice through a web of church-based and non-church-based organizations meeting together or collaborating in a variety of different ways.

Decision-Making

Decision-making structures

Like other kinds of voluntary organization, local churches use a variety of terms to refer to their key decision-making bodies. And the terms used do not necessarily tell you much about the authority and work of the bodies concerned. 'Councils' may have final authority or they may be little more than consultation forums for clergy. 'Management Committees' may or may not actually 'manage' work activities; they may just make broader policy decisions or suggest broad guidelines. The term 'trustees' can be particularly confusing. In some churches it refers to a group which manages a separate charity which to some extent is funding church activities. On the other hand, the 'trustees' may be in effect the church's local governing body. And then there are the 'committees', some of which may be sub-committees of a church governing body; some may have delegated powers from the governing body and/or clergy; and some of them may, in practice and theory, be little more than consultation forums or working groups with no authority or even power.

There are important implications for those studying local churches. Since the terms used to refer to internal groupings do not necessarily tell you much about their authority or power, we need to look beyond the terms and tease out:

- which are the key groupings which have authority to make decisions;
- whether there are any other groupings which seem to have the power to make decisions;
- what kinds of decisions groupings can make;
- what are the respective roles of clergy and lay people in each of the groupings;
- whether there is any difference between the official structures and those used in practice to make decisions.

One way to do this 'teasing out' is to ask 'what would happen if' questions which relate to extreme, although not impossible, situations. For example, in respect of any particular local church we might ask:

1   Who would talk to the mass media and police on behalf of the church if there were a serious accident or incident on church premises?

2 If the church were in danger of becoming unviable financially or in terms of membership numbers, where would be the internal forum(s) for discussing the problems? Who could and who would make a final decision about closing down or merger?

Stakeholders

The concept of 'stakeholding' – although somewhat overused in business talk – is useful for analysing decision-making within the local church. *Stakeholders* are those who have some kind of interest in an organization or in the outcome of a particular decision. In the business world that 'interest' will often be financial and relatively simple to identify and quantify. In local churches few, if any, of the stakeholders have a financial interest. Yet the consequences of not including a key stakeholder in a decision within a local church can be extremely serious.

We have discussed earlier in this contribution, the importance of identifying those individuals and groups who hold power, those who hold authority, and those who are part of the official governance structure. Few of these individuals and groups will need to be involved in every decision in the local church, or will want to be. At the same time, it can be important not to exclude people who see themselves as stakeholders. So identifying stakeholders for a particular decision is something which requires specific attention. For example, when decisions are to be made about designing the church kitchen, or the layout of chairs for worship services, or making changes to the liturgy, congregants who are not normally part of the 'inner core' or even particularly keen to express views, may suddenly evince a desire to be intimately involved in the decision-making and/or may argue that they have relevant specialist expertise to offer. Ignoring such stakeholders can lead to conflict, disaffection and even to people leaving the church altogether. In one congregation I studied, the organist (a category of volunteer that is hard to replace) left the congregation because he was not consulted about a decision to embark on a church building project. The decision to build meant that the church would not be able to afford a new organ for many years and nobody had thought to consult him about this.

Thus, for any particular decision, the relevant stakeholders need to be identified and ways found of consulting them and taking into account their perspectives. Conversely, when tracing back the reasons for a particular decision, no assumptions can be made about the myriad of pressures and influences which informed the final decision.

Conceptualizing decision-making

Research studies conducted in the past give a number of insights into the processes used in practice for making decisions in organizations. The different patterns of decision-making identified by researchers provide us with a useful toolkit for:

- analysing how a decision was made;
- planning how a decision will be made;
- enabling us to distinguish between the official decision-making processes and what happens in practice.

One distinction identified by researchers is between 'top-down' and 'bottom-up' decision-making; between decisions made at the apex of a hierarchy and 'trickled down' through that hierarchy for implementation, and decisions made at the 'coal-face' or 'grassroots' of an organization (Sabatier, 1986). The latter type of decision may take a while to become embedded into the higher echelons of an organization, even well after it is being implemented in practice. For example, in an Anglican church I studied, a group of congregants had taken the initiative in organizing 'healing services'. These services were held against the wishes of the priest who was opposed to them on theological grounds, but they continued and attracted increasing numbers of attenders, including some of the respected elders of the congregation. The priest eventually decided to 'turn a blind eye' and the services became, in effect, part of the congregation's portfolio of services.

Another useful distinction when analysing decision-making is between rationalism (or 'macro-rationalism') and incrementalism (or 'disjointed incrementalism'). This distinction derives from major studies by organizational and political researchers in the 1960s and 1970s (Braybrooke and Lindblom, 1963) which aimed to uncover both what people regard as a desirable way of reaching decisions and also what happens in practice in organizations.

We tend to assume that difficult or complex decisions are best made by taking a broad strategic approach; starting with the big picture and working inwards taking into account relevant variables (Kearns and Scarpino, 1996). This is the 'macro-rational' approach. But research found that in practice most decisions by individuals and groups are not taken like that at all. They are taken as small-step changes building on, or moving away from, previous decisions or states. 'Disjointed incrementalism' is a better description of what happens in practice. Further, researchers found that decisions made incrementally were generally just as organizationally effective as decisions taken any other way.

Conflict

Sources of conflict

One commonly offered explanation for conflict in any organization, including local churches, is 'personality differences'. Each of us has his or her own preferences for ways of doing things and when faced with pressures or situations which challenge our preferences, some of us get impatient or angry. This can play out in interpersonal battles which manifest themselves in ways ranging from private rows and vendettas through to internal organizational schisms. Individuals, and even whole groupings, can leave a local church as an end product of such 'personality differences'.

There can be similarly serious consequences of 'communication problems' – another common explanation for conflict. And here again, it is true that there can be major organizational implications accruing from a clergy person or lay leader failing to identify key stakeholders and failing to involve them in relevant decisions – or at least keep them informed.

Without wishing to downplay the importance of interpersonal difficulties and communication failures as explanations for conflict, those who study local churches should be aware that research has also shown that conflicts often find their deep roots in organizational structures, systems and cultures. They may manifest themselves as personality differences or 'lack of communication', but often there are elements in the organization itself which are fostering such manifestations of conflict.

It is true that working without conflict with other human beings requires a high degree of personal skill in such areas as self-discipline, listening, reading body language, anticipating problems. But it is also the case that the way in which organizations are structured and run can make the job of 'keeping the peace' more or less difficult.

Avoiding and resolving conflict

Some of the means for avoiding conflict in organizations have been mentioned in earlier sections of this contribution but bear re-examination under the current heading.

We drew attention earlier to the need to draw a distinction, when analysing organizations, between official statements (aspirations about what should be the case) and what is happening in practice. Yet this fundamental distinction is not widely understood and, indeed, can be found at the root of a number of conflicts which occur in voluntary organizations and churches. Congregants may be angered when they discover discrepancies and their attempt to get the church or other congregants 'back on track' and adhering to the official statements may sow seeds of conflict.

Even more difficult, congregants may have different understandings of the official statements and arguments can spring up over the 'correct' interpretation of them. For example, some congregants understand their local church to be primarily a place for community involvement whereas others see worship as the prime function and others still may be 'mission' churches focused on theological statements such as 'building God's kingdom' (Becker, 1999). The differing understandings remain implicit until such time as an individual or group is affronted by what they perceive as a discrepancy between their own understandings and those of others in the church.

Conflict might be avoided, or at least congregants might be reconciled, if forums can be provided in which these differences in perception can be teased out and debated. But providing such forums in congregations can itself be difficult. There is an element within Christianity which induces guilt feelings about expressing dissent from official statements, especially in public or in the presence of clergy. Moreover, by their very nature, local churches have what I have termed 'low goal ceilings' (Harris, 1998) – points beyond which debate is theologically unacceptable. To varying degrees, local churches can allow free debate on lower-level means and ends but, in comparison with secular voluntary associations, they have a low 'goal' ceiling; above that ceiling, organizational goals move up to a level at which they cannot be challenged, because to do so would call into question the fundamental premises and assumptions on which the local church has been established.

In spite of these very real barriers to open debate, there are likely to be benefits in terms of reducing conflict, for those local churches that do decide to provide opportunities for different expectations to be articulated and discussed in a safe environment. Studying as a group one of the research studies that have drawn attention to the different models and organizational images of local churches might be a route into such a debate, and might serve to 'give permission' for congregants to accept the legitimacy of varying expectations within the one church; expectations on which mutual toleration can be accepted rather than a necessary consensus (see for example, Becker, 1999; Dulles, 1978; Harris, 2001).

The need to think about ways in which varying models and expectations can be articulated – albeit within a safe environment in which neither guilt nor blame are attributed – applies equally to disputes between clergy and lay people. These can quickly develop into debates about who has the 'right' (or authority) to control whom.

In my own work on congregations, I developed a conceptual tool for understanding why disputes between clergy and lay people can often prove so intractable. I offer it here as a way of reassuring all parties that it is indeed exceptionally difficult for individual local churches to work out 'ways of operating' in this area; and as a way of showing how some mutual understanding between clergy and lay people can nevertheless be achieved within local churches.

Problems in the clergy–lay relationship in local churches are not necessarily just about personality differences or communication problems. Nor are they 'just' about differences in expectations as mentioned earlier in this section. Often they have deeper roots in the differing authority structures within which lay people and clergy are embedded by training and socialization.

Here again, it is useful to borrow some key concepts from classical sociologist Max Weber who, as we have seen in other sections of this book, distinguished between three different kinds of authority: 'traditional' (the kind held by monarchs descended from other monarchs); 'charismatic' (the kind held by people thought to have special qualities); and rational-legal (the kind that prevails within modern organizations in which people are appointed for their skills, and in which authority relationships between employees are clearly spelled out).

Using Weber's distinctions, we can say that clergy in local churches are seen by themselves and by lay people as having an authority that is different in quality and derivation from that enjoyed by lay people. Clergy carry 'charismatic' or 'traditional' authority, or some combination of the two; and this gives them, on the face of it, the 'right' to direct and control lay people and to interpret the overall purposes and values of the church. It also makes them feel answerable to higher authority systems beyond the local church. Lay people are not part of the clergy's authority structure. Their involvement in their working lives and their church lives is part of a 'rational-legal' authority structure. Rational-legal authority resides in hierarchies too but not in the same ones as the clergy are part of. So, in local churches, the two authority systems run in parallel with each other and there is no hierarchical apex or 'cross-over point' where disputes can be resolved because clergy and laity are operating in different authority worlds or systems; the traditional or charismatic one and the rational-legal one which is more familiar in secular voluntary organizations. Since the two systems run in parallel, ongoing disputes between clergy and laity about who has authority over whom are organizationally endemic in the local church. The respective parties are left to do the best they can to rub along together by common sense, politeness and, if possible, open debate about the nature of the problem.

What Questions Can Be Asked?

Here are some research questions you could explore using this contribution.

- What do denominational and local written documents say about who (individuals or groups) has the right to make decisions on key issues? You may wish to select just one key issue, e.g. appointment of new clergy; dismissal of clergy; changes to the physical fabric of the church building; budget-setting and monitoring; permission to form new church groups; changes to liturgy.
- Who are the key internal and external stakeholders of the church? Analyse the power they have in relation to one or more areas of the church's work. Try to explain why some stakeholders seem to have more power than others.
- Are there people or groups within this church whose wishes need to be attended to when key decisions are made – even though they do not have any position within the formal decision-making structures? What is the source of their power?
- How is your church linked into a broader church organizational structure? What mechanisms exist to ensure that your church conforms with the rules and wishes of that structure? What are the sanctions to which your church could be subjected if it 'strays'?
- Could your church become independent and locally autonomous?

What would be the advantages and disadvantages of becoming independent?

Case for Discussion

You are the minister of a new and small, but growing, church (Zed Church) which currently rents a village hall for worship and other meetings. The congregation is largely responsible for paying your salary. The congregation has been looking for a building to purchase for more than a year as this has been identified as a requisite for further growth. You have some promises of financial help for a purchase from your denomination and a couple of wealthy friends of the church with philanthropic inclinations.

One evening a member of the congregation phones you to say that he has found out that Saint A's, which has its own building, is merging with Saint B's. He guessed that their church building, which would be ideal for your own congregation, would soon be up for sale. So he had taken the step of making some discrete enquiries. As a consequence of what he had heard about the competition for buying the building, he had immediately put a deposit on the building from his own pocket. He felt that this was the only way to ensure that Zed Church secured this ideal building.

Questions on the Case:

- What does this tell you about power and authority in Zed Church?
- In the light of this experience, what organizational systems and structures would you put in place in Zed Church for the future?

Further reading

Becker, P. E. (1999) *Congregations in Conflict: Cultural Models of Local Religious Life*, Cambridge: Cambridge University Press
The author develops four congregational 'models'; ways of understanding the culture and outlook of local congregations. She uses these models to analyse the issues that faced more than 20 local congregations she studied.

Fried, S. (2002) *The New Rabbi: A Congregation Searches for its Leader*, New York: Bantam.
A fascinating account by a journalist congregant of the process by which a New Jersey synagogue sought and appointed a successor to

its long-serving rabbi. Includes excellent examples of informal and formal decision-making processes; and overt and hidden conflicts.

Harris, M. E. (1998) *Organizing God's Work: Challenges for Churches and Synagogues*, Basingstoke: Macmillan

Based on organizational research into three churches and a synagogue, the author attempts to explain organizational issues including problems surrounding power and authority and the relationship between clergy and laity.

Theological Strand – Power

Frances Ward

Introduction

In this contribution I seek to achieve three objectives. First, by using an extended case study of a research project I carried out in an inner-city congregation, St Barnabas, I show how issues of power can be researched in the local church, using methods from other disciplines. Second, I illustrate how questions of power can be explored from a theological point of view, using the three theological models, *praxis*, *critical correlation* and *corporate theological reflection* outlined in Section 2.2 above, so that a research project brings together creatively the insights of different disciplines with theological reflection. Third, I show how theological reflection can itself empower churches, shifting the focus from the researcher to the congregation as it thinks and reflects upon its ongoing life and practices.

The Research Project

What sparked my interest in studying a local church? I had read somewhere that the congregation could be understood as 'an embodied community that dares to call its body Christ's'. I wanted to explore the ways in which a church understood its corporate identity. As a working hypothesis, I took the notion of 'corporate identity' as what resulted from a complex interplay of 'unity' and 'diversity' in a congregation. And so I approached the *gate keepers* of an inner-city church I knew, called here St Barnabas. With a congregational membership from 11 different countries of origin, I wondered how this church sustained unity as they came together to worship, make decisions and do the other things that churches do.

As I got to know the congregation better what emerged was a dominant Anglo-Saxon culture in which some felt more at home than others. Although they still continued to come (obviously getting *something* out of it), many of the people I interviewed expressed a lack of fulfilment in the worship, or were silenced in decision-making processes, unable to make a full contribution. So my initial question about the nature of 'corporate identity' led me into theological questions of the nature of justice and equality, and to a consideration of the nature of power. I found myself considering the biblical injunction, 'There is no longer Jew or Greek, there is no longer slave or free, there is no longer male and female; for all of you are one in Christ Jesus' (Galatians 3.28). How did Paul address issues of power as he encouraged the nascent churches of his day (which were also very diverse in terms of class, ethnicity and gender) to express their unity in Christ? What does it mean to be an embodied community today that dares to call its body Christ's? Throughout the research project such theological questions were never very far away.

To investigate the corporate identity of a congregation, I used research methods from other disciplines. I spent time at St Barnabas as *participant observer* and used existing social data to set the congregation in its context. I studied *documents* and examined the *statistical* data available. I conducted *semi-structured interviews* with a proportion of the membership, selected carefully in order to capture the diversity present. It soon became clear that not all members had equal power in the ways in which the corporate identity of the congregation was constructed and sustained. The worship and decision-making processes in meetings were two practices in which the white leadership had stronger voices, while others from different ethnic backgrounds were often silent. Power was evidently central to the theological questions of diversity and unity that initiated the research.

The Shape of this Contribution

This contribution will be structured in the following way. There will be a text box which contains a brief description of St Barnabas with some excerpts from transcribed interviews that indicate a range of opinion about the worship and preaching at the church. I then show

how each of the three theological models outlined in Section 2.2 above can shape the theological reflection of the researcher:

- Praxis,
- Critical correlation,
- Corporate theological reflection.

To understand more carefully the power dynamics at the church, I drew upon the thinking of Michel Foucault, a French philosopher who wrote extensively on power. The specific way in which he understood power, as embedded in the relations between dominant and subordinated people within institutions, made his thought particularly relevant. So, below, you will find a box on his ideas about power.

The way in which this congregation struggled with its internal differences can be seen as a microcosm of the global dynamics of a post-colonial world. Many of the members at St Barnabas had come to Britain from former colonies responding to the government's appeal for labour in the 1950s. People also came as refugees and asylum seekers, having experienced some of the social and political upheavals of a globalized economic system. Post-colonial writing explores such changes in today's world. A notion that has emerged in this writing is that of *hybridity*. It is a technical term which will be explained in a box below. It is used in this contribution to suggest ways in which churches might work with issues of power and difference.

The church of St Barnabas

Here are some excerpts from interviews where the focus is upon preaching and the liturgy. In them something of the different perspectives on worship at St Barnabas emerges. The average attendance at the main Sunday morning service over the period of the research was 42, of whom 25 were black and 17 were white. Members of the congregation had been born in Antigua, Barbados, England, Germany, Ghana, Jamaica, Sierra Leone, St Kitts, Tanzania and the USA.

One black member, Raymond, said that the preaching was not what he was used to . . .

I never heard a sermon there yet. No.
Not what I call a sermon.
See. I class a sermon whoever, bishop, whatever preaching.
Quoting passages of the Bible, you know I like to hear. Is it in the Bible?

Next thing: those old folks they like to sing. I don't mean like 'O come all you faithful . . .'
When you go to church you want to hear a sermon. You never get that here.
The point is this. You got to hear a sermon: you got people crying. What I'm getting at.
In Barbados you'd hear the priest praising, and that was good.
You never hear that here.

Elizabeth, like Raymond, had been brought up in Barbados, and she too wanted stronger preaching . . .

What the church needs is hard preaching, hard preaching.
Sometimes people go up here and you can hardly hear what they are saying. Nothing of consequence, nothing to give you that feeling, you know, to hold onto and bring home with you. To say, now that was a good sermon.
Laughing and joking in between, yes, but you want something more forceful. Coming over. You know, put it over. Put it over.

These sentiments differed from those of white members, who did not want the 'strong' preaching desired by Raymond and Elizabeth. Marga-ret's perception was very different from Raymond or Elizabeth . . .

I wouldn't like to see the liturgy changed too much.
I like this style of worship.
The preaching, I always learn something from it, something to think about.
I always enjoy the sermon.
And it's always lively, always lively.

For Doreen, who was white and from the United States, sermons were secondary . . .

I listen to what's going on in the sermon but it's not why I come.
[I come for] the Gloria (a sung canticle in the service). . . . It's absolutely wonderful.

Greg, a white man from Britain, told me that the preaching did not inter-est him, rather . . .

Um, Christianity for me, or rather worship for me has become an icon, it's symbolic.

It represents something – I'm hunting for the expression – it's a bit of God coming to me through the liturgy.

I can't think of any other description than that it's an icon.

Something I can look at and appreciate in detail and so forth, and feed on, in the same way I can look at pictures and I think that sustains me.

Um, I do love worship.

It's a very different sort of feeding, feeding – except you're not just taking the bread and the wine – it's the whole thing.

And what it definitely is not is receiving verbal communication [. . .]

You have the old idea that the Catholic liturgy is for the poor who can't read, who haven't got much understanding, but who have something beautiful to look at – I suppose it's something like that.

I just switch my mind off and, um, allow the spiritual and aesthetic to soak in [. . .]

Theological Method One: Praxis

Using the *praxis* method of doing theology (*experience, exploration, reflection, new experience*), we can locate these excerpts within the *experience* stage with their focus on the real-life situation in the congregation. There is a real difference here between what satisfied, or didn't, the cultural expectations of members. Because this congregation was set within a denomination with a particular dominant Anglo-Saxon liturgical ethos, it might be expected that the desires of some would be subordinated to others. But need that necessarily be the case? To move into the next stage of *exploration*, to analyse further the relations of power, of dominance and subordination, I turned to the thinking of Michel Foucault.

Michel Foucault (1926–84) continues to be a highly significant thinker in a wide range of disciplines. He was influenced principally by Marx, Hegel and Nietzsche. He argued that power is not to be seen as a possession but rather permeates institutional life in complex and subtle ways. Instead of it being something you or I 'have', power more usefully describes the relationships of dominance and subordination within the different roles and functions that are exercised within organizations.

In his essay 'Pastoral Power and Political Reason' he wrote:

Power must be analysed as something which circulates, or rather as something which only functions in the form of a chain. It is never local-ised here or there, never in anybody's hands, never appropriated as a commodity or piece of wealth. Power is employed and exercised through a net-like organisation. And not only do individuals circulate between its threads; they are always in the position of simultaneously undergoing and exercising this power. They are not only its inert or consenting target; they are always also the element of its articulation. In other words, individuals are the vehicles of power, not its points of application. (Foucault, 1976/1980, p. 98)

Foucault studied how institutions used power to shape the lives of individuals. He examined the history of the hospital clinic (Foucault, 1963/1991) within western society, showing how it exercised institutional means to manage mad people. His book *Discipline and Punish* traced the development of the penal system and the ways in which prisoners were regulated into conformity by systems and routines. Foucault talked of 'docile bodies', bodies that become moulded by institutional power into 'normality'. People come to accept that things are the way they are, and so the status quo is established and sustained. Wherever institu-tional life is established – on a hospital ward, or in a voluntary organiza-tion, or in a congregation – particular discourses, or ways of thinking, doing and being, develop which strengthen and continue the status quo. Both those who are dominant and those who are subordinate are conditioned by the discourses of the institutions to which they belong.

For example, imagine you are in a hospital bed and the medical team are discussing your body and what is wrong with it in ways you don't understand. You feel very uncomfortable and out of place. However as you stay longer, you start to acclimatize to the routines, pick up the jar-gon. You find yourself feeling more and more at home. Your 'patient' role in that hospital starts to feel normal; you become defined by the labels that are used of you. Sometimes to such an extent that you do not want to leave. You become 'institutionalized'. It was these processes of insti-tutionalization that Foucault analysed with far-reaching influence.

Foucault argued, though, that these processes of normalization were not written in stone. He analysed the power of resistance and transgression: how the status quo could be challenged and its limits transgressed. He pointed out, too, that power has its compensations and pleasures – that for both the dominant and the subordinate their experience will not be perceived as malign, but often it has sufficient compensation to be worth becoming a docile body.

At St Barnabas, Foucault's theory of power gave me the means to analyse how dominant discourses, like the liturgical practices, were established within the congregation, and how they powerfully regulated members into a sense of corporate identity. Although some members expressed a lack of fulfilment in worship, and others found it difficult to engage in the dominant discourses of discussion and debate, nevertheless they stayed, illustrating Foucault's insight that there were compensations for docility.

Praxis: reflection

Having started with the *experience* of difference between congregational members, and *explored*, using Foucault, how different relations of power could be understood, I turned to Paul's first letter to the Corinthians to deepen my *reflection* on the question: If this local congregation is the 'body of Christ', what sort of body is it? What sort of body could it be? What parallels, if any, were there between the dynamics of power at St Barnabas and the struggles that emerge in Paul's writings?

Biblical scholars have argued that at Corinth the rich people offered meeting places for the Christians in their homes (see 1 Corinthians 16.15, 19). At 1 Corinthians 1.28 and 11.22 there are hints that there were poor and relatively rich people among the converts, so Paul was faced with the task of addressing the socially advantaged, and reminding them of their corporate unity with the poorer people. And it is probably the case that Paul himself, with his own relative lack of status, would have disturbed the existing power relations. His artisan status might well have been unacceptable to the wealthy social climbers at Corinth.

His strategy with the wealthy members of the Corinthian congregation was to use a fable by the Stoic Menenius Agrippa about the social body, which would have been familiar to his audience (Dunn, 1998, pp. 550–1). The fable was written to persuade those of lower economic status to submit to the authority of the more wealthy members for the sake of the whole body. Paul challenged the dominant at Corinth by a radical rereading of the original story. Reshaping Agrippa's original 'body', Paul now called it 'the body of Christ', and argued that each part of the body was equally important to the whole. In doing so, he challenged the powerful at Corinth, and also made the point that belonging to the 'body of Christ' was significantly different from other, former ways of living together corporately.

Using biblical material in this way helped me to reflect on how dominant categories of people (at Corinth, the rich; at St Barnabas, the white Anglo-Saxon ethos) were challenged by Paul to empty themselves of their power for the sake of the whole body. Paul held out to Corinth a different way to construct corporate identity. Perhaps different ways of living with diversity at St Barnabas could also show new ways of being the body of Christ in post-colonial times.

Praxis: *new experience*

At St Barnabas the opportunity to complete the *praxis* cycle by seeing how the ideas could lead to *new experience* was curtailed. A new minister came and the project had to come to an end. With hindsight, had I engaged with the congregation from the beginning using *action research*, the way my research was developing would have been shared with the members and they would have become active participants, influencing the directions of the project, and owning it in a way that would have been difficult to stop. But hindsight is easy! You'll see in the *corporate theological reflection* section below some ways in which the research could have been shared within the congregation.

Theological Method Two: Critical Correlation

The way in which I drew on Paul's writing to the Corinthians is an example of *critical correlation,* used here as an element in the *praxis* cycle. As a method it can stand on its own. *Critical correlation* brings together theology with insights from other disciplines – from contemporary cultural analysis, or literature and poetry, or, as here, from other sub-disciplines within theology – into a dialogue.

As I continued to reflect upon the diversity at St Barnabas, the ways in which post-colonial writers have thought about hybridity shaped my theological thinking.

Hybridity

Post-colonial literature has grown in the wake, primarily, of the work of Edward Said whose book *Culture and Imperialism* (1993/1994) is a good introduction to the field.

Homi Bhabha first used the term 'hybridity' to describe the ways in which different cultures come together, mix and create new identities. A hybrid identity is one which avoids the polarization between dominant and subordinated and is able to live creatively with differences of culture. Different power relations can also be recognized and negotiated in what he called the Third Space (Bhabha, 1995).

In literature, Salman Rushdie has explored hybridity. In writing about *The Satanic Verses*, he comments:

> Standing at the centre of the novel is a group of characters, most of whom are British Muslims . . . struggling with just the sort of great problems that have arisen to surround the book, problems of hybridization and ghettoization, of reconciling the old and the new. Those who oppose the novel most vociferously today are of the opinion that intermingling with a different culture will inevitably weaken and ruin their own. I am of the opposite opinion. *The Satanic Verses* celebrates hybridity, impurity, intermingling, the transformation that comes of new and unexpected combinations of human beings, cultures, ideas, politics, movies, songs. It rejoices in mongrelization and fears the absolutism of the Pure. Melange, hotchpotch, a bit of this and a bit of that is how newness enters the world. (Sandercock, 2004, p. 1)

Hybridity is a metaphor for new possibilities. The Third Space is a place of fluidity, where former fixities and unities are dissolved and reformed, so that new negotiations of power can occur between people of difference.

If the congregation is an embodied community that dares to call its body Christ's, I found myself asking: Could the notion of a *hybrid* body of Christ take us further? I considered two alternatives: Either the congregation could constitute a site where conflicts and struggles which are colonial in origin can continue to be played out in neo-colonial ways. Or post-colonial relations of power could be reconstructed by the space that is opened up by the notion of hybridity, the mixing and renewal of identity.

Other theologians had taken up the idea of hybridity. Kwok Pui-Lan, for example, spoke on 'Hybridity and Theological Imagination' at the American Academy of Religion conference, 19–23 November 1999, at Boston, Massachusetts. She explored the ways in which Christ can be seen as a fluid, destabilizing symbol. In a paper entitled 'Jesus the Hybrid', she says

> The most hybridized concept in the Christian tradition is Jesus/Christ. I am presenting this as a new construct. The space between

Jesus and Christ is unsettling and fluid, resisting categorization and culture. It is the borderland between the human and the divine, the one and the many, the historical and the cosmological, the Jewish and the Hellenistic, the prophetic and the sacramental, the God of the conquerors and the God of the meek and lowly. (Pui-Lan, 1999)

Kwok Pui-Lan argues that in the space of the slash (/) between Jesus and Christ all sorts of possibilities emerge – and have always emerged since the time of the early church. Such a hybrid notion allows the symbol of Christ to offer disruption to oppressive situations. An active Christ emerges, not a docile body rendered submissive within the dominant discourses of institutional life.

Foucault and post-colonial thinking enabled me to explore different theological understandings of 'the body of Christ'. As I considered 'power' in the local church, my whole thinking of the nature of this 'body' changed. If it is seen as 'hybrid', then the basis of the power relations could be transformed to displace set assumptions and fixed structures, and instead the congregation – not just St Barnabas, but any – could be a body that is always searching, always in transition, always different and alive because, as the cultural thinker Michel de Certeau explains (Ward, 2004; de Certeau, 1971/1997, p. 155), it has no other security than the living God. I came to the conclusion that it is discomfort and insecurity that become the clear signs of the presence of this body of Christ, for they indicate restlessness and movement, the position of not-having-arrived-yet, a desire for something different. Such an understanding of the body of Christ as a lively, hybrid body becomes a theological motif with transformative power.

When circumstances demanded, I withdrew from my role as participant observer at St Barnabas' church and concentrated on writing up the process and analysis. It was deeply frustrating not to be able to explore some of these ideas with the congregation: a good example of the messiness of doing such research (Ward, 2004). Had I been able, it might well have been along these lines, which takes us into the third method of theological reflection.

Theological Method Three: Corporate Theological Reflection

Corporate theological reflection is a method of doing theology as a group. It moves away from the lone theologian reflecting in his armchair to the possibilities and excitement of theological thinking and doing as an activity that belongs in the hands of the local congregation as the embodied community of faith. Something of its power to transform can be seen in Green's description of the knitting group (Green, 2000, p. 36).

For corporate theological reflection to happen some degree of emptying of power from those traditionally seen as 'the experts' needs to occur. At the same time those who have not always had the confidence or background to voice their faith sometimes need encouragement. Corporate theological reflection often requires a facilitator who has educational skills to enable adults or children to think, listen and talk in a group.

Let us imagine that I returned to the congregation of St Barnabas. Here are some ways in which the corporate reflection might have happened . . .

- A group of about eight to twelve people met regularly to discuss the ideas.
- I wrote a regular news bulletin throughout the research process and asked for responses to be shared.
- I gave feedback at decision-making meetings.
- I led an 'away day' to think about the future planning together of the congregation.

If a group had agreed to meet regularly over a number of weeks, here are some topics we might have explored. Depending on the nature of the group, I would give a lot of thought to introducing these ideas and making them accessible so that discussion opened up in ways that included all members. My own 'dominant role' would need attention, and it would be important to be honest and sensitive to issues of power at each stage of the corporate reflection.

Session 1:

- What does it mean to call the local church 'the body of Christ'?
- If we study together Paul's first letter to the Corinthians 12.12–27, and contrast it with Agrippa's fable, what do you think Paul wanted to achieve?

Session 2:

- If you look at this congregation, how would you describe it?

- What helps the congregation stick together?
- Who do you think is powerful? Who is not?
- Does it ever happen that someone wants to say something but can't?

Session 3:

- An accessible introduction to the thinking of Michel Foucault could be offered at this stage, and some exploration of how his ideas relate to the life of the congregation.
- What practices could be identified that shape the corporate identity?
- Who has most say in how those practices work?

Session 4:

- Again, depending on the group, the notion of hybridity could be explored in terms of a creative cultural mixing of different traditions and ways of worshipping. The group might then explore what could change in their liturgy and in their decision-making processes to reflect more fully the diversity of the congregation.

Session 5:

- Using the idea of Kwok Pui-Lan of the hybrid Jesus/Christ, the group could return to the initial question 'What does it mean to call this local church "the body of Christ"?'
- What sort of body is it that we 'embody'?

Session 6:

- The group could evaluate the ground it had covered and how the congregation as a whole could benefit from its work:
  – What have we learned from these sessions?
  – What do we want to change as a result in the way we congregate?
  – How might we go about sharing where we've got to?

Conclusion

This contribution has explored the notion of power in the local church, understood as dominance and subordination, by using three main methods of theological reflection, *praxis*, *critical correlation* and *corporate theological reflection* we have seen how theology can interplay in rich ways with other disciplines in studying the local church. Who does theology? And how? have also been questions I have considered, and I have shown how different ways of reflecting theologically can empower congregational members in the study of their own local church.

Further reading

Bernauer, J. and J. Carrette (eds) (2004) *Michel Foucault and Theology: The Politics of Religious Experience*, Aldershot: Ashgate.
Further exploration of Foucault's ideas as related to religion.

Browning, D. S. (1991) *Fundamental Practical Theology: Descriptive and Strategic Proposals*, Minneapolis, MN: Fortress Press.
A thorough exploration of the way in which theological values inform the work of the researcher of the local church, and some very good case studies.

Foucault, M. (1975/1991) *Discipline and Punish: The Birth of the Prison*, London: Penguin.
Foucault analyses institutional life and the practices that produce 'docile bodies'.

Graham, E. L. (2002) *Transforming Practice: Pastoral Theology in an Age of Uncertainty*, Eugene, Oregon: Wipf and Stock.
From a leading practical theologian, this book offers a fresh contribution to congregational studies, examining the power of faith communities to be transformational through practice.

Sandercock, L. (2004) *Cosmopolis II – Mongrel Cities in the 21st Century*, London and New York, NY: Continuum.
Addresses those concerned with the changing dynamics which affect post-colonial cities, and although not directly about churches and congregations, much of what she says about the context in which they are to be found is profoundly interesting as society faces the need to develop ways of living with difference and diversity.

4

Where Next in the Study of the Local Church?

You may have picked up and read this book for any number of reasons. Hopefully you have found some answers to your questions in the sections above, prompting you to think further about the context, worship and action, people and resources, and power relations of local churches. Here we offer some specific suggestions to different sorts of readers as to how you might develop your study of the local church once you've finished engaging with this handbook.

Local Church Leaders

Frances Ward

As a result of reading the book you should have a better idea about how to follow up and resolve issues that arise in the life of your church. The book has not attempted to cover everything, though, and if you want to take your interest in the local church further, the following suggestions might help you on your way.

Building communities of justice and equality

How might you do some further work on your own faith community, its internal dynamics and sense of vision? You might like to suggest that the decision-making body invite someone as a consultant to work with you. If you visit the website of this handbook, (*www.scmpress. co.uk/studyinglocalchurches*) you will find suggestions of people or organizations that can help you.

The changing shape of church and ministry

In the local church itself you may be interested in the changing shape of the church, and how ministry needs to adapt to reach out to society around. The report entitled *Mission-Shaped Church* (Mission and Public Affairs Council, 2004) is a good, accessible overview from an Anglican perspective of the different demands on church structures made by today's world and the mixed economy of ministry, lay and ordained, that needs to develop as a result. Questions of leadership within the local church could be taken forward by consulting the Centre for Innovative Church Leadership at *CICL@al-consulting. co.uk*.

The church and environmental issues

Increasingly issues to do with living in sustainable ways in the world will inevitably face local congregations. What more could your church be doing to 'go green' and care for the planet? The website of the Alliance of Religions and Conservation at *www.arcworld.org* offers a wealth of ideas and pragmatic approaches to living locally in a global world.

Working with government agencies

There is developing interest within political circles in the local faith community as a potential partner and resource for delivering what Robert Putnam called 'social capital': the voluntary work and service that societies rely upon, but which often lacks high profile. The report published in February 2004 by the Home Office Faith Communities Unit in Britain entitled *Working Together: Co-operation Between Government and Faith Communities* (Home Office Faith Communities Unit, 2004) (see *http://www.homeoffice.gov.uk/docs3/ workingtog_faith040329.pdf*) might well give you some good ideas about working with local agencies and political networks. You may need to start by familiarizing yourself with local government structures and reminding them of your presence and your voice in the community.

Interfaith issues

The world post-9/11 is a world of increasing distrust between people of different faiths, particularly between Christians, Jews and Muslims. What can the local church do to learn more about their neighbours of other faiths? You might find further resources to guide your thinking at the Inter Faith Network for the UK at *http://www.interfaith.co.uk/* More locally it could be a very interesting exercise to arrange a vicinity walk (see Section 2.3 above) with someone from the local mosque, or synagogue, sharing with each other what you see and how the neighbourhood appears through the eyes of different faiths. Or you could arrange a series of listening exercises with a group of people of different faiths, in order simply to grow in understanding of each other.

Further reading

There are two journals published in Britain today in the area of practical theology that will keep you aware of the issues of the day and offer you a theological perspective on contemporary concerns. Crucible is published quarterly, and is edited by John Atherton and Peter Sedgwick. If you wish to subscribe, contact subs@churchtimes.co.uk. The website of Contact, a journal in practical and pastoral theology, edited by Frances Ward, is www.contactpastoral.org.

For further reading on theological reflection, see Graham, E. L., H. Walton, et al. (forthcoming 2005) *Theological Reflection*, London: SCM-Canterbury Press.

For further resources, see Warren, R. (2004) *The Healthy Churches' Handbook*, London: Church House Publishing.

Ministerial Training Students

Philip Richter

This book has offered you perspectives and tools with which to study the local churches you are currently based within and those you will engage with in your future ministry. We have only begun to scratch the surface, but we hope we have whetted your appetite and have offered some glimpses of the potential usefulness of local church studies in resourcing the church's ministry and mission. You will be able to develop your skills and extend your awareness of this field of study by following up the leads we have given to other literature, especially within the further reading provided at the end of each section.

Practical implementation

You will also find it useful personally to try out some of the 'practical ways of studying the local church', in each section. It will be important to budget enough time for these practical exercises and to take account of the time involved in planning, securing people's co-operation, getting the permission of key 'gatekeepers', conducting your study, analysing your findings, and reflecting on the outcomes. You will have to fit this into what may be a very busy ministerial schedule. You may receive mixed reactions from your local church: some participants may query your use of time and you will need to consider how to justify your study. It will be important that what you do is seen not as your own personal 'hobby', but as something integral to the church's key values and mission priorities. It may become easier to justify your study of the local church once its fruits begin to be seen.

Continuing ministerial development

You will, naturally, be expected by the wider church to which you are responsible to be engaging in ongoing training and education. All the major churches now set a high premium on encouraging and enabling their ministers to continue being properly equipped for ministry, once initial ministerial training has been completed. Your continuing ministerial education or development, the terms used will vary between churches, may well include an Orientation Project in which you will be expected to analyse the church in which you will be ministering and its specific context when you first start your public ministry – in which case, this book should give you a headstart. Your continuing ministerial education programme for your earliest years in ministry may have to conform to a fairly inflexible curriculum but, if there is any room for negotiation, do try to make a case for including ongoing study of the local church.

Continuing ministerial education is meant to be part of a 'seamless robe' of training, which includes, but does not stop at the end of, initial ministerial training. Studying local churches as a student minister should help set up good habits for your ongoing ministerial development. Later in your ministry you might consider doing further formal academic study. We outline some possibilities below ('Students in Higher Education'). The field of local church studies, outside of the United States, is relatively new and underexplored, so there are within it lots of potentially fertile areas for further study. If you want some ideas as to what to research and would like your imagination stimulated, visit our website at *www.scmpress.co.uk/studyinglocalchurches*, where our contributors have outlined some of the gaps worth addressing in our understanding of local churches. The best research topics, however, will be whatever fascinates or puzzles you about the local church.

Whatever you decide to study about the local church, you will probably, as a minister, not simply be engaging in study for its own sake. It is likely that you will want to feed your findings back to the local church and, perhaps, to policy-makers in the wider church. This is not to suggest that your study should necessarily be narrowly geared to addressing specific problems affecting the local church. Even apparently general study may make serendipitous and providential connections with the life and witness of the local church.

Students in Higher Education

Douglas Davies

This introductory handbook is intended to help students in their first venture in studying the local church, probably an undergraduate dissertation or a placement report for those engaged in ministry training. If such a project has whetted your appetite where might you go next?

Taught Masters degree

The obvious possibility is a postgraduate qualification following your initial degree and the best route probably lies in a Masters degree: either a taught degree or by thesis only. Taught Masters degrees usually involve a large proportion of taught modules followed by a dissertation on the student's choice of topic. This extends the subject range of undergraduate work and adds thesis work under experienced super-

vision. This develops competence in research skills of bibliographi-
cal work, reading, note-taking, data-gathering and analysis, and the
composition and writing of a thesis. Such competences are strongly
preferred or even demanded by research funding bodies and it is very
difficult or impossible to gain grants for doctoral studies without
them.

A taught Masters degree is also a valuable way of changing academic
direction after your undergraduate degree or of focusing on one aspect
of earlier study. After an undergraduate degree in general studies or
social studies you might want to move to more detailed masters work
in anthropology, sociology, psychology, theology, religious studies,
history or law. Similarly, someone whose first degree was in theology
might wish to move into the social sciences. Similarly, the developing field of spirituality, which draws from a variety of disciplines and
frames them in distinctive ways, also offers a serious path of complementary further work.

Research Masters degree

People not needing research funding for doctoral work, and who have
sufficient background in research methods, might prefer a thesis-only
Masters degree. You would need to seek a university or college with
good supervision. Indeed, this applies to all because the quality of supervision is crucial for postgraduate work. A good supervisor possesses
general knowledge alongside detailed expertise. In today's academic
world it is realistic to expect that supervisors will have published some
significant material in a chosen field. This can be helpful for potential
students in giving them a sense of the supervisor's approach. The best
policy is to contact and, if possible, to meet with a possible supervisor
in advance of joining their institution. Still, students must have a realistic view of what supervisors can achieve. They cannot work miracles
and cannot write a thesis for you. At the end of the day your thesis is
your thesis. In other words, supervising and being supervised involves
a considerable degree of negotiation, open-mindedness and a readi-
ness for mutual learning.

Collaborative work

This handbook may, however, have stimulated your interest in interdisciplinary research and that, too, becomes even more possible at

postgraduate levels. A great deal of research needs doing in all areas associated with church and religious life, as this book has suggested. It is worth recalling the variety of academic disciplines sketched in Section 2.0 and which have not, otherwise, featured strongly in this book. For example, the geography of religion has played a relatively small part in the academic study of religion and yet many students will have studied geography at some level and could take its perspectives much further when studying the local church. There is a tremendous amount to be gained, whenever possible, from working collaboratively with people from different academic disciplines. One of my own most fruitful exercises was a large research venture, The Rural Church Project, involving scholars from geography, sociology, history and theology (Davies, Watkins, et al., 1991). Following that experience I have specifically engaged geography, sociology and history graduates as research associates in other projects (e.g. Davies and Shaw, 1995).

One feature of much professional life increasingly involves in-service training and professional development. One dimension of this involves Master of Ministry and Doctor of Ministry degrees. These are usually, though not necessarily exclusively, intended for church leaders. They may come at the outset of ministry or at some later stage. Many professional people often benefit from a serious period of study at some point in their career when they can pause to reflect on their busy lives. It is, however, particularly important to ensure that any qualification is offered by a serious institution and not some worthless mail-order degree factory. To engage in serious study while continuing one's job is not easy, but can be extremely valuable for self-appraisal and a sense of refreshed approach to routine activities.

Local Policy-Makers

Helen Cameron

We hope that this handbook has opened up options for working with local churches. You may wish to engage them in a consultation exercise or seek to involve them in a local initiative. You may wish to assess their potential for service delivery or community building. You may be seeking to evaluate what they currently do. Whatever the reason for your approach, it will be helpful to start by identifying their agenda. Has the church concerned undertaken a review of its activities? It may have been encouraged to use a particular review tool by its denomination, it may have come up with its own process, or it may be new to the whole idea of researching its practice. It is likely that you will find differences between the assumptions and approach of your agency and that of the church concerned. This section highlights two factors about working with local churches that we hope will help you as you plan your next steps.

Diversity

When we were discussing the cover for this book, we quickly agreed that we didn't want any visual representation of a church. No single image could represent all local churches. Most obviously, not all meet in church buildings: some meet in community buildings or in members' homes. The stereotypical church member is seen as a white middle-class older woman, yet many of the newest and most rapidly growing churches in the UK are being formed by black African immigrants. Most churches have to balance income with expenditure carefully, yet some are sitting on sizeable assets that are underused. A potential frustration in seeking to work with local churches is the variation in the ways in which they make decisions. The best guidance is to assume nothing and enquire carefully what processes any decision will need to go through and how long it will take. Your interest in local churches may be because you perceive them as a link into a local community. Again, it is worth enquiring whether this is the case. Some churches draw people from a wide distance, attracted by some particular feature of the church – this wider network may in itself be useful, but the church may not see its immediate locality as a priority for its mission.

A final and vital area of diversity concerns the theological beliefs of the local church. In particular it will be helpful to know how their beliefs about God inform their beliefs about their role in the local community. To give a few hypotheses as examples: one church may work with the community because members feel they are obeying instructions in the Bible; another because they feel it will open up opportunities to draw people into the Christian faith; yet another church may feel that there are injustices in the community they can play a role in correcting. You may feel you can work with some motivations and not others (Cameron, 2004).

Complexity

In comparison with public sector agencies, local churches are small organizations yet despite this they are unusually complex. People are connected to them in a range of ways, they undertake a range of activities, and they may have idiosyncratic ways of doing things that are cherished. An important contrast with most organizations is that the sub-groups of local churches are often focused on a particular goal or activity and the mechanisms for linking the different goals and activities together are likely to be weak. Representatives of the church who meet you may not have an in-depth knowledge of the workings of the activities or groups you are interested in – it is likely you will need to speak to several people rather than to one. This can seem inefficient and time-consuming, but it is this feature of churches that encourages activism and extends their networks, features that you may wish to access.

By contrast, people in local churches may find your world equally complex. If your job requires you to focus on outcomes, on what can be measured, on specific problems and needs, you may find a tension between your worldview and that of the local church. Local churches seek to build long-term and often lifelong and intergenerational relationships with people, so processes may be as important as outcomes.

By definition, churches value intangible and immeasurable things like faith, joy and peace and so may be reluctant to commit to performance indicators. Churches, like other membership organizations, attract people who want to be treated as whole people – body, mind and spirit – and not to be broken down into a bundle of clearly defined needs. This is not to say that dialogue is impossible, but rather that it is worth anticipating that patience will be required and that both sides may need several attempts to understand each other. In fact a message underlying this handbook is that collaborating on a piece of research may be a very good place to start building relationships with a local church.

Working with a local church can be a little like unpicking a knot – there is no entirely logical place to start – just make a start and follow the developing thread.

Conclusion

In chapter 3 we presented 16 different perspectives you could adopt when studying local churches. We investigated four dimensions of local churches – their global and local context; worship and action; resources and people; and power. Each of these dimensions was analysed from four different disciplinary perspectives – anthropology, sociology, organizational studies and theology. Although, for the sake of clarity, we have looked at each dimension of the local church through separate disciplinary lenses, in practice you will find that there is significant overlap and cross-fertilization between the different disciplines. Practical theologians, for instance, when using the methodological approach of 'critical correlation', might draw on all three other disciplines. The methods we described for studying local churches were generally not exclusive to individual disciplines. Ethnography, for instance, although a key method for anthropologists, can also be a useful tool for sociology, organizational studies or theology. The time line method, you will have noticed, was recommended by two of our contributors – from anthropology and organizational studies.

This book invites you to think outside of the boxes represented by the four disciplines we have covered, and to recognize the significant degree of overlap and interplay between them. We have found that no one discipline gives the full picture when studying local churches, and we have modelled interdisciplinary approaches. However, we have also been careful to avoid homogenizing the different disciplines. We have allowed each discipline its own voice and have reflected interdisciplinary diversity and, sometimes, tension. For instance, Stephen Pattison has critiqued the managerial assumptions of organizational studies on theological grounds. There is room for dialogue and critical exchange between the disciplines.

It is also important not to overlook the distinctive contributions of each discipline to the study of local churches: while organizational studies, for instance, may treat local churches as a type of 'voluntary organization', anthropology can, through ethnographic accounts, help to identify their distinctive organizational features. So, in practice, you will need to draw on all four disciplines as you study different aspects of local churches: sometimes you will find that anthropology, sociology, organizational studies and theology overlap and cross-fertilize; sometimes you will need to be alert to disjunctions and disagreement, and be ready to engage in critical dialogue.

In this handbook we have necessarily focused on a limited range of perspectives for studying the local church. We hope there is more than enough here to enable you to conduct your own study. But, however many different perspectives are applied to the local church, no single study can hope to do it complete justice. However much the local church is dissected and analysed, it turns out to be far more than the sum of its parts. The local church you study may contain people with insights and expertise going well beyond what is contained in this handbook – prepare to be surprised!

We hope you will enjoy studying local churches and make some interesting discoveries. But do try to resist the temptation to see yourself as 'superman' or 'superwoman', able to investigate and resolve, at a single stroke, the problems long wrestled with by sincere Christians in the local church. The theologian Sally McFague contrasts two ways of paying attention – the *arrogant eye* and the *loving eye* – and critiques the arrogant eye as 'disembodied, distant, transcendent, simplifying, objectifying, quick and easy' (McFague, 1997, p. 34). Wise researchers will cultivate a loving gaze towards the local church. Sally McFague offers two contrasting metaphors for investigating the world: *the map* and *the hike (without a map)*. We invite you to use the maps we have provided in this handbook, but to do your research into the local church in the spirit of:

Sellar . . . [who] went to India with a map . . . but ended up taking a hike, learning by paying attention to the lay of the land, ready for discoveries around the next bend in the trail, realizing that she was in an unknown place without a map, one that would require the full engagement of all her senses and skills. (McFague, 1997, p. 42)

Bibliography

Acker, J. (1992) *Gendering Organizational Analysis*, New York, NY: Sage Publications.

Albrecht, D. E. (1999) *Rites in the Spirit: A Ritual Approach to Pentecostal/Charismatic Spirituality*, Sheffield: Sheffield Academic Press.

Albrow, M. (1997) *Do Organizations Have Feelings?* London: Routledge.

Aldridge, A. (2000) *Religion in the Contemporary World: A Sociological Introduction*, Cambridge: Polity Press.

Ammerman, N. (1997) *Congregation and Community*, New Brunswick, NJ: Rutgers University Press.

Ammerman, N. T., J. W. Carroll, C. S. Dudley and W. McKinney (eds) (1998) *Studying Congregations: A New Handbook*, Nashville TN: Abingdon Press.

Arweck, E. and M. D. Stringer (eds) (2002) *Theorizing Faith: The Insider/Outsider Problem in the Study of Ritual*, Birmingham: University of Birmingham Press.

Atherton, J. (2003) *Marginalization*, London: SCM Press.

Aune, K. (2003) *Marginalised, Feminist or Called by God? Postfeminist Female Singleness in a British Evangelical Congregation*, British Sociological Association Study Day: Religion and Marginalisation, November 2003.

—— (2004) 'The significance of gender for congregational studies', in M. Guest, K. Tusting and L. Woodhead (eds) *Congregational Studies in the UK: Christianity in a Post-Christian Context*, Aldershot: Ashgate.

Avis, P. (ed.) (2003) *Public Faith? The State of Religious Belief and Practice in Britain*, London: SPCK.

Bacon, D. (2003) *Communities, Churches and Social Capital in Northern Ireland*, Coleraine: University of Ulster.

Baker, C. (2002) *Towards the Theology of New Towns: The Implications of the New Town Experience for Urban Theology*, University of Manchester, unpublished PhD Thesis.

Ballard, P. and J. Pritchard (1996) *Practical Theology in Action: Christian Thinking in the Service of Church and Society*, London: SPCK.

Bauman, Z. (1995) *Life in Fragments*, Oxford: Blackwell.

—— (2000) *Liquid Modernity*, Cambridge: Polity Press.

Becker, P. E. (1999) *Congregations in Conflict: Cultural Models of Local Religious Life*, Cambridge: Cambridge University Press.

Beckford, R. (2004) *God and the Gangs: An Urban Toolkit for those who won't be Sold out, Brought out or Scared out*, London: Darton, Longman and Todd.

Belbin, R. M. (1993) *Team Roles at Work*, Oxford: Butterworth-Heinemann.

Bell, J. (1993) *Doing Your Research Project: A Guide for First-Time Researchers in Education and Social Science*, Milton Keynes: Open University Press.

Bellah, R. N., R. Madsen, W. M. Sullivan, A. Swidler and S. M. Tipton (1985) *Habits of the Heart. Individualism and Commitment in American Life*, Berkeley, CA and London: University of California Press.

Bennett Moore, Z. (2002) *Introducing Feminist Perspectives on Pastoral Theology*, London: Sheffield University Press.

Berg, B. L. (2001) *Qualitative Research Methods for the Social Sciences* (4th ed.), London: Allyn and Bacon.

Berger, T. (1999) *Women's Ways of Worship: Gender Analysis and Liturgical History*, Collegeville, MN: The Liturgical Press.

Bernauer, J. and J. Carrette (eds) *Michel Foucault and Theology: The Politics of Religious Experience*, Aldershot: Ashgate.

Bhabha, H. (1995) 'Cultural Diversity and Cultural Differences', in B. Ashcroft (ed.) *The Post-Colonial Studies Reader*, London and New York, NY: Routledge.

Billis, D. (1993) *Organising Public and Voluntary Agencies*, London: Routledge.

Blaxter, L., C. Hughes and M. Tight. (2001) *How to Research* (2nd edition), Buckingham: Open University Press.

Block, P. (1993) *Stewardship: Choosing Service Over Self-Interest*, San Francisco, CA: Berrett-Koehler Publishers.

Block, P. (2000) *Flawless Consulting: A Guide to Getting Your Expertise Used*, San Francisco, CA: Jossey-Bass/Pfeiffer.

Bolton, G. (2001) *Reflective Practice: Writing and Professional Development*, London, California and New Delhi: Paul Chapman Publishing.

Booker, M. and M. Ireland. (2003) *Evangelism – Which Way Now?* London: Church House Publishing.

Bourdieu, P. (1977) *Outline of a Theory of Practice*, Cambridge: Cambridge University Press.

Bradshaw, P. F. (1992) *The Search for the Origins of Christian Worship: Sources and Methods for the Study of Early Christianity*, London: SPCK.

Braybrooke, D. and C. Lindblom (1963) *A Strategy of Decision and Policy as a Social Process*, New York, NY: Free Press.

Brierley, P. (2000) *The Tide Is Running out: What the English Church Attendance Survey Reveals*, London: Christian Research Association.

Brookfield, S. (1987) *Developing Critical Thinkers*, Milton Keynes: Open University Press.

Brown, C. G. (2001) *The Death of Christian Britain*, London: Routledge.

Browning, D. S. (1991) *Fundamental Practical Theology: Descriptive and Strategic Proposals*, Minneapolis, MN: Fortress Press.

Bruce, S. (1996) *Religion in the Modern World: From Cathedrals to Cults*, Oxford: Oxford University Press.

Cameron, H. (1998) *The Social Action of the Local Church: Five Congregations in an English City*, London School of Economics, unpublished PhD thesis.

——(1999) 'Are Members Volunteers? An Exploration of the Concept of Membership drawing upon Studies of the Local Church', *Voluntary Action*, 1 (2), 53–65.

——(2004) 'Typology of Religious Characteristics of Social Service and Educational Organizations and Programs – A European Response', *Nonprofit and Voluntary Sector Quarterly*, 33 (1), pp. 146–50.

Carroll, J. W., C. S. Dudley and et al (eds) (1986) *Handbook for Congregational Studies*, Nashville, TN: Abingdon.

Cartledge, M. (2003) *Practical Theology: Charismatic and Empirical Perspectives*, Carlisle, Cumbria and Waynesboro, GA: Paternoster Press.

Castells, M. (1989) *The Informational City*, Oxford: Blackwell.

——(1996) *The Rise of the Network Society*, Oxford: Blackwell.

——(1997) *The Power of Identity*, Oxford: Blackwell.

Centre for Research and Innovation in Social Policy and Practice (2003) *Unravelling the Maze – A Survey of Civil Society in the UK*, Newcastle: Centre for Research and Innovation in Social Policy and Practice.

Certeau, M. de (1971) 'How Is Christianity Thinkable Today?' *Theology Digest*, 19, pp. 334–45.

——(1971/1997) 'How Is Christianity Thinkable Today?', in G. Ward (1997) (ed.) *The Postmodern God: A Theological Reader*, Oxford: Blackwell.

——(1984) *The Practice of Everyday Life*, Berkeley, CA: University of California Press.

Chambers, P. (1997) '"On or Off the Bus": Identity, Belonging and Schism, A Case Study of a Neo-Pentecostal House Church', in S. Hunt, M. Hamilton and T. Walter (eds) *Charismatic Christianity: Sociological Perspectives*, Basingstoke: Macmillan.

——(2004) 'The Effects of Evangelical Renewal on Mainstream Congregational Identities', in M. Guest, K. Tusting and L. Woodhead (eds.) *Congregational Studies in the UK: Christianity in a Post-Christian Context*, Aldershot: Ashgate.

——(2004) *Religion, Secularization and Social Changes in Wales: Congregational Studies in a Post-Christian Society*, Cardiff: University of Wales Press.

Charity Evaluation Services (2003) *First Steps in Monitoring and Evaluation*, London: Charity Evaluation Services.

Chater, M. (1999) 'Theology and Management', *Modern Believing*, 40 (4), pp. 64–9.

Chrislip, D. D. (2002) *The Collaborative Leadership Fieldbook: A Guide for Citizens and Civic Leaders*, San Francisco, CA: Jossey-Bass.

Church of England Gazette (2002) 'Church of England Attendance and Membership', *Church of England Gazette*, 2 (5), http://www.gazette.cofe.anglican.org/articles/02_11_page6.html.

Churches Information for Mission (2001) *Faith in Life*, London: Churches Information for Mission.

Clark, D. (1971) 'Local and Cosmopolitan Aspects of Religious Activity in a Northern Suburb: Process of Change', in M. Hill (ed.) *A Sociological Yearbook of Religion in Britain, Vol. 4*, London: SCM Press, pp. 141–59.

——(1982) *Between Pulpit and Pew: Folk Religion in a North Yorkshire Fishing Village*, Cambridge: Cambridge University Press.

Clark, D. B. (1970) 'Local and Cosmopolitan Aspects of Religious Activity in a Northern Suburb', in D. Martin and M. Hill (eds) *A Sociological Yearbook of Religion in Britain, Vol. 3*, London: SCM Press, pp. 45–64.

Clark, E. (1996) *Making the Connections*, unpublished report.

Coffey, A. (1999) *The Ethnographic Self: Fieldwork and the Representation of Identity*, London, Thousand Oaks, New Delhi: Sage Publications.

Coghlan, D. and T. Branwick (2001) *Doing Action Research in Your Own Organization*, London: Sage.

Cohen, A. P. (1985) *The Symbolic Construction of Community*, London: Routledge and Kegan Paul.

Coleman, S. (2000) *The Globalisation of Charismatic Christianity: Spreading the Gospel of Prosperity*, Cambridge: Cambridge University Press:

Collins, D. (1998) *Organizational Change: Sociological Perspectives*, London: Routledge.

Connerton, P. (1989) *How Societies Remember*, Cambridge: Cambridge University Press.

Cray, G. (1992) *From Here to Where? The Culture of the Nineties*, General Synod Board of Mission, London: Church House Publishing.

Croft, S. (2002) *Transforming Communities: Re-Imagining the Church for the 21st Century*, London: Darton, Longman and Todd.

Csordas, T. J. (1997) *Language, Charisma and Creativity*, Berkeley, CA: University of California Press.

Dandelion, B. P. (2004) *The Liturgies of Quakerism*, Aldershot: Ashgate.

Davie, G. (1994) *Religion in Britain since 1945: Believing Without Belonging*, Oxford: Blackwell.

——(2002) *Europe: The Exceptional Case – Parameters of Faith in the Modern World*, London: Darton, Longman and Todd.

Davies, D. and A. Shaw (1995) *Reusing Old Graves: A Report on Popular British Attitudes*, Crayford, Kent: Shaw and Sons.

Davies, D., C. Watkins, M. Winter, C. Pack, S. Seymour and C. Short. (1991) *Church and Religion in Rural England*, Edinburgh: T and T Clark.

Davies, D. J. (2000) *The Mormon Culture of Salvation*, Aldershot: Ashgate.

——(2002) *Anthropology and Theology*, Oxford: Berg.

Davies, E. and A. D. Rees (eds) (1960) *Welsh Rural Communities*, Cardiff: University of Wales Press.

Dawson, C. (2002) *Practical Research Methods: A User-Friendly Guide to Mastering Research Techniques and Projects*, Oxford: How To Books.

Denscombe, M. (2002) *Ground Rules for Good Research*, Buckingham: Open University Press.

Dhooghe, J. (1968) 'Organizational Problems Regarding Different Types of Membership in the Church', *Social Compass*, 15 (2), pp. 93–9.

Dorsey, G. (1995) *Congregation: The Journey Back to Church*, New York, NY: Viking.

Douglas, M. (1970) *Natural Symbols*, London: Pelican Books.

Dowie, A. (1997) 'Resistance to Change in a Scottish Christian Congregation', *The Scottish Journal of Religious Studies*, 18 (2), pp. 147–62.

——(2002) *Interpreting Culture in a Scottish Congregation*, New York, NY: Lang.

DPHE (1999) *Key Health Data for the West Midlands 1999*, Birmingham: University of Birmingham Department of Public Health and Epidemiology.

Dudley, C. (ed.) (1983) *Building Effective Ministry: Theory and Practice in the Local Church*, New York, NY: Harper and Row.

Dudley, M. and V. Rounding (2002) *Churchwardens: A Survival Guide*, London: SPCK.

Dulles, A. (1978) *Models of the Church: A Critical Assessment of the Church in all its Aspects* (2nd edition), Dublin: Gill and Macmillan.

Dunn, J. (1998) *The Theology of Paul the Apostle*, Cambridge: William B. Eerdmans Publishing.

Dunn, N. M. (2003) 'Excluded Spaces: The Figure in the Australian Aboriginal Landscape', in S. M. Low and D. Lawrence-Zuniga (eds) *The Anthropology of Space and Place: Locating Culture*, Oxford: Blackwell, pp. 92–109.

Durkheim, E. (1915/1995) *The Elementary Forms of Religious Life*, New York, NY: The Free Press.

Durran, M. (2003) *The UK Church Fundraising Handbook: A Practical Manual and Directory of Sources*, Norwich: Canterbury Press.

Eastman, M. and S. Latham (eds.) (2004) *Urban Church: A Practitioner's Resource Book*, London: SPCK.

Eccleston, G. (1988) *The Parish Church?* London: Mowbray.

Farnsley, A. (2004) 'The Rise of Congregational Studies in the USA', in M. Guest, K. Tusting and L. Woodhead (eds) *Congregational Studies in the UK: Christianity in a Post-Christian Context*, Aldershot: Ashgate.

Fichter, J. F. (1953) 'The Marginal Catholic: An Institutional Approach', *Social Forces*, 32 (1), pp. 167–73.

Finneron, D. and A. Dinham (eds) (2002) *Building on Faith: Faith Buildings in Neighbourhood Renewal*, London: Church Urban Fund.

Finney, J. (1992) *Finding Faith Today*, Swindon: The Bible Society.

Flanagan, K. (1991) *Sociology and Liturgy: Re-Presentations of the Holy*, London: Macmillan.

Foucault, M. (1963/1991) *The Birth of the Clinic: An Archaeology of Medical Perception*, New York, NY and London: Routledge.

——(1975/1991) *Discipline and Punish: The Birth of the Prison*, London: Penguin.

——(1976/1980) 'Two Lectures', in C. Gordon (ed.) *Power/Knowledge: Selected Interviews and Other Writings 1972–77*, Hertfordshire: The Harvester Press, pp. 78–108.

——(1984) *The Foucault Reader*, London: Penguin.

Francis, L. J. (2003) 'Religion and Social Capital: The Flaw in the 2001 Census in England and Wales', in P. Avis (ed.) *Public Faith? The State of Religious Belief and practice in Britain*, London: SPCK, pp. 45–64.

Fried, S. (2002) *The New Rabbi: A Congregation Searches for its Leader*, New York, NY: Bantam.

Gabriel, Y. (ed.) (1999) *Organizations in Depth: The Psychoanalysis of Organizations*, London: Sage.

——(2000) *Storytelling in Organizations: Facts, Fictions and Fantasies*, Oxford: Oxford University Press.

Giddens, A. (1997) *Sociology*, Cambridge: Polity Press.

Gilchrist, A. (2004) 'Developing the Well-Connected Community', in H. McCarthy, P. Miller and P. Skidmore (eds) *Network Logic – Essay 11*, London: Demos.

Giles, R. (1999) (revised) *Re-Pitching the Tent: Reordering the Church Building for Worship and Mission*, Norwich: Canterbury Press.

Gill, R. (1994) *A Vision for Growth*, London: SPCK.

——(2003) (2nd) *The 'Empty' Church Revisited*, Aldershot, Hants: Ashgate.

Gorringe, T. (2002) *A Theology of the Built Environment: Justice, Empowerment, Redemption*, Cambridge: Cambridge University Press.

Graham, E. L. (1996) *Transforming Practice: Pastoral Theology in an Age of Uncertainty*, London and New York, NY: Mowbray.

—— (2002) *Transforming Practice: Pastoral Theology in an Age of Uncertainty* (2nd edition), Eugene, Oregon: Wipf and Stock.

Graham, E. L. and M. Halsey (eds) (1993) *Life Cycles: Women and Pastoral Care*, London: SPCK.

Graham, E. L., H. Walton and F. Ward (Forthcoming) *Theological Reflection: Methods (Volume 1)*, London: SCM-Canterbury Press.

Graham, E. L., H. Walton and F. Ward (Forthcoming) *Theological Reflection: Sources (Volume 2)*, London: SCM-Canterbury Press.

Gray, J. (2003) 'Open Spaces and Dwelling Places: Being at Home on Hill Farms in the Scottish Borders', in S. M. Low and D. Lawrence-Zuniga (eds.) *The Anthropology of Space and Place: Locating Culture*, Oxford: Blackwell, pp. 224–44.

Green, L. (2000) *Let's Do Theology*, London: Mowbray.

Greenwood, R. (2000) *The Ministry Team Handbook*, London: SPCK.

Grieve, J. (1999) *Fundraising for Churches*, London: SPCK.

Grimes, R. L. (1982) *Beginnings in Ritual Studies*, Washington, DC: University Press of America.

Grint, K. (ed.) (1997) *Leadership: Classical, Contemporary and Critical Approaches*, Oxford: Oxford University Press.

Griseri, P. (1998) *Managing Values: Ethical Change in Organizations*, London: Macmillan.

Grundy, M. (1998) *Understanding Congregations: A New Shape for the Local Church*, London: Mowbray.

Guest, M., K. Tusting and L. Woodhead (eds) (2004) *Congregational Studies in the UK: Christianity in a Post-Christian Context*, Aldershot: Ashgate.

Hadaway, C. K., P. L. Marler and M. Chaves (1993) 'What the Polls Don't Show: A Closer Look at US Church Attendance', *American Sociological Review*, 58, pp. 741–52.

Harris, M. (1996) 'An Inner Group of Willing People: Volunteering in a Religious Context', *Social Policy and Administration*, 30 (1), pp. 54–68.

—— (1998) *Organizing God's Work: Challenges for Churches and Synagogues*, Basingstoke: Macmillan Press.

—— (2001) 'Organising Modern Synagogues: A Case of Multiple Models', *European Judaism*, 34 (2), pp. 123–31.

Hauerwas, S. (1981) *A Community of Character*, Notre Dame, Indiana: University of Notre Dame Press.

Heelas, P., L. Woodhead, B. Seel, B. Szerszynski and K. Tusting (2005) *The Spiritual Revolution: Why Religion Is Giving Way to Spirituality*, Oxford: Blackwell.

Heskins, J. (2001) *Unheard Voices*, London: Dartman, Longman and Todd.

Higginson, R. (1996) *Transforming Leadership: A Christian Approach to Management*, London: SPCK.

Hilborn, D. and M. Bird (eds) (2002) *God and the Generations: Youth, Age and the Church Today*, Carlisle: Paternoster Press.

Hirst, R. (2003) 'Social Networks and Personal Belief: An Example from Modern Britain', in G. Davie, P. Heelas and L. Woodhead (eds) *Predicting Religion: Christian, Secular and Alternative Futures*, Aldershot: Ashgate.

Hoge, D. R. and D. A. Roozen (1979) *Understanding Church Growth and Decline 1950–1978*, New York: The Pilgrim Press.

Home Office Faith Communities Unit (2004) *Working Together: Co-operation between Government and Faith Communities*, London: Home Office.

Hopewell, J. F. (1987) *Congregation: Stories and Structures*, London: SCM Press.

Hornsby-Smith, M. (1989) *The Changing Parish: A Study of Parishes, Priests and Parishioners After Vatican II*, London: Routledge.

Hull, J. (1985) *What Prevents Christian Adults from Learning*, London: SCM Press.

Hunt, S. (2001) *Anyone for Alpha: Evangelism in a Post-Christian Society*, London: Darton Longman and Todd.

——(2003) *Alternative Religions*, Aldershot: Ashgate.

——(2004) *The Alpha Enterprise: Evangelism in a Post-Christian Era*, Aldershot: Ashgate.

Hunt, S., M. Hamilton and T. Walter (eds) (1997) *Charismatic Christianity: Sociological Perspectives*, Basingstoke: Macmillan.

Inge, J. (2003) *A Christian Theology of Place*, Aldershot: Ashgate.

Inglehart, R. (1997) *Modernization and Postmodernization. Cultural, Economic and Political Change in 43 Societies*, Princeton, NJ: Princeton University Press.

James, W. and D. H. Johnson (eds) (1988) *Vernacular Christianity*, Oxford: JASO.

Jamieson, A. (2002) *A Churchless Faith*, London: SPCK.

Jamieson, P. (1997) *Living at the Edge: Sacrament and Solidarity in Leadership*, London: Mowbray.

Jeavons, T. H. (1994) *When the Bottom Line Is Faithfulness: Management of Christian Service Organizations*, Indianapolis: Indiana University Press.

Jenkins, T. (1999) *Religion in English Everyday Life*, New York, NY and Oxford: Berghahn Books.

Katz, D. and R. L. Kahn (1978) *The Social Psychology of Organizations*, New York, NY: John Wiley.

Kay, W. K. and L. J. Francis (1996) *Drift from the Churches: Attitude Toward Christianity During Childhood and Adolescence*, Cardiff: University of Wales Press.

Kearns, K. and G. Scarpino. (1996) 'Strategic Planning Research: Knowledge and Gaps', *Nonprofit Management and Leadership*, 6 (4), pp. 429–40.

Kelley, D. M. (1977) *Why Conservative Churches Are Growing*, New York, NY: Harper and Row.

Kumar, K. (1995) *From Post-Industrial to Post-Modern Society*, Oxford: Blackwell.

Lartey, E. Y. and J. N. Poling (2003) *In Living Colour: An Intercultural Approach to Pastoral Care and Counselling* (2nd edition), London: Jessica Kingsley.

Levitt, M. (1996) *Nice When They Are Young: Contemporary Christianity in Families and Schools*, Aldershot: Avebury.

Lewis, I. (1986) *Religion in Context*, Cambridge: Cambridge University Press.

Lischer, R. (1995) *The Preacher King*, New York, NY: Oxford University Press.

Lovell, G. (1994) *Analysis and Design: A Handbook for Practitioners and Consultants in Church and Community Work*, London: Burns and Oates.

Lukes, S. (1974) *Power: A Radical View*, Basingstoke: Macmillan.

Lyall, D. (2001) *Integrity of Pastoral Care*, London: SPCK.

Lynch, G. (2002) *After Religion: 'Generation X' and the Search for Meaning*, London: Darton, Longman and Todd.

Lynd, R. S. and H. M. Lynd (1929) *Middletown*, New York, NY: Harcourt, Brace, Constable.

Lyon, B. (2000) 'What is the Relevance of Congregational Studies for Pastoral Theology', in J. Woodward and S. Pattison (eds) *The Blackwell Reader in Pastoral and Practical Theology*, Oxford: Blackwell, pp. 257–71.

Malinowski, B. (1948/1974) *Magic, Science and Religion*, London: Souvenir Press.

Martin, D. (2002) *Pentecostalism: The World their Parish*, Oxford: Blackwell.

Maximus (1982) *The Church, the Liturgy, and the Soul of Man: The Mystagogia of Saint Maximus the Confessor*, Still River, MA: St Bede's Publications.

May, T. (1997) 'Social Surveys: Design to Analysis', in T. May (ed.) *Social Research*, Buckingham: Open University Press, pp. 81–108.

McFague, S. (1997) *Super, Natural Christians*, London: SCM Press.

McGavran, D. A. (1955) *Bridges of God*, New York, NY: Friendship Press.

McGrail, P. (2004) 'Display and Division: Congregational Conflict Among Roman Catholics', in M. Guest, K. Tusting and L. Woodhead (eds) *Congregational Studies in the UK: Christianity in a Post-Christian Context*, Aldershot: Ashgate.

McGuire, M. (1982) *Pentecostal Catholics: Power, Charisma, and Order in a Religious Movement*, Philadelphia: Temple University Press.

McLellan, D. (ed.) (1977) *Karl Marx: Selected Writings*, Oxford: Oxford University Press.

Michonneau, G. (1950) *Revolution in a City Parish*, Oxford: Blackfriars.

Milbank, J. (1997) *The Word Made Strange: Theology, Language, Culture*, Oxford: Blackwell.

Mission and Public Affairs Council (2004) *Mission-Shaped Church: Church Planting and Fresh Expressions of Church in a Changing Context*, London: Church House Publishing.

Mitchell, J. and S. Marriage (2003) *Mediating Religion: Conversations in Media, Religion and Culture*, London: Continuum.

Moon, J. (2000) *Reflection in Learning and Professional Development: Theory and Practice*, London: Kogan Page.

Morgan, G. (1997) *Images of Organization*, London: Sage.

Morisy, A. (2004) *Journeying Out: A New Approach to Christian Mission*, London: Continuum, Morehouse.

Muir, C. (2003) *The Speechless Song: A Hymnological Portrait of Two Congregations*, University of Manchester, unpublished MA thesis.

Niebuhr, H. R. (1957) *The Social Sources of Denominationalism*, New York, NY: Meridian.

No attributed author (no date) *The Church as Text in George Herbert's Temple and Country Parson*, Sheffield: Early Modern Literary Studies, Sheffield Hallam University (see www.shu.ac.uk/emls/iemls/pd/herbarch.html).

Office of National Statistics (2001) *Social Capital: A Review of the Literature*, London: ONS.

Osborn, L. (1988) *Dear Diary: An Introduction to Spiritual Journalling*, Nottingham: Grove Books Limited.

Pagden, F. (1968) 'An Analysis of the Effectiveness of Methodist Churches of Varying Sizes and Types in the Liverpool District', in D. Martin (ed.) *A Sociological Yearbook of Religion in Britain, Vol 1*, London: SCM Press.

Pahl, J. (2003) *Shopping Malls and Other Sacred Spaces: Putting God in Place*, Grand Rapids, MI: Brazos Press.

Palmer, B. (1997) *Congregational Profiling: Developing the Concept*, London: Leo Baeck College. November 1997.

Parker, M. (2002) *Against Management: Organization in the Age of Managerialism*, Cambridge: Polity Press.

Parsons, G. (1993) 'Filling a Void? Afro-Caribbean Identity and Religion', in G. Parsons (ed.) *The Growth of Religious Diversity: Volume 1, Traditions*, London: Routledge, pp. 243–74.

Paton, R. (2003) *Managing and Measuring Social Enterprises*, London: Sage.

Pattison, S. (1994) *Pastoral Care and Liberation Theology*, Cambridge: Cambridge University Press.

——(1997) *The Faith of the Managers: When Management Becomes Religion*, London: Cassell.

——(2000) 'Organisational Spirituality: An Exploration', *Modern Believing*, 41 (2), pp. 12–20.

——(2004) 'What Are You Afraid of? Reflections on Institutional Change', *Change – Friend or Foe: Report on the Annual Study Conference of the College of Health Care Chaplains 2000* (R. L. Richards), pp. 44–57.

Pattison, S. and J. Woodward (2000) 'An Introduction to Evaluation in Pastoral Theology and Pastoral Care', in J. Woodward and S. Pattison (eds) *The Blackwell Reader in Pastoral and Practical Theology*, Oxford: Blackwell.

Peacock, A. (2000) *The Project Worker: A Guide to Employing Staff in Church Projects*, London: The Church Urban Fund.

Peshkin, A. (1984) 'Odd Man Out: The Participant Observer in an Absolutist Setting', *Sociology of Education*, 57 (October), pp. 254–64.

Putnam, R. D. (2000) *Bowling Alone: The Collapse and Revival of American Community*, New York, NY and London: Simon and Schuster.

Ramshaw, E. (1987) *Ritual and Pastoral Care*, Philadelphia: Fortress Press.

Rappaport, R. (1979) *Ecology, Meaning and Religion*, Richmond, CA: North Atlantic Books.

Reader, J. (1994) *Local Theology: Church and Community in Dialogue*, London: SPCK.

Reed, B. (1978) *The Dynamics of Religion: Process and Movement in Christian Churches*, London: Darton, Longman and Todd.

Reissman, C. K. (1993) *Narrative Analysis*, Newbury Park, London, New Delhi: Sage.

Resourcing Mission Office. (2001) *Pilgrims Way*, Manchester: The Methodist Church.

Rhodes, R. (1997) *Understanding Governance*, Buckingham: Open University Press.

Rich, A. (1991) *An Atlas of the Difficult World: Poems 1988–1991*, New York, NY: W. W. Norton.

Richter, P. and L. J. Francis (1998) *Gone but not Forgotten: Church Leaving and Returning*, London: Darton, Longman and Todd.

Roberts, R. H. (2002) *Religion, Theology and the Human Sciences*, Cambridge: Cambridge University Press.

Robertson, R. (1995) 'Globalisation: Time-Space and Homogeneity-Heterogeneity', in M. Featherstone et al. (eds) *Global Modernities*, London: Sage.

Sabatier, P. (1986) 'Top-Down and Bottom-Up Approaches to Implementation Research: A Critical Analysis and Suggested Synthesis', *Journal of Public Policy*, 6 (1), pp. 21–48.

Said, E. W. (1993/1994) *Culture and Imperialism*, London: Vintage.

Sandercock, L. (2004) *Cosmopolis II – Mongrel Cities in the 21st Century*, London and New York, NY: Continuum.

Schon, D. (1983) *The Reflective Practitioner*, New York, NY: Basic Books.

Schreiter, R. (1997) *New Catholicity – Theology Between the Global and the Local*, Maryknoll: Orbis Books.

Sheldrake, P. (2002) *Spaces for the Sacred: Place, Memory and Identity*, London: SCM Press.

Sheppard, D. (1983) *Bias to the Poor*, London: Hodder and Stoughton.

Smith, W. C. (1963) *The Meaning and End of Religion*, New York, NY: Macmillan.

Smith, W. R. (1889/1927) *Lectures on the Religion of the Semites*, Edinburgh: A and C Black.

Soja, E. (2000) *Postmetropolis*, Oxford: Blackwell.

Southcott, E. W. (1956) *The Parish Comes Alive*, London: Mowbray.

Stacey, M. (1960) *Tradition and Change: A Study of Banbury*, London: Oxford University Press.

Steven, J. (2002) *Worship in the Spirit: Charismatic Worship in the Church of England*, Carlisle: Paternoster Press.

Stringer, M. D. (1999) *On the Perception of Worship*, Birmingham: University of Birmingham Press.

Stromberg, P. (1986) *Symbols of Community: The Cultural System of a Swedish Church*, Tucson: University of Arizona Press.

The Methodist Church (2003) *The Constitutional Practice and Discipline of the Methodist Church*, Peterborough: Methodist Publishing House.

Thomas, R. (2003) *Counting People in: Changing the Way We Think About Membership and the Church*, London: SPCK.

Thompson, J. D. (1967) *Organizations in Action: Social Science Bases of Administrative Theory*, New York, NY: McGraw-Hill.

Tisdale, L. T. (1997) *Preaching as Local Theology and Folk Art*, Minneapolis MN: Fortress.

Tönnies, F. (1955) *Community and Association (Gemeinschaft und Gesellschaft)*, London: Routledge and Kegan Paul.

Toulis, N. R. (1997) *Believing Identity: Pentecostalism and the Mediation of Jamaican Ethnicity and Gender in England*, Oxford: Berg.

Troeltsch, E. (1931) *The Social Teaching of the Christian Churches*, London: Allen and Unwin.

Turner, H. W. (1979) *From Temple to Meeting House: The Phenomenology and Theology of Places of Worship*, The Hague: Mouton Publishers.

Turner, V. (1969) *The Ritual Process*, London: Routledge and Kegan Paul.

Tyson, R. W., J. L. Peacock and D. Patterson (eds) (1988) *Diversities of Gifts*, Urbana and Chicago: University of Illinois Press.

Wagner, C. P. (1976) *Your Church Can Grow*, Glendale, CA: Regal Books.

Walker, A. (1985) *Restoring the Kingdom*, London: Hodder and Stoughton.

Walter, T. (1990) 'Why Are most Churchgoers Women?' *Vox evangelica*, 20, pp. 73–90.

Ward, C. K. (1958) 'Some Elements of the Social Structure of a Catholic Parish', *Sociological Review*, 6 (1), pp. 75–93.

Ward, F. (2000) *Writing the Body of Christ: A Study of an Anglican Congregation*, University of Manchester, unpublished PhD thesis.

——(2004) 'The Messiness of Studying Congregations Using Ethnographic Methods', in M. Guest, K. Tusting and L. Woodhead (eds) *Congregations in the UK: Christianity in a Post-Christian Context*, Aldershot: Ashgate.

——(2005) *Lifelong Learning: Supervision and Theological Education*, London: SCM-Canterbury Press.

Ward, P. (2002) *Liquid Church*, Carlisle: Paternoster Press.

Warner, S. (1992) *New Wine in Old Wineskins: Evangelicals and Liberals in a Small-Town Church*, Berkeley, Los Angeles, CA and London: University of California Press.

Warren, R. (1995) *Building Missionary Congregations: Towards a Post-Modern Way of Being Church*, London: Church House Publishing.

——(2004) *The Healthy Churches' Handbook: A Process for Revitalizing Your Church*, London: Church House Publishing.

Watts, F., R. Nye and S. Savage (2002) *Psychology for Christian Ministry*, London: Routledge.

Weber, M. (1947/1964) *The Theory of Social and Economic Organization*, New York: Free Press.

——(1963) *The Sociology of Religion* (First English Translation), Boston, MA: Beacon.

White, J. (1990) *Introduction to Christian Worship*, Nashville: Abingdon Press.

White, S. (1997) *Groundwork of Christian Worship* revised, Peterborough: Epworth Press.

Wickham, E. R. (1957) *Church and People in an Industrial City*, London: Lutterworth Press.

Widdicombe, C. (2000) *Meetings that Work: A Practical Guide to Teamworking in Groups*, Cambridge: Lutterworth.

William Temple Foundation (Forthcoming) *Regenerating Communities – A Theological and Strategic Critique*, Manchester: William Temple Foundation (see www.wtf.org.uk).

Wilson, B. (1982) *Religion in Sociological Perspective*, Oxford: Oxford University Press.

Woodhead, L., M. Guest and K. Tusting (2004) 'Congregational Studies: Taking Stock', in M. Guest, K. Tusting and L. Woodhead (eds) *Congregational Studies in the UK: Christianity in a Post-Christian Context*, Aldershot: Ashgate.

Woodward, J. and S. Pattison (eds) (2001) *The Blackwell Reader in Pastoral and Practical Theology*, Oxford: Blackwell.

Wootton, J. H. (2000) *Introducing a Practical Feminist Theology of Worship*, Sheffield: Sheffield Academic Press.

Wright, N. (1997) 'The Nature and Variety of Restorationism and the "House Church" Movement', in S. Hunt, M. Hamilton and T. Walter (eds) *Charismatic Christianity: Sociological Perspectives*, Basingstoke: Macmillan.

Wright, S. (ed.) (1994) *Anthropology of Organizations*, London: Routledge.

Zuckerman, P. (2003) *Invitation to the Sociology of Religion*, New York, NY: Routledge.

Index of Subjects

abuse, 133, 194, 203

action, 2, 5, 18, 21, 23, 24, 26, 40, 41, 42, 45, 49, 56, 68, 69, 71, 74, 85, 89, 90, 91, 93, 96, 119, 122, 127, 128, 131, 134, 156, 157, 179, 180, 181, 184, 186, 199, 203, 234, 243

action research, 22, 26–7, 123, 158, 228

activism, 159, 161, 242

activity, 14, 29, 39, 63, 64, 70, 71, 80, 89, 92, 98, 106, 109, 110, 113–14, 115, 118, 122, 126, 133, 143, 152, 160, 162, 174, 188, 192, 210, 231, 242

administration, 64, 71, 128, 131, 160, 203

adult education, 25, 83

age, 8, 15, 52, 101, 146, 149, 150, 160, 201

Alpha course, xiii, 129, 200

anthropology, xvi, 1, 9, 12, 13–14, 19–20, 29, 37, 43, 44, 89, 90, 92, 93, 123, 180, 186, 188, 189, 191, 193, 197, 239, 243, 244

art, xiv, xv, 12, 174

artefacts, 27, 135, 140, 141, 144, 145

assets, 67, 135, 159, 160, 165, 167, 168, 169, 171, 241

association, 62, 69, 84, 85, 110, 211, 217

associational, 58, 64, 110, 111, 114, 152, 200

attender, 148, 150, 153, 160, 167, 171, 215

authority, 8, 49, 51, 65, 66, 67, 68, 69, 70, 75, 92, 100, 109, 110, 116, 117, 125, 132, 150, 163, 188, 189, 194, 195, 196, 198, 200, 202, 203, 204, 208, 209, 210, 211, 212, 213, 214, 218, 219, 220, 221, 227

beliefs, 14, 15, 21, 27, 29, 31, 39, 45, 49, 66, 68, 69, 70, 79, 90, 100, 101, 103, 106, 114, 123, 126, 127, 129, 134, 142, 143, 149, 157, 158, 159, 187, 188, 189, 190, 192, 194, 198, 241

belonging, 4, 9, 45, 49, 51, 81, 111, 129, 131, 133, 144, 145, 146, 152, 153, 182, 227

Body of Christ, 45, 47, 131, 133, 179, 193, 227–31

boundaries, 45, 47, 50, 55, 61, 66, 81, 104, 108, 129, 152–4, 179, 182, 198, 200, 204, 205, 208

boundary-spanning, 72, 86

buildings, 37, 50, 53, 71, 84, 86, 87, 89, 110, 114, 117, 119,

buildings (*cont.*):
123, 124, 130, 135, 141,
145, 160, 165, 167–8, 170,
173, 175–87, 191, 193,
205, 207, 214, 219, 220,
249
bureaucracy, 110, 200

catholicity, 43, 76–7, 87
cell churches, 126
change
church, 2, 24, 26, 36, 41, 50,
62, 66, 73, 91, 109, 113,
123, 127, 143, 151, 161,
166, 169, 175, 204, 207,
214, 216, 219, 232
individual, 4, 41, 60, 151,
189, 207, 224, 232
social, 2, 7, 10, 13, 20, 22, 51,
57, 66, 78, 79, 84, 86, 87,
106, 150, 158, 193, 201,
223
charisma, 49, 67
charismatic, 44, 49, 50, 59, 63,
91–4, 97, 98, 100, 102,
108, 122, 134, 188, 193,
200, 218–19
charismatic movement, xv, 63,
92, 108, 126, 208
children, 18, 35, 113, 129, 132,
143, 149, 150, 155, 162,
176, 180, 183, 196, 231
Christ, 81, 126, 128, 129, 130,
131, 145, 222, 229–30
church architecture, xiv, 12, 174
church café, 44, 49, 176–8
civic, 7, 10, 156, 191, 212
civil society, 85–6, 87, 88
class, 52, 80, 137, 145, 151,
152, 201, 203, 222, 241
clergy, 9, 60, 67, 68, 70, 71, 72,
117, 132, 160, 161, 163,
164, 167, 195, 202, 203,
208, 211, 213, 216, 217,

218, 219, 221
cohesion, 14, 56, 84, 99, 106,
198, 199, 203
commitment, 51, 66, 72, 73, 83,
105, 121, 129, 161, 162,
189, 200, 204, 209
communal, 10, 82, 100, 106,
110–11, 120, 152, 155,
156, 157, 184
communion, 107, 108, 126,
193, 196
community, 45, 81, 99, 129,
146, 153, 168, 183, 208,
240
church, xiv, xv, 3, 17, 24, 47,
49, 51, 74–5, 82, 83, 87,
89, 100, 110, 111, 122,
131, 151, 179, 182, 221,
222, 229, 231, 234, 235
local, 2, 6, 7, 9, 10, 51, 52–3,
54, 55, 71, 82, 83, 84, 86,
87, 105, 110, 119, 120,
127, 128, 130, 132, 133,
135, 156, 157, 160, 170,
173, 175, 176, 177, 178,
180, 184, 185, 187, 204,
205, 207, 208, 217, 241
global, xv
moral, 45, 81–3, 100
Iona, 126
community service, 7, 114
comparative, 19, 20, 27, 90, 169
confidentiality, 38–9
conflict, 14, 15, 49, 53, 115,
118, 137, 193, 194, 198,
199, 211, 214, 216, 217,
253
congregational identity, 8, 146,
205
consultancy, 22, 27–8, 165
consumerist, 51, 152, 190
context, 2, 3, 30, 82, 83, 106,
129, 133, 135, 156, 158,
163, 237

global, 54, 63–4, 233
language, narrative, 47, 48,
   92, 95
local, 2, 7, 9, 35, 50, 54,
   55–6, 61–2, 68, 86, 87,
   110–11, 157, 208, 222
national, xiii, 43, 51, 54, 56–
   7, 62–3, 65, 135, 200
organizational, 68, 118, 122
western culture, 54, 57–8, 59
contextualization, 46, 57, 60–1
control, 36, 68, 69, 78, 79, 116,
   120, 121, 149, 192, 195,
   196, 199, 203, 218
   behaviour, 188, 191–4
   by church, 60, 131, 193, 207
   individual, 3, 16, 31, 39, 101
   social, 14, 15, 100, 198, 204
conversion, 48, 76, 129
Corinthians, 179, 227, 228, 231
corporate identity, 34, 137, 221,
   222, 227, 228, 232
corporate theological reflection
   – see theological reflection
critical correlation – see
   theological reflection
cultural, 6, 8, 9, 10, 13, 19, 20,
   29, 45, 46, 47, 51, 54, 55,
   57, 58, 59, 60, 61, 62, 63,
   64, 77, 79, 103, 104, 106,
   122, 124, 136, 193, 198,
   201, 204, 205, 225, 228,
   230, 232
culture, 9, 16, 18, 20, 44, 46,
   49, 50, 54, 57, 58, 59, 63,
   64, 68, 72, 79, 80, 89, 98,
   99, 101–5, 108, 111, 117,
   128, 130, 141, 153, 175,
   187, 203, 204, 220, 222,
   229, 230

deacon, 2, 203, 204, 207
decision-making, 38, 50, 67, 82,
   117, 121, 124, 128, 130,

131–2, 154, 187, 195, 209,
   210–11, 213–16, 219, 221,
   222, 231, 232, 234
decline, 10, 52, 55, 56, 57, 58,
   60, 61, 62, 64, 69, 73, 84,
   85, 87, 105, 137, 147, 149,
   161, 173, 174, 185, 204,
   206, 207
denomination, xiv, 1, 2, 3, 27,
   45, 59, 65, 67, 71, 74, 75,
   148, 152, 160, 165, 166,
   177, 200, 211, 220, 225,
   240
deprivation theory, 190
discipleship, 82, 126, 129, 179
disclosive practice, 123
discourse, 8, 81, 87, 102, 137,
   139, 154, 195, 198, 226,
   230
diversity, xv, 11, 76, 77, 79, 81,
   86, 96, 221, 222, 228, 232,
   233, 241, 243
docile body, 226, 230
dominance, 78, 149, 225, 233

ecumenism, 66, 71, 83, 106, 117,
   119, 129, 132, 153, 200
Eden project, 82–3
education, 1, 2, 53, 71, 89, 103,
   111, 113, 126, 128–9, 231,
   149, 190, 237
embodiment, 179, 192, 197
emic, 20, 29, 107
empower, 26, 99, 132, 158, 221,
   233
equality, 78, 222, 234
ethics, xv, 16, 17, 18, 24, 38,
   52, 81, 82, 90, 107, 109,
   134, 169, 206
ethnicity, 8, 146, 149, 151, 201,
   222
ethnographic, 8, 10, 20, 44, 54,
   91, 94, 98, 107, 109, 123,
   186, 244

ethnography, 20, 27, 29, 45, 52, 89, 146, 243

etic, 20, 29

evaluation, 4, 5, 26, 29–30, 86, 166, 240

evangelical, 7, 48, 53, 63, 91, 105, 108, 129, 208

evangelism, 82, 113

experience, 7, 10, 25, 26, 35, 51, 77, 83, 91, 92, 109, 188
 – see also praxis under theological reflection
 reflection on, 33, 83, 175, 186,
 of worship, 93, 94, 95, 96, 100–4, 123, 189, 194, 197

exploration, 12, 18, 19, 23, 25, 26, 76, 108, 111, 113, 123, 127, 128, 134, 206, 225, 232

fellowship, xiii, 71, 131, 153, 200, 201

feminist theology, 122, 133, 179

fieldwork, 20, 29, 107, 207

finance, 114, 115, 155, 168

focus group, 31, 145

functionalism, 13, 99

functionalist, 13, 14, 99

function, 46, 47, 56, 80, 98, 100, 101, 123, 124, 133, 138, 168, 191, 217, 225

gay people, 131, 154

gender, 8, 52, 86, 101, 146, 149, 201, 222

generation, 58, 72, 139, 150, 193, 242

global, 34, 43, 44, 46, 51, 54, 55, 59, 63, 64, 65, 71, 74, 76, 77, 78, 79, 80, 81, 83, 85, 87, 88, 103, 133, 223, 235

global issues, 71, 133

globalization, 8, 51, 76, 79, 80, 81, 88

goal, 4, 49, 71, 90, 112, 115, 119, 120, 156, 217, 242

governance, 67, 70, 86, 117, 210–12, 214

grid, 192

groups, xiii, 3, 4, 10, 20, 24, 25, 28, 31–2, 33, 36, 44, 46, 66, 70, 71, 76, 79, 83, 86, 87, 98, 100, 106, 110, 113, 114, 115, 116, 117, 124, 125, 126, 128, 129, 130, 131, 151, 153, 155, 167, 188, 189, 190, 191, 193, 194, 195, 198, 199, 200, 202, 203, 206, 207, 211, 213, 214, 216, 219, 242

growth, 1, 7, 18, 23, 52, 55, 60, 62, 63, 74, 75, 84, 87, 92, 173, 174, 185, 203, 220

habitus, 49, 50

healing, 63, 84, 133, 179, 191, 193, 215

hierarchy, 46, 51, 92, 100, 188, 202, 215

history, xiii, xiv, 2, 10, 18, 27, 30, 34, 46, 47, 49, 64, 69, 77, 78, 80, 87, 101, 135, 177, 226, 239, 240

hybridity, 76, 223, 228–9, 232

ideal-type, 82, 194, 200

identity, 8, 45, 87, 99, 103, 105, 153, 180
 congregation, 2, 8, 9, 34, 39, 72, 77, 81–6, 101, 111, 113, 123, 128, 145, 151, 157, 178, 202, 205, 221, 222, 227, 228–9
 denominational, 83, 102, 135, 137, 138, 139–43
 ethnic, 54, 151

individual, 40, 107
national, 56, 150
social group, 6, 10, 46, 73,
    99, 154, 187
ideology, 16, 68, 156, 194, 201
imagery, 125, 128, 177, 178
imagination, 79, 137, 184, 185,
    229, 238
inclusion, 48, 81, 99, 113, 129,
    131
individual, xv, 14, 25, 26, 30, 31,
    38, 46, 49, 58, 95, 96, 103,
    105, 110, 113, 129, 131,
    134, 139, 155, 164, 188,
    189, 195, 196, 202, 217
injustice, 130
institution, 71, 161, 163, 195,
    239, 240
interaction, 14, 15, 31, 33, 70,
    71, 96, 106, 153, 205
interdisciplinary, 7, 17, 186,
    239, 243
interview, 30–1, 52, 62, 64, 87,
    97, 104, 106, 107, 119,
    134, 144, 157, 177, 196,
    206, 222, 223

jural power, 195, 196
justice, xv, 88, 130, 131, 222,
    234

kairos time, 124
knowledge, 4, 9, 13, 18, 26, 35,
    36, 77, 80, 88, 92, 95, 99,
    104, 128, 129, 156, 162,
    239, 242

language, 45, 47, 49, 68, 87, 90,
    95, 99, 109, 116, 154, 189,
    195, 216
leader, 2, 28, 36, 49, 70, 100,
    104, 122, 125, 127, 129,
    159, 164–5, 189, 193,
    194–6, 216

leadership, 2, 23, 24, 25, 70,
    102, 111, 113, 126, 132,
    149, 153, 154, 156, 165,
    175, 176, 187, 188, 189,
    194–6, 200, 201, 202, 203,
    204, 222, 234–6
learning, 1, 18, 33, 38, 128,
    129, 239, 244
leavers, 61, 151–2, 158
liberation theology, 24, 83–4,
    130, 190
liminal, 143
literature, 175, 228, 229
    academic, 1, 6, 7, 8, 9, 24,
    25, 63, 102, 144, 153, 159,
    165, 228, 236
liturgical seasons, 124
liturgical space, 123, 183
liturgy, 47, 86, 91, 94–5, 102,
    108, 122–8, 135, 139, 143,
    174, 188, 195, 214, 219,
    223, 224–5, 232
local, 4, 10, 51, 55–6, 61–2, 77,
    80–1, 84–5, 87, 152, 186,
    211
locality, 10, 51, 84, 87, 151,
    167, 168, 170, 174, 184,
    185, 186, 241

managerialism, 16, 66, 68, 75
meaning, 8, 14, 21, 45, 48, 53,
    58, 92, 95, 96, 99, 100,
    101–5, 107, 108, 123, 177,
    181, 183, 187, 194, 199
mega-church, 55, 105
member, 49, 56, 67, 84, 85,
    102, 104, 106, 110, 111,
    119, 124, 129, 132, 160–2,
    163, 164, 165, 166, 169,
    176, 179, 183, 192, 202–3,
    223, 241
membership, 49, 100, 112, 138,
    146, 147–9, 153–4, 161–2,
    185, 193, 214, 242

memory, 46, 48–50, 80, 87, 96,
    137, 139, 140, 141, 150,
    183, 184
method, 12, 19, 20, 24, 25, 26–
    35, 37–40, 56, 64, 89, 93,
    103, 106, 123, 133, 143,
    145, 156, 170, 173, 175,
    186, 221, 225, 228, 230,
    239, 243
Methodism, 59, 67, 106, 144,
    148, 170
methodology, 12, 19–26, 52, 83,
    90, 93, 134, 158
minister, 36, 38, 111, 114, 119,
    120, 123, 142, 151, 175,
    183, 186, 194, 202, 203,
    204, 207, 220, 228, 237,
    238
ministry, 1, 2, 3, 17, 18, 36, 75,
    142–3, 175, 177, 185, 235,
    236, 237, 238, 240
mission, 2, 37, 53, 63, 67, 81,
    83, 105, 108, 114, 118,
    121, 128, 129–31, 155,
    157, 158, 159, 166, 168,
    169, 170, 173, 175, 176,
    198, 204, 205, 206, 207,
    217, 236, 237, 241
mobility, 51, 149
Mormonism, 30, 196–7
Muslim, 142, 229, 236
mystical authority, 96, 183,
    194–6
myth, 14, 72, 98, 112

narrative, 8, 43, 46–8, 49, 50,
    54, 66, 70, 72, 82, 84, 87,
    146, 179
neo-tribalism, 81
network, xiii, 10, 43, 56, 65,
    66, 71–2, 74–5, 84, 85–
    6, 114, 132, 136, 153–4,
    161, 198, 204–5, 208,
    212

paid staff, 159, 164, 210
Parochial Church Council, 120,
    202
participant observation, 14, 19,
    20, 44, 52, 64, 89, 92, 93,
    94, 95, 106, 107, 109, 206
partnership, xiv, 4, 5, 26, 86,
    109, 116–18, 121, 176,
    177, 212
pastoral, 2, 79, 113, 124, 132,
    133, 153, 155, 176, 179,
    180, 184, 204
pastoral care, 71, 124, 128,
    132–3, 134
pastoral cycle, 23, 25
pastoral theology, 9, 17, 236
pastorate, 127
Paul, 179, 222, 227, 228, 231
Pentecostal, 44, 49, 63, 91, 92,
    93, 97, 122, 146, 148, 208
Pentecostalism, 54, 92, 126
performance, 16, 22, 93, 96,
    108, 135, 141–3, 166, 242
personality, 49, 67, 70, 155,
    216, 218
place, xiii, xiv, 3, 11, 40, 45, 46,
    50, 51, 53, 56, 72, 73, 80,
    84, 96, 128, 135, 140, 144,
    145, 149, 151, 168, 174,
    175, 176–7, 178, 179, 180,
    181–3, 184, 185, 186, 187,
    191, 217, 229, 244
planning, 2, 35, 39, 118–19,
    149, 215, 231, 237
plausibility structure, 99
polity, 65, 74, 117, 203, 211
post-colonial, 76, 223, 228, 229,
    230, 233
power, 8, 43, 59, 66, 76, 77, 83,
    87, 96, 99, 100, 101, 104,
    121, 124, 126, 131, 132,
    138, 149, 165, 187, 188–
    97, 189, 190, 191, 193,
    194, 195, 196, 197–208,

209–21, 221–33, 234, 243

practical theology, 12, 17, 18, 19, 23–6, 37, 134, 135, 175, 236

practice, 4, 8, 18, 24, 25, 32–3, 45, 68, 72, 86, 100, 101, 113, 114, 118, 119, 121, 123, 124, 127, 133, 135, 137, 139, 140, 142, 143, 145, 147, 149, 158, 169, 175, 180, 189, 206, 210, 227, 232, 233, 240

praxis – see theological reflection

preaching, 122, 124, 127, 128, 188, 222, 223, 224

precommitments, 18, 23, 25, 32

profane, 45

prophetic, 92, 130, 133, 230

protest, 130, 144

Protestant, xiv, 48, 50, 102, 106, 188, 189

pseudonym, 52, 130, 145, 170, 175

psychology, 14, 123, 133, 158, 239

purity, 154, 192, 193

purpose, 22, 27, 30, 36, 37, 39, 40, 41, 42, 70, 93, 112, 117, 120, 123, 126, 130, 160, 163, 167, 168, 177

Quakerism, 126, 136, 137, 139, 140, 142, 145–6, 195

qualitative, 21, 44, 170

quantitative, 21, 44, 60, 170

questionnaire, 33, 38, 52, 64, 106, 127, 134, 157

race, 131 – see also ethnicity

rationalism, 215

rationality, 49, 66, 67, 68, 69, 70, 77, 79, 81

Reformation, xiv, xv, 56, 76, 91, 125, 188

regeneration, urban, 4, 72, 84, 87, 98, 168

religious marketplace, 62, 206

resistance, 80, 83, 198, 203, 204, 226

resources, xiv, 6, 24, 37, 43, 48, 53, 66, 67, 71, 74, 83, 101, 110, 111, 114, 115, 116, 117, 118, 121, 122, 123, 125, 131, 135, 136–46, 146–59, 151, 155, 159–73, 165–9, 173–87, 198, 202, 203, 205, 207, 236

rhetoric, 79, 83, 92

rite, 94, 95, 96, 102, 149, 189, 190, 193

rites of intensification, 189, 190

rites of passage, 84, 124, 130, 149, 189, 197

ritual, 14, 49, 50, 71, 89–98, 98–101, 103, 107, 108, 109, 124, 143, 161, 178, 187, 189, 191, 193, 194, 195, 196, 197

role, 18, 27, 64, 70, 100, 101, 102, 103, 104, 109, 154, 159, 162–3, 164–5, 203, 213, 225, 226, 230, 231, 241

Roman Catholic, 6, 50, 63, 67, 76, 84, 91, 94, 98, 100, 102, 109, 143, 144, 147, 148, 167

sacred, xiv, 45, 47, 62, 64, 90, 100, 103, 124, 179, 181, 183, 184, 187

sanctuary, 176–83

sects, 43, 77, 153, 154, 189, 192, 193, 200

secular, xiv, 54, 67, 68, 71, 74, 83, 99, 100, 114, 122, 132, 133, 153, 156, 165, 168, 185, 187, 217, 219

secularism, 78
secularization, 10, 58, 147, 176,
    207
see, judge, act, 23
sermon, 28, 30, 46, 47, 91, 107,
    125, 127, 129, 154, 193,
    223–4
service – to others, 105, 114,
    116, 129, 130, 132, 160,
    161, 165, 170, 240
services – worship, 28, 39, 47,
    98, 102, 104, 107–8, 120,
    122, 123, 124, 126, 129,
    148, 153, 189, 191, 193,
    195, 215, 223–5
shopping, 55, 71, 180
silence, 141, 143, 185, 193
social action, 4, 8, 14, 51, 71,
    98, 103, 106, 168, 198, 199
social capital, 7, 9, 10, 57, 105,
    106, 146, 153, 155–6, 157,
    198, 205, 206, 235
social life, xv, 14, 46, 49, 89,
    136, 188, 198, 205
space, 44, 45, 55, 77, 80, 81,
    84, 85, 87, 88, 93, 96, 100,
    103, 108, 123–4, 126, 135,
    136–7, 174, 175, 176–7,
    181–7, 229, 230
spirit possession, 29, 189, 190,
    191, 197
spirituality, 58, 66, 72, 114,
    187, 239
stability, 53, 66, 73, 113
stakeholder, 66, 67, 121, 211,
    214–15, 216, 219
statistics, 21, 33, 41, 44, 62,
    147, 148, 156, 170–3, 174,
    222
status, 103, 109, 112, 149, 153,
    163, 189, 190, 191, 198,
    199, 202, 207, 208, 226,
    227
stories, 14, 22, 43, 46, 48, 49,

65, 72, 74, 127, 131, 185,
    189
story, xv, 8, 47, 48, 53, 62, 66,
    73, 75, 97, 101, 131, 174,
    176, 177, 227
sub-group, 73, 110, 112, 115,
    119, 121, 153, 169, 202,
    203, 242
subordination, 116, 225, 233
supervision, 132, 238, 239
survey, 21, 28, 33–4, 52, 57, 62,
    75, 89, 147, 148, 157, 158
symbol, 82, 99, 125, 183, 187,
    191, 193, 194, 229, 230
symbolic, 83, 99, 100, 113, 124,
    128, 137, 193, 197, 198,
    204, 205, 208, 225
symbolism, 14, 108, 197

Taizé, 126
task, 70, 80, 82, 110, 111, 112,
    113, 117, 120, 151, 163,
    205, 207, 227
team, 64, 70, 75, 100, 117, 120,
    132, 153, 159, 164–5, 175,
    195
temple, xiv, 177–9, 182–3, 185,
    196–7
text, 24, 25, 44, 48, 91, 92, 93,
    127, 139, 141, 182
theological reflection, 5, 23–6
    corporate theological
        reflection, 18, 19, 25, 127,
        128, 129, 130, 134, 175,
        186, 221, 223, 228, 230–1
    critical correlation, 18, 19, 25,
        133, 135, 175, 185, 186,
        221, 228, 243
    praxis, 18, 19, 23–4, 25,
        33, 77, 82, 123, 175, 221,
        225–8, 233
time, 11, 20, 26, 35, 36, 37, 38,
    44, 45, 51, 65, 66, 72–3,
    80, 81, 90, 124, 126, 135,

147, 154, 155, 163, 164,
174, 180, 181, 185, 186
timeline, 34, 73, 145, 186, 243
tradition, xiv, 5, 10, 18, 25, 27,
49, 65, 66, 67, 68, 70, 72,
73, 81, 99, 102, 103, 113,
125, 127, 128, 141, 151,
159, 164, 175, 181–3, 188,
198, 208
transcendence, 126, 188

unity, 4, 66, 76, 118, 145, 181,
221, 222, 227

values, 8, 14, 18, 21, 39, 56,
57, 58, 69, 71, 73, 74, 80,
86, 93, 100, 101, 102, 103,
111, 112, 113, 114, 117,
119, 120–1, 123, 126,
128, 130, 131, 153, 161,
162, 163, 170, 173, 190,
192, 194, 199, 218, 233,
237
vicarious religion, 144
voluntary, xiv, 7, 51, 69, 71,

105, 106, 112, 116, 157,
161, 166, 168, 173, 204,
211, 235
organization, 15, 16, 71, 106,
112, 116, 160, 164, 165,
166, 173, 210, 213, 217,
219, 226, 243
sector, 16, 71, 166, 210
volunteers, 71, 155, 160, 163,
164, 214
vulnerability, 105, 132

walk, 35, 62, 87, 156, 180–1,
186, 236
William Temple Foundation, 87,
88, 106
worldview, 29, 98, 99, 103, 183,
199, 242
worship, 8, 39–40, 44, 49, 50,
51, 70, 71, 73, 76, 83, 84,
85, 89–98, 98–109, 113–
14, 119, 120, 122–35,
137, 142–3, 151, 154, 168,
177, 178, 179, 217, 223–5,
227

Index of Names

Acker, Joan, 69
Albrecht, Daniel E., 93, 97
Albrow, Martin, 69, 112, 121
Aldridge, A., 154, 158
Ammerman, Nancy T., 7, 34, 35, 55, 57
Aune, Kirsten, 149, 154, 201
Avis, Paul, 158

Bacon, Derek, 77, 106
Baker, Chris, ix, 76–88, 84
Ballard, Paul, 19, 24, 26
Bauman, Zigmunt, 80, 81, 153
Becker, Penny Edgell, 10, 111, 217, 218, 220
Beckford, Robert, 25
Belbin, R. Meredith, 164
Bell, J., 42
Bellah, R. N., 56
Bennett Moore, Zoe, 133
Berg, Bruce L., 32
Berger, Teresa, 126
Bernauer, James, 233
Berry, Jan, ix, 122–35
Bhabha, Homi, 228, 229
Billis, David, 110, 116
Bird, M., 150
Blaxter, L., 158
Block, Peter, 28, 165
Bolton, G., 33
Booker, M., 113
Bourdieu, Pierre, 49, 50
Bradshaw, Paul F., 125
Branwick, T., 27

Braybrooke, D., 215
Brierley, Peter, 57, 62, 147, 148, 151
Brookfield, Stephen, 33
Brown, C. G., 149
Browning, Don S., 7, 8, 25, 122, 123, 130, 233
Bruce, Steve, 147, 149, 154

Cameron, Helen, ix, 4, 15, 22, 35–42, 65–75, 71, 135, 159–73, 163, 240, 241
Carrette, Jeremy, 233
Carroll, Jackson W., 7, 34, 35
Cartledge, Mark, 122, 134
Castells, M., 80, 81, 83, 85, 88
Chambers, Paul, ix, 52, 198–208, 202, 203, 204, 205, 207, 208
Chater, Mark, 68
Chrislip, D. D., 165
Clark, David B., 8, 203
Clark, Elizabeth, 157–8
Coffey, Amanda, 32
Coghlan, D., 27
Cohen, A. P., 146
Coleman, Simon, ix, 44–54, 59
Collins, David, 16, 73, 75, 135, 136, 201
Collins, Peter, ix, 135, 136–46
Collins, Sylvia, ix, 135, 146–59, 200, 201, 205
Cray, Graham, 88, 129
Croft, Steven, 126

Csordas, Thomas, J., 92, 93, 98

Dandelion, Ben Pink, 143
Davie, Grace, 144, 149, 152, 158
Davies, Douglas J., x, 3, 13, 19, 72, 124, 132, 161, 188, 197, 202, 208, 238, 240
Davies, Elwyn, 208, 240
Dawson, C., 42
de Certeau, Michel, 35, 180, 187, 230
Denscombe, 42
Dhooghe, J., 162
Dinham, Adam, 167
Dorsey, G., 185
Douglas, Mary, 191, 192, 197
Dover, Graham, xi, 74–5
Dowie, Alan, 9, 205, 208
Dudley, Carl S., 7, 34,
Dudley, M., 67
Dulles, Avery, 218
Dunn, J., 227
Dunn, Nancy M., 180, 186
Durkheim, Emile, 45, 46, 54, 56, 99, 100, 199
Durran, M., 165

Eastman, M., 77
Eccleston, G., 152

Farnsley, Arthur, 6
Fichter, J. F., 161
Finneron, Doreen, 167
Finney, J., 151
Flanagan, K., 91, 94, 95, 96
Foucault, M., 199, 223, 225, 226, 227, 230, 232, 233
Francis, Leslie J., 61, 148, 152, 155, 158
Fried, S., 220

Gabriel, Y., 16, 72, 75
Giddens, Anthony, 198

Gilchrist, A., 86
Giles, Richard, 167, 173
Gill, Robin, 167, 173, 206
Gorringe, Timothy, 183, 184, 186
Graham, Elaine L., 8, 26, 32, 74, 123, 133, 134, 233, 236
Gray, John, 180, 187
Green, Laurie, 19, 23, 24, 25, 26, 231
Greenwood, Robin, 70, 75, 164
Grieve, Jane, 165
Grimes, Ronald L., 93
Grint, Keith, 165
Griseri, P., 112, 121
Grundy, Malcolm, 110, 111, 121
Guest, Mathew, x, 5–10, 6, 9, 53, 64, 98–109, 161, 207

Hadaway, C. K., 148
Halsey, Margaret, 133
Hamilton, Malcolm, 208
Harris, Margaret, x, 7, 112, 121, 163, 209–21, 217, 218, 221
Hauerwas, S., 82
Heelas, Paul, 57, 58, 64
Heskins, Jeff, 29
Higginson, Richard, 68
Hilborn, David, 150
Hirst, Rob, 205
Hoge, D. R., 60
Hopewell, James F., 6, 8, 9, 53, 72, 75, 101
Hornsby-Smith, Michael, 57
Hughes, C., 158
Hull, John, 129
Hunt, Stephen, 129, 200, 208

Inge, John, 174, 187
Inglehart, R., 57, 58, 63
Ireland, M., 113

James, Wendy, 98
Jamieson, A., 152
Jamieson, Penny, 165
Jeavons, T. H., 114, 122
Jenkins, Timothy, 8, 53, 55, 56, 202, 203
Johnson, Douglas H., 98
Johnson, Ian D., xi, 170–3
Jordan, Stuart, x, 109–22

Kahn, R. L., 16
Katz, D., 16
Kay, W. K., 148
Kearns, K., 215
Kelley, D. M., 60
Kumar, K., 77, 78, 88

Lartey, E. Y., 133, 134
Lawrence-Zenuga, Denise, 186
Levitt, M., 149

Lewis, Ioan, 190, 197
Lindblom, C., 215
Lischer, 182
Lovell, George, 28
Low, Setha M., 186, 187
Luckett, Virginia, xi, 120–1
Lukes, Stephen, 198
Lyall, David, 127, 133
Lynch, Gordon, 150
Lynd, H. M., 6
Lynd, R. S., 6
Lyon, B., 9

Malinowski, Bronislaw, 89, 90, 91, 95
Marler, P. L., 148
Marriage, S., 153
Martin, David, 59
Maximus, 181, 182, 183
May, T., 34
McFague, Sally, 244
McGavran, D. A., 7
McGrail, Peter, 99

McGuire, Meredith, 100, 101, 108
McLellan, David, 199
Michonneau, George, 6
Milbank, John, 82
Mitchell, J., 153
Moon, Jennifer, 33
Morgan, Gareth, 16
Morisy, Ann, 155
Muir, Craig, 127

Needham, Paul, 195
Niebuhr, H. R., 154, 200
Nye, R., 154, 158

Osborn, Lawrence, 32

Pagden, Frank, 203
Pahl, John, 187
Palmer, Barry, 73
Parker, Martin, 16
Parsons, G., 151
Paton, Rob, 166, 173
Patterson, Daniel, 197
Pattison, Stephen, x, 16, 30, 65–75, 68, 73, 75, 133, 243
Peacock, Alison, 164
Peacock, James L., 197
Peshkin, Alan, 109
Poling, James N., 133, 134
Pritchard, John, 19, 24, 26
Pui-Lan, Kwok, 229, 230, 232
Putnam, Robert D., 10, 85, 105, 106, 155, 156, 235

Ramshaw, Elaine, 124
Rappaport, R., 103
Reader, John, 24
Reed, Bruce, 7
Rees, Alwyn D., 208
Rhodes, R., 212
Rich, Adrienne, 184, 186
Richter, Philip, x, 3, 14–15, 20–1, 61, 152, 158, 236–8

Roberts, Richard H., 69
Robertson, R., 81
Roozen, D., 60

Sabatier, P., 215
Sandercock, L., 79, 229, 233
Savage, S., 158
Scarpino, G., 215
Schreiter, R., 76, 88
Seel, Benjamin, 64
Shaw, Alistair, 240
Sheldrake, Philip, 181, 187
Sheppard, David, 130, 191
Smith, Wilfred Cantwell, 27
Smith, William Robertson, 90, 94, 95
Soja, E., 78
Southcott, E. W., 6
Stacey, Margaret, 55
Steven, James H. S., 93
Storrar, William, x, 135, 174–87
Stringer, Martin D., x, 8, 89–98, 95, 97, 98, 146
Szerszynski, Bronislav, 64

Thomas, Richard, 161
Thompson, J. D., 115
Tisdale, Leonora Tubbs, 127, 134
Toulis, Nicole R., 54, 146
Troeltsch, Ernst, 154, 200
Turner, Harold W., xiv
Turner, Victor, 90, 93, 94, 194, 197
Tusting, Karin, 6, 9, 53, 64

Tyson, Ruel W., 197

Wagner, C. P., 7
Walker, Andrew, 201
Walter, Tony, 149, 208
Walton, Heather, 26, 32, 236
Ward, C. K., 6
Ward, Frances, x, 2, 9, 17–19, 23–6, 32, 33, 76, 77, 221–33, 230, 234–6
Ward, Graham, 247
Ward, Pete, 88, 161
Warner, S., 65, 107, 109
Warren, Robert, 1, 118, 129, 236
Watkins, Charles, 132, 202, 208, 240
Watts, F., 154, 158
Weber, Max, 49, 51, 67, 103, 199, 200, 209, 218
White, James, 123, 124
White, Susan, 123, 124, 126, 135
Wickham, E. R., 6
Widdicombe, Catherine, 23, 164, 173
Wilson, Bryan, 147, 198
Winter, Michael, 132, 208
Woodhead, Linda, xi, 53, 54–65, 57, 58, 64, 200
Woodward, J., 30, 133
Wootton, Janet H., 122, 135
Wright, Nigel, 204
Wright, Susan, 16

Zuckerman, P., 158